30
32
51

FROM RENOIR TO PICASSO

The Author by Picasso

FROM RENOIR TO PICASSO

Artists in Action

by

MICHEL GEORGES-MICHEL

With fifty illustrations by or of those artists

TRANSLATED BY
DOROTHY AND RANDOLPH WEAVER

HOUGHTON MIFFLIN COMPANY BOSTON
The Riverside Press Cambridge
1957

FIRST AMERICAN EDITION 1957

LIBRARY OF CONGRESS CATALOG CARD NUMBER: 57-9025
FIRST PRINTING

The Riverside Press
CAMBRIDGE • MASSACHUSETTS
PRINTED IN THE U.S.A.

CONTENTS

AUTHOR'S NOTE

I wish to thank Messrs. Albin Michel and Brentano (under the direction of Robert Tenger) for their courtesy in allowing me to reproduce in an expanded form several passages from previous books in order that the present work should be more complete.

FOREWORD

It has not been my intention in these pages to write either a book of art criticism or a series of biographical sketches. My aim has been simply to record some of the conversations I have had over the last fifty years with a great many artists at different periods of their lives. Most of them were good enough to give me an idea of their views and theories on art in general, and at the same time to explain to me some of the details of their respective techniques. It is my hope, therefore, that this book may serve as a kind of History of Contemporary Painting, and indicate the various trends and movements which have so violently affected it from time to time.

I have purposely dwelt to some extent on the picturesque side of the lives of certain painters, and have included any feature which I thought might help to recapture the atmosphere of their environment and time. By allowing them to express, in their own words, their doubts and aspirations, their minds and characters, one can often convey something of the essence of their work.

If some readers accuse me of having given too much space to anecdotes, I must reply that I have, after all, only written about what I have personally seen and heard. Though an anecdote may be objectionable in a painting when it takes precedence over the painting itself, it can, nevertheless, be of value in writing. In fact, a well-chosen anecdote, or even an epigram, will sometimes give better insight into the mentality of a human being than a dozen chapters of psychological analysis.

If these few lines, then, should amuse, interest and instruct the reader, I shall feel that I have accomplished my purpose and I shall rest content.

M. G.-M.

From Monsieur de Gas to Count Toulouse-Lautrec

DEGAS

I WAS NOT yet twenty when I went to call on Monsieur Degas. "He may eat you alive," I had been warned. But he received me cordially enough in his studio in the rue Victor-Massé. His famous servant Zoé had let me in because of my youthful appearance.

"What can I do for you?" Degas inquired.

I swallowed hard; for this was Degas, whom even the boldest never dared to address as anything but "Monsieur de Gas";[1] the impeccable draughtsman, who, though a disciple of Ingres, had supported the realist movement by his paintings of ethereal little ballet girls, and raged whenever he was classed with the Impressionists, as Petit Larousse has him listed even today! True, he had given the Impressionists the support of his great authority at the time of their first exhibitions in 1874 and '75, at Durand-Ruel's, for he realised their importance and, besides, Monet had sponsored them. But after that Degas had retired to his studio, which, in his opinion, was the only place for a painter to do his painting. . . . I remembered his biting *mots* and devastating quips, which were the talk of Paris.

[1] Degas' family name. He was the first to call himself Degas. [*Translator's note.*]

"What do you want?" he asked me again.

"To see you," I mumbled.

"Oh? Some people come to see my painting; but you come to see me. Who sent you?"

"No one. I——"

He doubtless forgave me on account of my youth, for he said quite gently:

"Well, sit down."

He began to hunt around among his portfolios, glancing at me over his shoulder as he did so. Finally, he said:

"Well, now you've seen me. Are you a painter?"

"No—— Yes—— No——"

"Ah. You're afraid to admit it?"

"I like painting too much to try to paint."

"So. You love God too much to go to church——"

"I go to art galleries."

"Well, if you go to church, you ought to pray. If you go to art galleries, then you ought to paint. In fact, at your age, that is the only place where you should do your painting."

* * * * *

I did not have occasion to see him again till some time afterwards. It was when I went to the exhibition of Claude Monet's *Water-lilies*, which today line the walls of the Orangerie. I was with Henri Bernstein, and, just as we were entering, we ran into Degas, wearing his "Kronstadt" hat and flowing cape, as he has so often been depicted.

"Well, well!" Bernstein said to him. "I thought you had quarrelled with Monet and all the other Impressionists."

"Nonsense," replied Degas. "I wanted to see these *Water-lilies* he's been working on for so many years. Everyone's been telling me about them."

"And how do you like them?"

"Well, as I said to him, 'Your little cups of camomile aren't so bad'."

"Indeed? But that certainly can't have brought about a reconciliation!"

"Bah! I made it up with him just to have the chance of saying that."

LAUTREC

One afternoon in the spring of 1901 I was standing near the entrance of Ollendorf's bookshop when I heard the girl at the cash desk exclaim:

"Oh, look! Here come the three beavers!"

The girl, who was young and pretty, looked very much like a Lautrec drawing herself, with her coils of hair piled up on her forehead, her waist pinched in by her corsets, her skirt swaying about her hips, and her high-buttoned bootees reaching half-way up her calves.

I glanced towards the door and saw the three "beavers" coming in, looking like actors out of an Offenbach comedy. The one on the left was Thadée Natanson, editor of the *Revue Blanche* and founder of the *Cri de Paris*; on the right was Tristan Bernard, whose beard was still black at that time; while in the middle, his top-hat barely level with their shoulders, was a sort of dwarf with short twisted legs, a long straight body, and massive arms which ended in enormous hands with well-trimmed nails. From the high, stiff collar at the top of the body emerged an incredible head. The slightly protruding eyes, which were very gentle in their expression, gazed out through pince-nez perched on a long red nose; and the lips were two folds of purple flesh in a dark circle of beard.

But no one thought of laughing at the dwarf; first, because his two companions showed him such marked respect, and secondly, because, although he was deformed, his whole being radiated a sense of purpose and a natural distinction which was entirely devoid of affectation.

I don't know why his extremely dignified bearing reminded me of Verlaine, whom one of our professors had taken us to see at the Café du Rocher. The recollection I have of Verlaine is not the one ascribed to him by legend, but of a figure sitting up very straight in front of the paper he was reading. I have no idea what he was drinking. But I recall my surprise, when an acquaintance went up to speak to him, at the distant way in which the poet greeted him—with the back of his hand, as if to wave him away.

I was well acquainted with two of Lautrec's "models", La Goulue and Yvette Guilbert, of whom I have written at some length in another book.[1] Neither of them was in the least aware of the tremendous talent of the man who was painting them, nor had they any notion of the fame that would one day be his. Yvette Guilbert, for instance, once sent back to Lautrec one of the portraits he had done of her, with these words scribbled across it: "You little monster, you have made me out a perfect horror!" It is true that at a later date Yvette confessed to me that she had refused to pose for Burne-Jones, the painter. "I've enough portraits of the kind you turn out as it is," she had informed him.

As for La Goulue, I sometimes went to see the famous music-hall artist in her circus caravan, for in her later years she became a lion-tamer.

One day she said to me:

"By the way, my lad, you haven't got eight hundred francs, have you? Even five or six hundred would do. I've got to pay for my lions' keep, and I'd be glad if you'd take off my hands those rolls of canvas I've had lying about here for so long."

The "rolls of canvas" were none other than Lautrec's *Moulin*

[1] *Cinquante ans de Gloires Théâtrales* (Édition A. Bonne).

Rouge, with the portraits of Valentin-le-désossé (Valentin, the Boneless Wonder), Fénéon, Oscar Wilde and Tapié de Céleyran.

Before 1914, eight hundred francs, or even five hundred, represented quite a sum for a young man of my age. I went back to the office of *Gil Blas*, the paper I was working for at that time, and told them about my interview. I was always listened to seriously when I talked to my colleagues about painters, not because I happened to know many artists personally, but because of an incident that had once occurred on my return from a visit to Rodin: on that occasion, the whole staff had thrown themselves on me and tried to snatch away the handful of drawings the sculptor had tucked under my arm as I was leaving.

In the editorial room there was a young man who had been listening to my story. Without saying a word he slipped away, ran downstairs, went into a jewellers' which was in the same building, and bought himself a watch on credit. (I don't know if he ever paid for it; but he married the jeweller's sister.) I have often wondered whether he pawned or sold the watch. In any event, the fact remains that he had enough money to go that very day and buy La Goulue's "rolls of canvas", which he then sold to Messrs. Barbazanges and Hodebert, who cut them up into eight pieces, not counting some "scraps". (In spite of all that wealth of canvas there were no collectors of Lautrec's work in those days!)

At a later date it was possible to put the pieces together without too much difficulty. And the two canvases now hang in the Louvre Annexe, in the Jeu de Paume building. Thanks to Paul Boncourt, Robert Rey and François-Poncet, the French Government was induced to buy them from M. Hugues Simon, in 1929, for the sum of four hundred thousand francs. Hugues Simon and Georges Bernheim, each of whom owned them for a time, had both refused three million francs which Germany offered for them.

* * * * *

The painter Heuzé once told me a rather touching anecdote about Lautrec.

He happened to be sitting alone one night in a Montmartre café, when a poor old flower-woman came up to him to offer her wares. The artist refused politely, whereupon the woman said:

"You don't drive me away brutally the way the others do. And you call me 'Madame'. You must be a real gentleman, a great gentleman, or else a great artist, because they are the only ones who are polite to poor people! I once knew a great artist. I even posed for him. You may have heard of him?"

The painter in question was Manet, and the old woman herself was Victorine Meurant, who had posed for Manet's *Fife-player* and *Olympia* . . .

* * * * *

Romain Coolus, another of Toulouse-Lautrec's friends, often used to talk to me about the artist and, if I repeat some of his anecdotes here, it is only because, so far as I know, they have never appeared in print before. Moreover, they may add to our knowledge of the character of that very great little man.

It was only a short time before Coolus's death. I chanced to be visiting an exhibition of Lautrec's work, admirably organised by Julien and Michel Florisoone, and I was looking at a portrait, done in pink-and-blue hatchings, of a man with a vivid complexion and piercing, ironic eyes, when I heard someone behind me say:

"I've changed a bit since then, haven't I?"

I turned round. It was Coolus himself, his moustache bristling despite his eighty-two years, his sardonic and humorous mouth twisted into the sort of grin which had once caused Tristan Bernard to remark: "Coolus is the only man who can kiss a woman on the mouth and murmur sweet nothings into her ear at the same time."

"That portrait was painted in 1898," Coolus told me. "Lautrec had already done several sketches of me, one of which was reproduced on the programme of the *Comédie Parisienne*—afterwards the *Athénée*—when I put on the five-act play *Raphaël* there at the same time that Oscar Wilde was putting on his *Salômé*. I had met Lautrec at the Natansons' *Revue Blanche*, and I met him again at Thadée's house at Villeneuve-sur-Yonne. One morning, while we were staying there, the painter knocked at my door, and said:

" 'Come on downstairs. I want to do an El Greco portrait of you.' "

(It turned out to be more like a Van Gogh in pastel, with hatchings like the Japanese prints which had influenced the Dutch painter.)

"It took him two morning sittings. What a delightful man he was; so appreciative of any courtesy and sensitive to the slightest rebuff. He suffered terribly because of his ugliness, his deformed legs and his moist, protruding lips.

"But he was kindness itself. He always remained the artist and the distinguished gentleman, especially in those 'houses' where he painted and where I lived with him. The inmates all adored him."

"Did he really live in those 'houses'?"

"No. He had a large studio in the rue de Tourlaque, where he kept open house. He knew all about making cocktails long before the Americans did. Ah, those cocktails of Lautrec's! I remember one wild party at the Natansons' when he got even Vuillard and Bonnard drunk. The adjoining room had been transformed into a hospital, where we were looked after by his cousin, Dr. Tapié de Céleyran, the assistant of the noted surgeon, Dr. Péan, who used to operate in a frock-coat, and invented the forceps that were named after him.

"Lautrec and I had our work-table in a room no one else ever entered, in a 'house' in the rue des Moulins, just opposite where Rodier's stores used to be. In the evening we would go up to the 'parlour' and treat the 'ladies' who weren't 'working' for the moment to a 'marquise' or a bottle of champagne. Then Lautrec would play faro with them. Or else he would ask them to pose for him. Whenever one of them tried to discuss art or politics with him, he would say:

" 'Now, don't you bother about that. It's not your business. What I'm interested in is that gargoyle of a face of yours.'

" 'All right, Monsieur le Comte. Sorry. Here's the gargoyle. Do you want it front view or side?'

"The only thing he lived for was to draw and paint. We often went together to see Hervé's *Chilpéric*. Lautrec went simply to watch Marcelle Lender, especially her back. Just as Renoir had a passion for skin that 'took the light', so Lautrec, who also loved fine textures, such as the grain of leather or wood, admired Lender's back because of the way it absorbed and reflected the colours of the footlights and because of its incomparable modelling; it was like balm to the crippled little man's eyes. How many times he painted Marcelle Lender and Marcelle Lender's back; how he loved and adored that back; it sent him into a sort of platonic swoon. . . . For, you see, although Lautrec was first and foremost a painter of music-halls and brothels and the girls he found there, he was, nevertheless, supremely pure, as pure as the slightest of his sketches. . . ."

Lautrec: Self-portrait

To shadow he brought the gift of new colours
Each hour saw him born to a brighter world
He died in a rainbow

From Monet's Rainbow Palette to Renoir's Rosy Flesh-Tints

CLAUDE MONET

It was Georges Clemenceau who took me to see Claude Monet at Giverny.

I was certainly glad of the chance to go with such a sponsor to pay a visit to the most celebrated of the Impressionists, the group which had been the first to perceive that a shadow is not uniformly black and that objects appear to change colour according to the time of day and the variations in the atmosphere. In fact, it was chiefly Monet, Sisley, Pissarro, Renoir (for a while) and Berthe Morisot who, following Manet's method, began painting light tones on a light background and did away with "prune-juice" and "lumps of shadow" on their canvases. Monet had already demonstrated these two ideas in his London pictures, his *Haystacks* series, his *Débâcles* and his famous studies of Rouen Cathedral. Gone were the days when he had had to tell Durand-Ruel that he would be only too glad to sell him three canvases for a hundred francs apiece. In 1883 he had bought a beautiful estate in Normandy, with gardens and "Japanese" ponds which were the envy of many an artist.

Clemenceau's car stopped at the foot of the hill; and I can still see the great political leader energetically climbing the side road up to the painter's home with the aid of his cane, his gay little hat, so common among painters of the period, pushed back from his rugged forehead, and his moustache bristling. He rang the bell at the gate and a servant came out and told him that Monet was working near the "new pond".

"Good, good," said Clemenceau, as the porter opened a little gate for us on the other side of the road. We crossed the railway line, circled a clump of trees and discovered Monet with his back to us, brushing in a large canvas in front of his water-lilies. He did not look round, evidently thinking that it was a member of the household who had come out to speak to him. We halted some distance away and Clemenceau made a sign to me not to move. Then, when he saw that Monet had paused in his work for a moment, he quietly approached and put an arm round the painter's shoulder.

Monet rose to his feet in surprise. He was smaller than Clemenceau and heavily built. I noticed that he was wearing a velveteen jacket, over the front of which flowed his thick, brilliant beard. After I had been introduced, Clemenceau exclaimed enthusiastically:

"What a subject you've got there!"

"Yes," the artist agreed, "they will all turn pink and orange soon. They are the kind of flowers that develop slowly. But when they are fully formed. . . . Come and see."

We followed him back across the road to the main gate where Clemenceau had rung the bell. On either side of the long garden walk was a rectangular flower-bed filled with glowing flowers, which several gardeners were tending. At the end of the walk was a low-roofed pink house with green blinds. We did not enter it directly, but first passed through a large out-building where we saw two immense panels of his *Water-lilies* which he had already completed.

"I am going to extend them all round the room," said Monet, "so that one will get the impression of being in the centre of a lily-pond."

Hat in hand, his body bent slightly backward, and leaning on his cane, Clemenceau gazed at the murals from under his bushy brows. All at once he said:

"Now, Monet, what about the Academy?" But seeing the painter's expression, he added with a quick gesture of the hand, "Oh, no. I haven't come as a delegate. . . ."

Monet replied in a mild, grave voice, which was a trifle gruff, though there was no trace of bitterness in it.

"The Academy——" he began; then, pausing, he said, "Look——" and pointed towards the garden. After a moment, he went on: "I have already refused a decoration. And now it's the Academy. . . . What would I be doing making social calls and talking twaddle with all those people who have continually opposed us? They don't understand us yet, even if they have begun to accept our painting. What attitude could I adopt towards those people in their drawing-rooms? Me, in a drawing-room—— Why, I'm an out-of-door painter. Was Boudin a member of the Academy? Or Cézanne? No, no. That sort of thing is not for me."

"What are you going to do with those?" inquired Clemenceau, indicating the two large panels which were fastened on the wall with strips of wood.

"Just let me finish a dozen or so first. I'm thinking of having a large octagonal studio built for myself on the other side of the house so that I can have the whole set arranged the way I want it."

"Wouldn't you like to present them to the Government in exchange for a seat in the Academy?" Clemenceau asked with a laugh.

"To the Government? That's another matter. I'd prefer that to a so-called art-collector. But I want to keep them for myself, first. Then, provided they're not put away in some official store-room . . ."

"Oh, come now," protested Clemenceau. "Do you think I would allow that?"

"Well, if you will take the responsibility——" replied Monet to the man who had made the Louvre accept Manet's *Olympia*. Then, changing the subject, he said, "Let's go and have something to drink."

* * * * *

We entered the little house. Monet led the way up several steps to the dining-room, passing through a room hung with Japanese prints, including the *Cedars* and the *Tokaïdo* by Hiroshige, which had doubtless served as inspiration for his own "series".

The dining-room was done in rustic style and painted light green and yellow. A maid brought in a bottle of local white wine, which she served in handsome glasses on a check table-cloth. As I got up for a moment to examine the Hiroshiges, Monet said to me:

"If you are fond of paintings, you must see the ones in my bedroom. You should also take a look in the room next to it because you'll find my best picture there."

"That's not a favour he grants everyone," said Clemenceau.

"No. But not everyone comes here with Clemenceau, either," he replied.

The bedroom upstairs was lighted by windows looking out on to the garden. To the left of the fireplace my eye was caught, first of all, by Cézanne's famous *Château Noir*, which Monet had bought from the artist himself; on the other side hung a *Vue de l'Estaque* and below it a *Baigneurs*. On the back wall were a Degas pastel of a *Woman in the Bath*, two Pissarros, and a Berthe Morisot; while over a desk, on which there was a Corot portrait, hung a breathtaking Renoir, full of colour and swarming movement, *The Casbah at Algiers*.

Over the head of the bed were other Renoirs: one of Mme. Monet alone, dressed in blue and reclining on a divan; the other of Mme. Monet with her son Jean, seated on a lawn. It was apropos of this latter canvas that Manet is said to have dropped a brick. For he had once painted the mother and son when visiting the Monets, and it so happened that, while he was working on his picture, Renoir, who was a young man at the time, dropped in unexpectedly. He was so taken with the subject that he immediately wanted to try his hand at it too. He asked Monet for canvas and paints, and forthwith set up his easel not far from Manet's. The other, growing nervous at this intrusion, presently left his work and went over to look at Renoir's. After gazing at it for a minute, he called Monet aside and said:

"Monet, Renoir is a friend of yours, isn't he? If I were you, I should advise him to give up painting."

I went into the adjoining room and found only one picture

there, and that unframed: Cézanne's *Boy in a Red Waistcoat.* I stood looking at it for a long time. All at once I was aware that Clemenceau and Monet had also come in, and I heard the painter say in his deep, beautiful voice:

"Yes, Cézanne is the greatest of us all. . . ."

RENOIR

Renoir! With the exception of Cézanne, Renoir was without any doubt the greatest painter of his generation. Like Cézanne, he has too often been classed with the Impressionists. He started out with them and he retained a few traces of their teachings or, rather, of their discoveries. But his personality went beyond all their theories, and expressed itself with a passion, a sensuousness and a love of art that none of the others ever equalled.

How often he used to say to me, as he said to many others:

"Theories? Study Nature, and you'll see how they all go to the devil. The open air? Yes, all right for your lungs. But for your work, the studio's the place. That's where you can see everything best."

Les Collettes, his home at Cagnes: the sun blood-red behind the Estérels, lighting up the whole garden; the olive trees twisted like deformed giants; the orange trees; the tiled balustrade; the roses, "red as a baby's bottom"; and Renoir's statues, with full, pouting lips and thick ankles, like the figures in his canvases. Gazing at it all, one might say to oneself:

"All of Despiau, all of Maillol, came out of that Renoir sculpture. But for that matter, the whole landscape is Renoir. Do you imagine that you are looking at Nature here? Not at all. Look again and you will see that it is Renoir who painted it all—even the song of the fountain. . . ."

* * * * *

The red sun behind the Estérels. . . . How often have I seen Renoir painting, seated in his wheel-chair, his brush bound to his hand between two fingers, but fastened to the back so that he could hold the brush perpendicular to the canvas, like a twig, his gaze fixed on his subject, murmuring to himself, as he took in the luminous landscape:

"*Merde*, but it's beautiful! *Merde*, but it's beautiful!"

I was moved to repeat the same words, and in the same tone, when I happened to come across an especially fine canvas of his many years later; and again subsequently, when I went to an exhibition of his work that Duveen put on in New York. A friend, who had joined me at that moment, added:

"It's as beautiful as Raphael. There is the same magic of jubilant colour, the same buoyant atmosphere. And the flower-like smiles of the Parisian girls are as *spirituel* as the smile of the Virgin."

"My wife and I are motoring over to see Renoir," one of his art-dealers said to me in Monte Carlo on a morning in 1918. "I'm taking him some sugar and a bottle of Napoleon brandy. Would you like to come along?"

"I would, indeed."

We went round the Baie des Anges in Nice, bathed in sunshine, crossed the Var, reached Cagnes, and, after mounting the steep hill, arrived at *Les Collettes*. It was just at the season when the anemones were coming into bloom, and they were everywhere, even along the side of the road; for Renoir had given orders for them not to be picked, as he wanted them left in their natural state.

The painter received us in the dining-room, which opened out on the terrace with its tiled balustrade. On the mantelpiece was the terra-cotta medallion he had made of his youngest son, Claude, otherwise known as "Coco", together with some of the glazed pottery he had done.

Renoir was huddled in his portable chair; but all at once his little grey-green eyes glanced sharply out of their hollow sockets and began to sparkle. The art-dealer was examining a picture of a nude, which had just been finished and placed on the floor against the wall. After admiring it ecstatically, he asked:

"Who posed for that?"

"The baker's wife," replied Renoir, with a chuckle. "She had a bottom—— Oh, forgive me," he added, though quite unembarrassed by the presence of his guest's wife. "But it's true. It was so beautiful! The whole town would have like to dance round it . . .!" He hesitated a moment, then said, "But you're staying for lunch, aren't you? I must let them know. Will you go out on to the terrace while we're waiting? There's a beautiful picture out there. It makes me happy just to look at it all day long."

The picture in question was the one I mentioned earlier: the sea beyond the olive trees, all shimmering blue and white; the Estérels, with their tops clearly outlined, as in Japanese screens, one behind the other, and ash-gold in hue.

"Monsieur Renoir," said the art-dealer, returning to the dining-room, "I am thinking of buying the Deudon Collection that is up for sale in Nice. There are six of your canvases, ranging from 1875 to 1880: *The Rose-garden*, *The Vargemont Road* and *The Sewing-woman*, among others; and also several Manets, Sisleys, and Monet's *Gare Saint-Lazare*."

"You can't do that! You must be mad!" exclaimed Renoir.

"Why?"

"Because I sold them for a hundred francs apiece. Think of the price you'd have to pay now just because they belong to my 'blue period', as they call it. Do you think the porcelains I once did for six francs a day, or the fans I decorated with Watteau's *Embarkation for Cythera* in my early days, or even the window-shades and signs I did, are worth more than what I am painting now? It's just a fashion. Don't buy those pictures. I'd rather sell you some of my others."

"I'd be only too delighted. . . . But, Monsieur Renoir, doesn't it give you a certain satisfaction to know that your canvases are selling for such high prices?"

"Not in the least—except to know that it annoys the academicians, whose work doesn't sell for much even at public auctions. The Hôtel Drouot, you know, is the barometer of art. When a work brings a high price at an auction sale, it proves that the artist has won the approval of the public."

"That reminds me of one of Picasso's remarks," retorted the art-dealer. " 'For a picture to be really beautiful,' he said, 'it has to be very expensive; otherwise, no one appreciates it.' "

"Yes, that's right."

"I've got one of Picasso's latest canvases with me here. Look——"

"Take that filth away!" cried Renoir.

"Why, you surprise me!" protested the art-dealer. "Corot turned down Manet when he was proposed for the Salon's selection committee. And Manet, in turn, didn't appreciate your talent. Now you are acting in the same way!"

"How you infuriate me! I am Renoir. I paint and I intend to remain Renoir. If I wanted to paint pictures like that one [and he pointed to Picasso's *Christmas Night*], I would paint them. But I paint for my own pleasure. Now, shut up, will you? Lunch is ready. I've told them to make us an omelette-au-rhum."

The huge omelette was brought in and placed, sizzling and golden, in front of us.

"Well, how do you like it?" Renoir asked the company.

"Excellent, Monsieur Renoir," said the art-dealer.

"What, only excellent, eh? So it should be. Why, I told them to put all your brandy in it!"

"Oh, Monsieur Renoir—in an omelette? Why, that's almost the same as if I were to hang your pictures in my—bathroom!"

"You are tiresome! Didn't you give me the brandy as a present? Haven't I the right to use it in any way I like, and no strings attached?"

After lunch we went out to Renoir's studio at the back of the garden, where the artist worked when he did not want to be disturbed by inquisitive people, whom he always received courteously enough, in spite of his notoriously grumpy manner. On the floor was a clutter of canvases, which glowed like precious stones. In the centre of the studio there was a couch, with a canopy over it, where he put his models; while in one corner of the room was a straw hat, with paper flowers on it, which he would place askew on the head of this or that model, first rumpling their hair before they posed.

Renoir was working on a *Judgement of Paris* at the time.

"What a beautiful, gay religion the Greeks had," he said. "Whenever their gods got bored, they could come down and have a good time on earth."

"Are you pleased to have been made a Commander of the *Légion d'Honneur*?" inquired the art-dealer's pretty wife.

"No. Only when I go anywhere, because then people know that I'm not an upstart. And," he added, with a wink, "it makes the others furious." But he said it without malice.

* * * * *

I remember one of Renoir's remarks about Monet to the effect that "Monet painted the 'passing hours' instead of painting each time 'an eternal hour' ".

I also recall how pure and pagan Renoir was in his attitude, for instance, towards the human body and flowers.

"Look at those anemones," he said on one occasion. "Don't you think they look like a woman's sex-organs?"

And again:

"I think I have at last found the exact 'place' for the breast. I was never quite sure before. . . ."

* * * * *

It was in August 1919 that Paul Rosenberg invited me out to his house at Vaucresson.

"Renoir is coming to lunch," he informed me. "I've also invited Jeanne Borel of the Opéra Comique, because he likes music."

Renoir came with his model Catherine Hessling, the young woman who later played Nana in the film of that name, which his son Jean produced. How thin the painter was: he looked as though he weighed nothing at all as he sat there in his chair. And his face was cadaverous under his cap, which he had pulled down over his ears. But his eyes were alert, and so was his mind.

Glancing at a large tree that was growing in the centre of the lawn, he remarked:

"Why, it's a regular monkey-tree! By the way, where is Vollard? Well, never mind: we can manage without him for one day. . . . He often comes in the morning. He puts on my socks for me."

At lunch Renoir did justice to the food, the wine and the champagne. He did not get drowsy until the singer, who had come especially in his honour, began to sing.

We drove him back to Paris. Rosenberg asked him if he wanted to go by way of Bougival, or to take the shorter road.

"Yes, by Bougival," answered Renoir.

When we came to Fournèse's, at the place where the artist had painted *Le Déjeuner des Canotiers* in 1881, Renoir ordered the chauffeur to stop and, in a sort of religious silence, he contemplated the landscape as though he were gazing at a picture of his youth. We could detect no sign of emotion on his face; yet what memories must have filled his heart! Suddenly, he said sharply,

"Let's go now!" And his reverie dissolved.

But he did not speak again till we arrived at the door of his studio in the Boulevard de Clichy, near the Cirque Medrano.

* * * * *

I was to see him once more, a short time before his death. It was at Cagnes again, at the beginning of winter. On my arrival I was told that he was working in his studio at the back of the house on a *Baigneuses* (now in the Louvre). I decided to wait for him in the garden. I could imagine him sitting at the easel he had had specially made so that the canvas could be raised or lowered or moved from side to side at will; this enabled the artist, who could not move about himself, to reach any part of the picture he wanted to work on. Presently I caught sight of him through the trees being carried along in his portable chair, his long hooded cloak hanging almost to the ground. The sun was setting in a red ball, spreading a mellow glow over the whole countryside. Renoir beckoned to me.

"I'm going for a little walk," he said, as I came up to him. "Come and walk along beside me."

He was lifted up high so that he could see the flowers, and he looked as though he had been hoisted on to a shield, making a sombre silhouette against the sky. As he went by, the gardeners and everyone else he passed all lifted their caps and greeted him respectfully, saying,

"Good evening, Monsieur Renoir."

If only he could have painted the scene, what a companion-piece it would have made to Courbet's *Good Morning, Monsieur Courbet!*

Matisse: Self-portrait

In the Claws of the Fauves

MATISSE

I WENT TO SEE Matisse on the advice of my friend Vignier. It was in the days before he had become the most celebrated of the Fauves, and at that time he was living on the Quai St. Michel, not far from the bookshop belonging to Vanier, where Verlaine used to buy his books. It was an old building, with staircases all over the place. Marquet, Flandrin and Marval also had studios there, looking out over the roofs towards the Préfecture, with Notre-Dame and the wonderful vista of the Seine nearby.

As he opened the door, the artist at first looked at me uneasily, but he motioned me to come in, examining me furtively all the while. He already had a few wrinkles on his forehead, which gave him a worried expression, and his gaze was critical behind his glasses. He had a short nose, somewhat like Zola's, and his fleshy lips were tightly compressed in the midst of his beard.

"This is what I'm working on now," he said, as he brought out a canvas to show me. It was a view of one of the bridges over the Seine, with the water leaden and smooth.

"What beautiful pigment," I said.

"Yes, the pigment must be beautiful," he replied; "that's really essential. The colours must harmonise. But when they are violent and luminous it is a difficult and delicate matter. I have to experiment for a long time, often for a very long time."

And that was all there was to my first interview with Matisse.

That same year I met him again, this time on the terrace of a café in the Place St. Michel. He was sketching a scene on the quayside with a short, thick pencil, making careful little strokes without any corrections—but only after studying the subject thoroughly before tracing a single line.

I got to know him better through the Russian Ballet many years later. Matisse had by then become the leader of the Fauves,[1] who had revolted against the Impressionists' small touches of harmonious colour by using large, violently coloured surfaces. Later on, the Cubists or Constructors revolted in their turn by introducing a third dimension into their works, first breaking down the pictorial volumes, then making a new synthesis of these fragments. Matisse was influenced by all these to the point where he was producing canvases with drawing that was almost schematic.

Meanwhile, Serge Diaghilev, the impresario of the Russian Ballet, had commissioned Matisse to do the settings for Stravinsky's *Rossignol*, and had persuaded him to go to London, where the première was to take place, to execute them, as Matisse did not want anyone else to enlarge them from his maquettes.

Diaghilev had rented a place as big as a barn on the eighth floor of a building in London's theatre district, and the only way you could get to it was by climbing an interminably long, narrow ladder, holding on to a side-rail with one hand and carrying a lighted taper in the other. When I went to see the painter there, he asked me for some practical advice on several points.

"I've never done stage scenery before," he explained.

I told him what I knew about it, and advised him to leave a fraction of an inch of bare canvas between each colour because, in the glare of the footlights, every detail shows up as clearly as a miniature under a magnifying-glass, even when seen from the gallery.

"I'm planning to have a curtain as white as porcelain," said Matisse. "For it's to be a Chinese curtain, after all, isn't it? There will be as few lines as possible.[2] As for the décors, those Russians expect something violent, don't they? Well, they're not going to

[1] Matisse, Marquet, Rouault, Desvallières, Derain, Vlaminck, Othon Friesz, Van Dongen, Puy, Rouveyre, de Waroquier, Crotti, Camoin, and Charles Guérin.

[2] Matisse used the same technique again when he did the decorations for the well-known Chapel of the Rosary at Vence.

get it. I'm going to teach them the proper proportion of colour according to French tradition: pure white, pale pink, light blue. And they can take it or leave it."

One evening, while we were working, a huge fire broke out in a neighbouring loft and lit up the whole studio. Matisse, who was not at all alarmed by the sparks flying in our direction, suddenly exclaimed:

"Look how the pink reflections turn to orange against my blue. That's a good idea: I'm going to make the costumes pink."

I often went for long walks with Matisse while we were in London. Sometimes we went to the National Gallery together. On either side of the main staircase, just inside the entrance, there used to be two large canvases, one by Whistler and the other Turner's *Fighting Téméraire*.

"I can't stand Whistler," said Matisse. "But Turner, yes: the quality of his pigment is beautiful. In painting, that is everything, you see. No matter what the subject and the drawing are like, if your pigment, your material, is beautiful—as beautiful as enamel, for instance—you look at it with pleasure, and it is good."

One night, when we had strayed quite far in the London drizzle, Matisse said to me:

"Do you understand the Cubists? I must say I can't make head or tail of them."

He told me of an incident that occurred when Diaghilev was directing a rehearsal of *Parade* by Erik Satie and Jean Cocteau, for which Picasso had done the settings, and he asked the choreographer,

" 'When that little ballerina skips and then falls down and kicks her legs in the air, what is that supposed to mean?'

" 'Why, it's quite simple,' said Diaghilev, shocked. 'That's the *Titanic* disaster.'

"No," repeated Matisse, "I must say I can't make head or tail of them——"

We were practically lost in the downpour, and, holding the umbrella well over us, I finished the sentence for him,

"——any more than certain people can understand why you give your figures hands three times their natural size, and asymmetrical eyes and——"

"Oh, but that's the way I feel them," he retorted. But then, as he had a sense of humour, instead of explaining his theories of balance or his deliberate distortion of academic forms, he went on:

"It is true that if I ever met the kind of woman I paint coming along the street, I should probably have a fit." And he chuckled in his beard, his eyes twinkling behind his glasses.

* * * * *

But it was in his studio in Nice that I got to know him really well. Ah, Nice, when it is out of season, with the streets almost empty; the sea nearly black, so intense is its blue; and the view from Matisse's apartment in the Place Charles-Félix, overlooking the Old Market, the beach and the sea!

The apartment was behind the Ponchettes gallery, near the Romanesque church of Saint-Suaire, on an upper floor of a handsome old building in the Italian style: square, ochre-coloured and with a fine pediment. His door was at the top landing of a wide flight of stone stairs, with frescoes painted on the walls on either side. A card stuck over the bell read: "M. Henri Matisse: Ring twice".

You entered by a hall, at the end of which was a window with a view of the sea. On the right was a room with two windows hung with net curtains. Between the windows stood a little dressing-table with white lacquered panels and an oval mirror. On the mantel was a replica of Michelangelo's *Slave*, at whose feet were such assorted objects as oranges, a bird cage and a gramophone with a pink flower-shaped horn, which Matisse used to play while he worked.

The walls were covered with ordinary paper with a commonplace flower design on it. On the floor were an Arab tabouret and several packing-cases, while close by stood his famous screens with their cut-out paper patterns, Arab style, which he reproduced so often in his pictures. Above them, extending across the room, was stretched a wire, on which hung an oil-lamp with a makeshift shade.

Behind a screen one of his models was cleaning his brushes with kitchen soap. On the far side of the room a violin hung on the wall between two of his latest canvases, both of them still-lifes.

The first day I went to see him there, Matisse was painting by one of the windows. He was wearing a raw-silk shirt and he had on his gold-rimmed glasses. Presently he went over to the wall and began pinning up some bits of cloth which, when they caught the sunlight, became like brilliant jewels of colour.

"So that's your wonderful striped material?" I said.

"The sunlight cleans everything," he replied, and pointed out of the window towards the dusty city, sparkling under the sun. "Come along. Let's go and have some lunch."

Just as he opened the door, he found himself face to face with two Germans.

"Monsieur Matisse?"

"Yes."

"You remember me, don't you? I'm the director of the —— Gallery."

"Yes. But I have nothing for you."

"We only want to buy two canvases—anything you have on hand."

"I have nothing on hand just now."

"Couldn't you let us see——"

"I have nothing for the moment."

"May we come back later, then?"

"I have nothing," he answered them quietly but firmly.

Most days Matisse went out to lunch at Camus's, a local restaurant in a dark little street in the Old Town, between the Municipal Casino and the sea. A table was always reserved for him.

"Why didn't you want to sell anything to those two fellows?" I asked, as we sat down.

"They would certainly have given me my price," he said.

"Well, then? Your apartment is full of canvases, after all."

"Yes, but it's not a good time. Those two rascals will come back, don't worry. I shall see them again soon enough."

The proprietor of the restaurant brought us a *salade niçoise*, in which the tomatoes gleamed and the green peppers looked dark against the light green of the lettuce, which was dotted with black olives.

"Now, that is really beautiful," declared Matisse, who seemed more interested in gazing at the dish than in eating it.

"Is it true, Matisse, that you keep your canvases in a safe in one of the banks here?"

"Certainly. Why not? They're my securities."

"Securities that will go up in value. . . ."

"That's why a safe in a bank is just the place for them. It is the best protection for them, too. Whenever I go away, or even when I'm here, my canvases are safe from any accident that might happen in the house, not to speak of fire or theft. Waiter, bring us our coffee quickly. It is five minutes to, and I've got a model coming at two o'clock. I want to get back on time."

He was prompted by an old habit of his, inherited from the days when a model was expensive for him. Or perhaps it was just self-discipline.

We quickly climbed the two long flights of stairs. Matisse set out the Arab tabouret and arranged the materials on the divan.

"Do you see that large mirror over there? I like to use it to check on the model from time to time."

The bell rang. It was an old woman with a note: the model was ill and couldn't come. Matisse did not seem very put out.

I had begun to do a drawing of him in my sketch-book, whereupon he said,

"Let me have a sheet, will you?"

"Here's another pad," I said. And he set to work to do a picture of me.

We went out on to the balcony to work. The sun dusted with light the few palm trees along the water-front where the sea glittered brightly.

I can't remember what brought up the subject of Lautrec in our conversation, but I happened to mention the many tracings the latter had done for some of his pictures.

"Have you seen the collection of them in the museum at Albi?" I asked Matisse. "For the poster he did of Jane Avril, and for his woman clown, he made at least twenty tracings before he was able to get the correct angle for the spread of the legs."

"Do you think I don't carefully draw the paper flowers in my backgrounds dozens of times beforehand?" demanded Matisse, peering at me over his glasses.

"Even those you do in a 'z' or a cross, with a couple of brushstrokes?"

Matisse by the Author

"Yes, even those I do with just two brush-strokes. But after I have drawn them in detail twenty or thirty times, I get the knack of it automatically in my hand, and then I can do them exactly, with just two strokes. Look here, for instance——"

He brought out a dozen heavy albums of fine vellum paper. Turning the pages slowly, he showed me hundreds and hundreds

The Author by Matisse

of drawings done in absolutely pure lines, without a single re-touching.

"If it weren't in the safe at the bank, I would show you a canvas, *Europa and the Bull*, on which I have worked for three years, and I shall probably have to work on it for quite a while longer. Some people imagine that you can turn out canvases like mass-produced cars. For that picture alone I have already made three thousand sketches—yes, three thousand. I often do them while my model is resting."

The doorbell rang again.

"Don't bother," said Matisse. "I'm not at home—unless that's the house-painter. I've taken the apartment upstairs and I'm joining it on to this one."

It was the house-painter. He came in with his ladder over his shoulder.

"Look out for my pictures!" Matisse warned him. Then, turning to me, he went on, "Now, as I shan't be able to work any more, I'm going to do a larger picture of you."

He took up one of his albums and began drawing with his fountain-pen. At that moment the house-painter came back through the room with his ladder and jogged Matisse's elbow. The result was a large blot on my cheek in the drawing.

"Oh!" I exclaimed, in dismay.

"It doesn't matter," said Matisse. "It will have to stay that way now. Blame it on Fate." And he went on with his drawing.

ROUAULT

If it wouldn't be accurate to call Rouault taciturn, he is certainly not loquacious.

To those who asked him why, after having begun his career in a Raphaelesque style, he portrayed all judges as monsters, and almost all women as loathsome creatures, with loose, bluish flesh, like creatures straight from Hell, he could hardly have replied, as Matisse did,

"Because I see them as they are."

He went out to lunch with me one day at the time he was working on the stage-sets for *The Prodigal Son.*

How well I recall the terrace of the Sporting Club, which was then situated in the Champs Elysées, and the quiet, self-effacing man who was with me.

He told me many of the things I already knew about him: namely, that he had been a glass-worker and painter of stained-glass windows; that that profession had influenced his colour far more than Gustave Moreau's school had done; and that he had not been able to give up the "leading", which separated his colours and brought out their values. He said, moreover, that the rather affected Moreau (almost all of whose "pupils"—Matisse, Desvallières, Marquet, Maurice Denis and Rouveyre—became Fauves)—was in fact extremely liberal-minded, and did not expect those who studied under him to paint as he did.

"I agreed to do these décors," he explained, "because I felt that

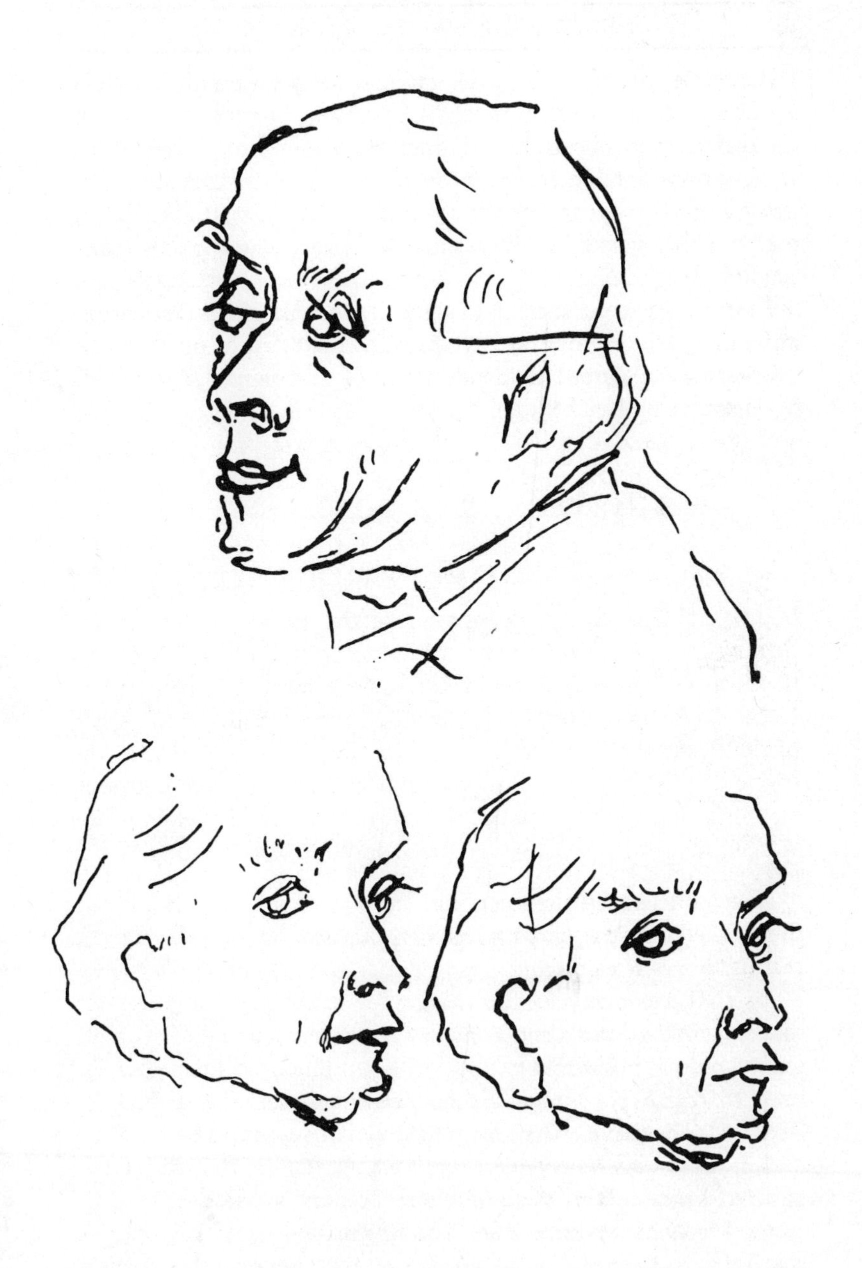

I should be painting immense stained-glass windows. The light would be caught in them instead of passing through. But that is the difference between stained-glass and stage-settings, and I had to give considerable study to the problem. And this time I'm going to have to work quickly, feverishly. It is something new for me, as I often take five years to paint a canvas, scraping it out, doing it over again. . . ."

Rouault was good enough to allow me to make the little sketches of him reproduced in these pages; and as I felt that he might find it awkward if we continued to talk of this or that painter, I respected his discretion. But I regret it now.

THIRTEEN, RUE BONAPARTE: SEGONZAC

Before the First World War, I lived for some years in a building at No. 13 rue Bonaparte, on the corner of the rue des Beaux Arts, just opposite the charming cour Gaillon. From my windows on one side I could see, lower down, the room where Oscar Wilde had died; and on the other, the magnificent courtyard of the Beaux Arts, where, at the beginning of June each year, the horde of students from the *Quat'z' Arts* ball would mill around riotously in the early hours of the morning before dispersing. We were always awakened by their band and their bawdy songs:

On dit, bien souvent, au Village
Qu'un casque, ça n'sert à rien du tout
Rien du tout
Ça sert à donner du courage
A ceux qui n'en ont pas du tout
Pas du tout
De loin, ça prend des airs fanta-ouasques
Et chacun crie en les voyant
En les voyant
Ah! Qu'ils sont beaux avec leurs ca-ousaques
Ils ont vraiment l'air épatant-tant-tant-tant. . . .

Zim balaboum la lai-re
Zim balaboum lalaire

Zim la boum la boum lala
Zim la boum
Zim lala
Lalala . . .

On dit, bien souvent, à l'École
Qu'une femm', ça sert à rien du tout
Rien du tout
Ça sert à donner la v . . .
A ceux qui ne l'ont pas du tout
Pas du tout
De loin, ça prend des airs bona-ouasques!

A chorus of savage yells would follow, and suddenly, stripping off their tinselled finery, their Roman togas, their Chaldean robes and all the rest, two thousand harum-scarums would rush forward, climb the iron fence and dance about madly in the courtyard. The women—mostly models—who were practically naked or else daubed with paint, then took the fountain by storm, and fought for the privilege of sitting on the jet of water spouting from it.

Many of the crowd swarmed into the café owned by Père Establet, a rough-and-ready Provençal, who brought out bottles of Tavel and Châteauneuf-du-Pape. The bench at the back was reserved for the third-year students, the one in the centre for the second-year ones, and the tables set with napkins for members of the *Institut*.

The house at No. 13 was kept by old Mère Michon, whose two pretty daughters were friends of ours. Hanging on the wall of her room just inside the entrance could be seen the resplendent uniform of one of the Horse Guards of the Republic, which had belonged to a relative of the good woman, who so often came to the aid of the poorer students. The landlord was in his own way a man of letters, a Parisian and a collector of beautiful tapestry cartoons.

In the same building, in which the poet Paul Géraldy had written *Toi et Moi*, lived two painters who were in complete opposition to the Beaux Arts. One was Dunoyer de Segonzac and the other was Derain.

Segonzac—what clear eyes he had!—counted among his visitors such artists as Luc Albert Moreau, Dufresne, de la Fresnaye,

Mare, Boussingault and La Patellière. All of them, being of peasant stock, talked with each other in the strong peasant dialect of the French countryside.

An American newspaper printed a friendly, but far too American, article on Segonzac, in which it was stated that the painter always drank eight bottles of red wine before starting work.

It is true that Segonzac and his friends often foregathered round a bottle or two of good French wine. Like the peasant accent they were so fond of, it was their way of rebelling both against the nouveau-riche mentality of the time, and against its cosmopolitanism. The spirit and art of the group were, above all, essentially French.

* * * * *

Segonzac had great influence on the younger painters because, having escaped from the *ateliers* of Luc-Olivier Merson and Jean-Paul Laurens, he had skirted the Cubists, though taking note of what they had to teach, and had then returned to the great tradition of Courbet. Yet all this did not prevent his following the more important Parisian trends, and he produced, in consequence, his admirable series of studies of Isadora Duncan and Nijinsky, his portraits of Colette and Thérèse Dorny, and the illustrations for Dorgelès' *Croix de Bois* and an edition of the *Georgics*.

In his engravings, which he executed with such loving care, Segonzac was completely honest. He would not rub out his provisional lines because they made the movement all the more vivid.

Once Forain, who was slightly jealous of him, remarked spitefully,

"Yes, since he draws hundreds of lines, one of them is bound to be right."

A friend of Segonzac's, whom I know well, reproved Forain with the rejoinder,

"You make hundreds of lines, too, before you get the right one, but you're so clever you rub out the others."

* * * * *

All at once Segonzac got his reward, and a rather dangerous reward at that; for one of his still-lifes, a beautiful golden-brown loaf of bread on a table, fetched an unheard-of price at the time:

seventy-four thousand francs. Immediately all those who owned Segonzacs, collectors as well as dealers, began to "dream", as they say in the art world, and asked such fantastic prices for his work that for a short time no one could be found to buy his paintings.

Anyone else perhaps would have gone under during the lull. But there was nothing bogus about his kind of painting. The demand for it soon began again, and the artist was deluged with orders.

Being of solid peasant stock, Segonzac was not in the slightest thrown off balance by all this. Quite the contrary. He packed up his easel, and set off for Provence to bask in the sun so loved by Cézanne and Monticelli.

Segonzac was no more dazed by the sun than he had been by the rise in prices for his work; but he was sufficiently captivated by the Côte d'Azur to buy a villa and settle down there.

He did not give up his technique of using umber tones; he put more blue into his compositions and made his nudes more sensuous. He transmuted the richness of nature into a still finer richness, in which the quality of pigment counted for more than wealth of colour. He mastered the problem of light rather than let himself be enslaved by it, as so many other painters had done, even the greatest.

And those same Americans who had wanted to play up the picturesque side of his life, and who in 1933 gave him the Carnegie Award for his *Winter in Provence*, would be surprised, if they met André Dunoyer de Segonzac, to find that he is an amiable, reserved gentleman, whose eyes are as blue as the skies in his landscapes, a trifle distrustful and ironic, perhaps, yet smiling and friendly towards those who deserve and win his confidence. They would find in him the man who, with a pen as exact and incisive as his etching-needle, wrote the following:

"One of the most important elements in a work of art is its balance. Its balance is what gives a work its homogeneity, its unity and strength. It is the proof of having 'mastered the subject'; of being able to give each thing its proper importance. That holds true for architecture, for painting, for sculpture, for all the arts. It is the 'balance' of Greek sculpture that strikes us first of all, and enables us to take it in instantly and entirely; and it is what makes it superior to decadent works. It is from this 'balance' that we get a sense of rhythm and harmony, and the complete satisfaction that certain works of art convey."

Dunoyer de Segonzac might have written those words about himself.

DERAIN

And now for Derain. Bulky and impassive in appearance, like the trees he painted, and like them, arched a little, and bowed.

He always dressed in grey and wore a bowler hat. He had a prominent nose, and eyes that had a piercing, all-enveloping gaze. His chin was long and determined.

"I can't understand the kind of painting he does," said our concierge, Mère Michon, "but they say it's good. And he seems a respectable sort of man."

Derain had, in fact, already become taciturn and introspective. It was the period when he was doing his pictures of cathedral-like forests.

But he was also fond of the female face. Aline, his wife, was a pretty brunette, with firm flesh and a delicate profile, and she only needed a sprig of myrtle in her hair to turn her into a pure Corot.

He must have loved Corot very much.

One day, when someone asked me what I thought of Derain, I replied, "He is Corot's natural son; but his son, nevertheless." And Derain, with whom I had not exchanged three words in ten years, overhearing this remark, came up to me and shook my hand, nodding his approval.

He was always quick with a rejoinder. Modigliani, being a little drunk one day, had gone to see Derain, and had begun to make a nuisance of himself. Derain was busy working; but, as he liked Modi, he didn't want to send him away. Derain was wearing a sailor's cap at the time, and to annoy him Modi remarked,

"I see you're our pilot now."

"Don't talk to the pilot," advised Derain, pointing to the words written on the ribbon of his cap.

Modigliani drew himself up, and retorted as he went out of the door,

"You manufacturer of masterpieces!"

I had occasion to meet him more often during the great days of the Russian Ballet, after I had moved away from the building we had both been living in. Not only had he become interested, like everyone else, in that great explosion of art, but he had, along with Picasso, Matisse, Braque and many others, become one of its most brilliant exponents. And his enthusiasm was such that he himself went to the costumiers' to choose materials, and even helped with the fittings in the theatre workrooms.

One evening, worn out, probably, by all the social fuss made of him, he invited me to go with him to a strange little eating-place in Montmartre, where one could get anchovies, Norwegian herrings, roll-mops, and other salted dishes, as well as Danzig eau-de-vie, flecked with gold.

"I love this kind of food," he said, as he savoured each dish slowly. And those were about the only words he uttered for a long while. But at one moment he held up a little iridescent fish between thumb and forefinger and, turning it about in the light, glanced at me to see if I was appreciating its delicate colours. Then he put the whole fish in his mouth, skinning it with his teeth as a rough young sailor would have done, and swallowed it down.

VLAMINCK
ROBERT DELAUNAY

While the Fauvist movement was growing, interesting developments surprised the public: other experimenters besides the first Cubists were trying to give still greater intensity to colour.

At one painters' dinner I went to at the time I encountered a tall young man, with flushed face and clear eyes, who kept staring at me in an odd way.

"What's the matter?" I finally asked him.

"I'd like to know you," he said familiarly, as if we had been students at the Beaux Arts together, or had met at Establet's place. From his voice and manner, I couldn't at first tell whether he was hostile or friendly.

"That's Robert Delaunay," said my neighbour, the water-colourist, Degaillaix, who was later to do the beautiful panels for the *Normandie*. "He's the man who 'dislocated' the Eiffel Tower. He's a kind of acrobat, himself; a Simultanist, an Orphist, but especially a Dynamist. And what a colourist! What an inventor!"

"Very well," I said, addressing the young man again. "I'd be glad to have a talk with you later, when the dessert is served."

In due course he came to find me, his pipe in one hand and a dark-haired young woman in the other—or that was the impression he gave, so large and powerful were his hands.

"I should like to know you," he informed me, "because you seem so alive. I watched you while you were talking, I saw your eyes light up. You didn't argue: you just fought. This is my wife Sonia; she's Russian by birth but French by nature. She does designs and creates new shades for textiles. If you ever go to Rodier's, you will see some of them there. I sell ideas."

"Are you a painter?"

"A painter? What is a painter, if he hasn't got ideas? He's a dauber, a photographer, a man who trots around a box of paints and wears corduroy trousers. Now, I sell ideas. I've just come back from America. Over there I sold one a day. Ideas not only for painting, but for anything and everything. They used them in any way they wanted to: for good or for bad, for paints or for chocolate, for dreams or for dollars. What difference did it make to me? The important thing for me is to produce new things. Some of them get lost; that's the law of life. Out of the millions of eggs a fish lays, only a few hundred escape the sharks, the ocean currents or their own mother. But some of them hatch out. I produce ideas the same way. And since I need money, I sell them.

"Now I'll say good-bye, because Sonia is tired and we live some distance away. But we'll see you again. Did you know that I was a gunner with your brother during the War? I hope to see you again soon."

We have seen each other off and on, here and there, for the last thirty years. He is always in a hurry, running like a flame and just as restless; looking after his wife's affairs as well as his own; and blowing down his pipe as if he was trying to put it out. His *Eiffel Tower* now hangs in the entrance-hall of the Paris Museum of Modern Art.

It was at that same banquet that I made Vlaminck's acquaintance. We became friends almost at once. With his light checked suit and his large sensitive face, he seemed rather precious, in spite of his robust figure, resembling a sort of Oscar Wilde, but only in that poet's healthy Anglo-Saxon aspect. And when I told him so, he replied:

"I prefer that to being compared eternally to a racing cyclist, even though I was one, for my own amusement, when I was young. People don't understand anything. It's the same with my pictures. They imagine that I paint a canvas as if it were a photo, whereas, in fact, before I set up my easel anywhere, I study my landscape sometimes for a month in order to get a good impression of it in my mind, which is important, and to take it in to the last detail, which is important, too. Then, when I've got the 'feel' of it in every way, I set to work. And then something else begins . . ."

OTHON FRIESZ

Friesz: how well he represents three different periods in painting! Seemingly so calm, with his rugged old Norman's face, and his Norman origin which he defends so ferociously: it is the only subject on which he is ever heated.

"Pure Norman; and my name, Othon, is pure Norman. Friesz

is, too. Norwegian? You're joking. A Norman from 'way back': the son of Normans; grandson of one of the captains of the Trans-Atlantic Company's first big ships, the *Eugène Pierre* and *Ville de Paris*. It was my grandmother—who was a La Chenez-Eudes—who gave me my Christian name. And my painting, too, is entirely in the French tradition: Impressionist in 1901; Fauve in 1905; and then a return to composition in 1908. I may have a corsair's mug, but I'm more Deauville than the Maharajah of Kapurthala or the Dolly Sisters."

We were talking together in the countryside near Honfleur, where the sky is often threatening, yet clear; he paints that kind of sky as delightfully as those of the Midi, where he has a villa, *Les Jarres*, near Toulon.

"Northern skies," the Scandinavian painter Diricks once remarked to me, "and Northern waters are much more transparent than those of the tropics."

Friesz had also been in the East, in Tunisia and all over North Africa. But he had come back to his native soil and sky.

"We feel perhaps a deeper, more instinctive emotion at home," he said.

When in Paris, Friesz lives in a studio at the back of a garden in the quiet rue Notre-Dame-des-Champs, which is full of convents and roomy old houses. The visitor is amused or interested by the terracotta busts and pieces of majolica, which catch his eye as he approaches the artist's studio. Once inside, he immediately notices that Friesz has unostentatiously hung on his walls examples of each of his different periods, which, to him, are very moving souvenirs.

I went to call on him there to announce the good news that he had been made a Commander of the *Légion d'Honneur*. I had just come from a talk with the Minister who, only the evening before, had bought, unknown to Friesz, one of the painter's finest canvases. Unfortunately, Friesz was out of town at the time. But as a motor ride of three hours did not seem too unpleasant, especially for the purpose of delivering such good news to a friend, I decided to go to Honfleur at once.

Mais aux frais matins de l'Hellade
Parfumés d'amande et de fleurs

Si je préfère la balade
De la rude route d'Honfleur.

Dufy, dessous ses blancs pommiers
Balance son fauteuil rustique
Sur le port, avec les pompiers
Friesz fait de la gymnastique . . .

"If Monsieur Friesz hasn't gone up to the Côte-de-Grâce," they told me at the *Cheval Blanc*, "he should be out there on the jetty."

And there indeed he was, standing foursquare to the wind, with a pea-green jacket on and a mauve-coloured hat—yes, mauve—gazing at the beautiful line of the hills of Le Havre, blue beyond the estuary.

I gave him the news of his honour, and then we started reminiscing together.

"I ran into Dufy yesterday," he told me. "What memories he brought up! He recalled how one day, when we were living in Montmartre and hadn't enough to eat, he came up to me, flushed with excitement.

" 'I've found a dealer at last!' he said. 'I'm going to buy a car and go on a cruise to India. Come along, and I'll introduce you.'

"The dealer, who had only a tiny box of a shop, was a little woman—and by 'little woman' I mean small in size—called Berthe Weill. She had prints by Willette and Balluriau hanging from clothes pegs on a wire stretched across the room, and along with them a resplendent water-colour by Dufy.

"Dufy introduced us to her, and it wasn't long before we were all sharing the honours of the wire: Marquet, Girieud, Balluriau, Vlaminck, Utrillo, Pascin, Picasso, Van Dongen, Jacqueline Marval.

"The collectors began to buy, and among them Marcel Sembat, the husband of the painter Agutte, Denys Cochin, Olivier Saincère and Albert Sarraut.

"How we had to fight at times to get an advance! One night Picasso came in and threw his *navaja* [1] down on the table; and poor

[1] A long Spanish knife. [*Trans. note.*]

Berthe tried to offer it to me next day as payment for one of my landscapes.

" 'I can't eat wood,' I told her; 'I'm not a sword-swallower, even of Spanish swords. I want money!'

"Without a word little Weill turned round, pulled up her skirt, took a note out of her stocking, and handed it to me."

Among Berthe Weill's customers there was a man called Druet, who owned a café on the corner of the Place de l'Alma and the Avenue Marceau. In matters of art, this amazing collector was advised by one of his customers, with whom he played chess every evening. The customer's name was Rodin—none other than the great sculptor himself.

When Rodin was turned down by the Salon in 1910, Druet said to him:

"What would you say to exhibiting your work in a tent, if I put one up for you in the Cours-la-Reine? I'll do my best to get permission from the City Council, and we'll ask a franc a head as entrance fee."

Rodin agreed to the plan, and his exhibition caused an immense sensation all over the world.

"It was in that same place," resumed Friesz, "that the Independents' show was held, but our group had to use lots of publicity to attract the public. And the entire exhibition was bought up by Druet on the advice of Rodin.

"Then Rodin said to him, 'Why don't you open a gallery yourself? There are plenty of galleries for the old hack painters, but none for the younger men. Only a Norman like you could compete with a Bernheim.' "

Druet gave up his café. And, as he dabbled in photography as well as paintings, he prudently set up a photographic studio next to his gallery, in order to have something to fall back on. The premises were near the gallery Paul Guillaume was to direct several years later.

Strangely enough, it was the photographic studio that failed, and the gallery that prospered. From the Faubourg St.-Honoré Druet moved to the rue Royale, which was more central, and there he showed, in groups, the work of most of the younger painters, ranging from Maurice Denis to Flandrin, and Desvallières to Gauguin.

Friesz was given a place of honour among them; and Druet introduced a young woman-painter named Jacqueline Marval, whose fresh colours were the delight of all Paris.

Druet took on a young art-director, the writer Alfred Athis, the husband of Marthe Mellot and brother of Thadée Natanson, just as the Bernheim-Jeunes had engaged in an advisory capacity—and it was a good precedent—the scholarly and sensitive Félix Fénéon, of whom Lautrec had often made sketches.

One of the first to break away from Impressionism, Friesz had gone on developing on his own. And many of the younger painters followed him. Friesz weaned them of the theory of "the value of values", and taught them the law of contrasts. He advised them against "the moment" in painting, which, he claimed, belonged to photography.

Of the many conversations I had with him, the one that impressed me most, I think, was on the subject of Monet. But let me repeat his words. When I asked Friesz if he had been a pupil of Bonnat's at the Beaux Arts, he replied:

"Yes. But Bonnat hardly ever bothered about us. Luckily, his teachings didn't amount to much. He was a man of few words; as a rule, all he would say was: 'This is good. That is bad. That sketch is better than the last one you did.' No, he never bothered about us—except when he discreetly put a hundred-franc note into the hand of one or other of us, whom he knew to be hard up.

"Like many other students, when I'd had enough of the childish little dodges at the École, such as putting big rocks in the foreground and little blue landscapes in the background, to give a sense of distance, I began to suspect that, in spite of appearances, painting must be more difficult than that. . . . We were in the midst of Impressionism, the very Impressionism which, at that time, represented revolt, and against which our whole generation has since rebelled. I myself realised the weakness of Impressionism one day after seeing in an exhibition twelve paintings by Claude Monet of the same landscape, each done at a different time of day. I was overcome with admiration until I happened to see one of them by itself. The twelve together had seemed to complement each other, and were very satisfying. But the one by itself struck me as being 'lost', incomplete, 'hanging in space', as it were. Then I understood all that Cézanne's work teaches us—a single picture of his always appears well established, definite, self-sufficient and sufficient in what it represents. And so all of us—Derain, Matisse, Rouault, Braque, Vlaminck, Picasso—made an effort to get away from Impressionism, which had influenced even music and poetry. Of course, we immediately went to the other extreme—that is to say, the use of violent tones and aggressive pictorial orchestrations: what is called 'fauvism'. Then each of us began to develop his own personality. Being French, I returned by new paths to the French tradition, though following my own inspiration and developing along the lines of the discoveries I had made. I think that the most important law is the observation of contrasts, and not of values—another of those phrases derived from the futilities of the École. Also, one must get rid of the accidental. And so, what I am painting now . . ."

Instinctively, I glanced towards his easel and palette.

"No," said Friesz; "I'm painting in my head at the moment. I steep myself in my subject; I make a choice of typical details; I note the geometric lines of construction, the light, the colours. When I feel saturated with them, full of them, seething with them, then they must come out. I stand in front of my canvas here at home. Note that I said in front of my canvas, and not in front of the subject. Then only what is essential comes out, and I am able to 'realise' a work that is at once an abstraction and yet a complete whole. Yes, I have come to the conclusion that a painter should not try to seize or reproduce the impression of a given moment; but, on the contrary, when he is realising a landscape or even a face, he should do them in recollection, timelessly, as they will always appear. The exception is never eternal."

RAOUL DUFY

Raoul Dufy was also a Norman, and of the same period as Friesz. But Dufy's was a different kind of painting—French, in the style of the great decorative painters, but full of innovations.

"No, I don't divide the sea into two colours; nor my canvas, either. I try to put light in places where people don't usually put it. If one part of the English Channel is indigo and another part old Bordeaux red, it is simply because of the contrasts of light. In fact, that is what the sea is like. I emphasise the contrasts; the important thing is that the relations between them should be right,

and in harmony. This Norman countryside, which Monet loved so much, is more colourful than Gauguin's islands."

We were talking together in the villa where Dufy was living at the time, on the coast between Deauville and Honfleur, overlooking the beach. Seen from that height, the sea was indeed a wonderful sight. The waves looked as though they had been edged with white lace by the women sitting in their deck-chairs along the shore.

Dufy had settled there in order to finish the series he was doing on Honfleur and Deauville: the white sails of the regattas against the blue skies of France; the sea leaving a white tracery along the sides of the estuary; and the "Races", the aesthetic aspects of which he had brought into vogue again—a risky thing to do, after Degas and Lautrec. But Dufy overturned all the old conceptions, restored the nobility of lines by recreating them, and, instead of superimposing light on colour, he coloured the light.

"I have just discovered a new medium—the Maroger—which makes it possible to paint as the old masters did, the real old masters, the Van Eycks. And I shall use it when I start work on the largest panel that has ever been done: a *History of Science.* The Government have commissioned it, and it will have four hundred figures!"

I saw him working on the composition of that astonishing fresco, which was well over a hundred and fifty feet long. With the help of documents, Dufy first got together the "heads" of the different personages, and made notes for their clothing; then he planned various groups of scientists, with their instruments in front of them, and arranged them around a central motif in poses appropriate to their characters. And when he finally began the actual painting, he executed the panel in sections, without enlarging it by squaring up and transferring. Having his values already in his head, he worked with incredible speed, and produced that wonderful, luminous painting, which was one of the marvels of the 1937 Exhibition.

Dufy was already represented in art galleries all over the world; but all at once he won universal acclaim. I know of few artists whose rise to fame was so rapid.

In New York, Raoul Dufy's water-colours and little narrow canvases were worth a hundred dollars in 1940. When I returned there in 1945, they were fetching anything from twelve to fifteen hundred dollars; and some of them are worth double that today.

Dufy personally witnessed this rise in prices when he went to America for treatment for his rheumatism. All the principal galleries in New York—Rosenberg, Knoedler, Durand-Ruel in 57th Street, and Wildenstein in 69th Street—seemed to be gay with the canvases of Raoul Dufy. And his red and ochre horses could be seen prancing in all their windows.

* * * * *

I saw Dufy again at his last retrospective exhibition at Carré's. He was in his wheel-chair; his face was a trifle fatter, and his eyes were clear and bright. And his gestures, as well as the apparent ease of his painting, were those of a *grand seigneur*. His curly blond hair still covered his high forehead, and his smile was frank and open.

There were a good many of his earlier canvases in the show, and Dufy was pleased about that.

"Push me along in front of my pictures," he said. "I want to see my *Summer* again."

We went to look at his gay painting of a bandstand in the midst of a garden, with light, airy trees, and figures like actors on a stage, so realistic and charming. The whole scene seemed swept by great strokes of colour.

"It is really better than I thought," Dufy remarked, with a smile. "But I should also like to look at my *Concert*; it was the first I did in oils."

"By the 'Maroger' method?" I asked.

"Yes. But my new canvases are done with a mixture of turpentine. I've gone back to it. The Maroger medium opened up new possibilities that I should never have discovered in any other way. But now I want to get what I am trying for without it. You shouldn't be satisfied merely with beautiful pigment and brilliant effects; if you are, you're apt to tend towards the artificial. At present I am trying to be more *tonal*. I can do without the contrast of complementary colours. I want my colours to blend, without mingling, when placed next to each other. That's my work for the future."

* * * * *

The whole room was full of his friends, and they followed in the path of this artist, who, with a boldness rarely seen before, had found a new way of making light serve colour, and so avoid what he called "a loss of light".

Gazing at his remarkable version of Renoir's *Moulin de la Galette*, Dufy exclaimed with a laugh:

"It's really very funny. I say that because I haven't seen that canvas for a long time; I can look at it as if it had been done by someone else, or by another 'me'."

"Did you really like the Renoir picture so much?"

"Yes. Perhaps it was a coincidence. I mean, there must have been some sort of affinity between two rheumaticky people . . ." Then, pointing to his *Orchestra*, he continued: "That canvas is not really finished. But it doesn't matter. By wanting to finish a thing one often spoils it: one tries to put too much in."

One afternoon I went out with Dufy to the Paris suburb of Montfort-l'Amaury. He wanted to see once more the magnificent stained-glass windows in the old church there. His eyes opened wide, as though trying to absorb all the light and colour of the glass, and he murmured,

"No one will ever do better than that. . . ."

VAN DONGEN

A Fauve in a gilded cage, with a short nose and a long beard half-covering a pink, ascetic face, in which sparkled the blue eyes of a child—Delft blue, to be exact, since he was Dutch—this super-Parisian habitué of Deauville, Longchamp, Biarritz, Cairo and Cannes. And when some collector once referred to him as a "society-painter", he retorted:

"I, 'society'? Why, I began my career making varnish for horses hooves out of boiled snails. And look at this——" And he pointed to his coat and cap, which were those of a lock-keeper.

We were sitting at the Bar du Soleil, drinking port, each glass of which cost as much as the price of a dinner in Paris, and among the guests "Kiki" (a nickname derived from Van Dongen's christian name of Kees) had invited, there were as many duchesses as whores and as many horsy people as people who liked to paint horses.

"How did you happen to come to Deauville?"

"Well, I wanted to stay in Paris, which I don't really know well, even after sixty years. But my dog began to sulk, and I don't like that. He wanted to go to the country. But where? We might have tried China, but things haven't been very quict thcrc lately. Or New York. But there you have to go to the cinema. So I preferred this charming spot on the English Channel, where the women are pretty, and you can put on a dinner-jacket to go to the Casino."

"I thought you only wore a dinner-jacket when you washed your car."

"Oh, it has to be used for something else, of course. And then, say what you like, you've got the sea here, too. And yachts. I rather like seeing those white spots moving along the horizon. They are like brush-strokes moving about, and constantly making corrections. They do the work for me, you see."

"Aren't you doing any painting?"

"Painting? Oh, yes. You have to earn a living, don't you? Rolls-Royces are expensive, even if you've only got a Citroen. I've painted in Egypt; I've painted in Montmartre; I've even painted in Deauville. After all, the sea is the same moist light everywhere, as Baudelaire said: a little more violent here, more gently whispering farther north. But wherever you go, the lines are 'written down', and set in blue. That's the way I see it, at any rate. Another person sees it differently—luckily for us both."

"Monsieur Van Dongen," one of the women present inquired, "why did you paint a green dog in one of your canvases? There are no green dogs in Nature. . . ."

"That is true. But why have you dyed your hair mauve? Is hair mauve in Nature?"

"You're quite right, of course. But I should like to see your dog."

"My dog?"

"Didn't you just say that if you were in Deauville . . ."

"Oh, yes. But to tell you the truth, I haven't got a dog. I invented one so that I could go about with society people. . . . Fido, Fido! Down, boy, down!"

Why had he painted the dog green? Why did he make the shadows in his faces green? The Impressionists put their light areas in a soft setting of complementary colours. Van Dongen has gone a step farther. He shadows a pink face with green. The important thing is that he should do it successfully, and not make a mistake.

He only jokes with people who don't understand painting. With them he prefers to talk about something else, or to answer evasively. At heart, he is like all the other great ones: eternally seeking.

"In a few years I feel that I may succeed in doing what I am striving for. Yes, you saw me brush in the portrait of Maud Loti in a quarter of an hour (a quarter of an hour—and thirty years, as Whistler would have said). But take this canvas I've been working on for twelve years. I've spoiled it several times; taken it up again; painted it over; re-done it. It won't be any better, perhaps, than some others I've done in two sittings; but you should work away all the same, of course, because when you work, you always find something, you change your direction, even if it is only some simple technical detail of colour that you've discovered."

Yes, he works quickly. Once we went to Venice together—I, to work on a novel (I went there for seven consecutive seasons to gather material for my *Dans la Fête de Venise*), he, to paint.

As Van Dongen did not appear the morning after our arrival, I knocked at his door and went in. There he was, with seventeen large canvases drying out on the hotel balcony, which overlooked the Salute: a gondola with lovers in it; San Giorgio; the Salute, all grey in the moonlight, and the moon itself, with a ring round it.

"Let's go for a walk," he said, as he dried his hands. "I've worked enough for the time being. I must give my brushes a rest."

We went out to the Piazza San Marco, strolling along under the arcades of the Zecca. St. Mark's was all sparkling behind its flag-poles hung with banners. The pigeons suddenly whirled up, frightened by the sound of the midday cannon.

"Are you going to do a picture of St. Mark's?" I asked him.

"No; it's been done to death already. I'm leaving that to the young English girls."

"You did the 'Salute' very well," I remarked.

"Yes. But the 'Salute' is beautiful because of its mass and architecture. It's the detail of St. Mark's that counts."

We arrived at the Doges' Palace.

"And what about that?" I asked.

"Yes. I shall do that. But I want to wait till that rubbish is gone."

By the word "rubbish" Van Dongen was referring to a huge warship alongside the quay, hardly thirty feet away from the Palace, whose delicate rose colour seemed crushed by the mass of metal.

"On the contrary, you should take advantage of it," I pointed out. "The contrast would be very 'Van Dongen'."

"Well, yes. I suppose you are right," he agreed.

He stopped, half-closed his eyes, and remained thus for a minute or two. Then he said:

"There. It's all done."

(And as a matter of fact the next day he produced one of his finest canvases in grey and rose.)

"Now let's go to Florian's. I want to do some sketches of the officers there, and have a vermouth, and look at the sights of the place. This afternoon I'm going to sit in the bandstand and make some notes on St. Mark's."

I had an engagement for lunch. Later, when I returned to meet "Kiki", I was greeted by a comic spectacle. For there he was, sitting in the middle of the bandstand, just as the band arrived for the afternoon concert.

"That's a beautiful picture you're doing," the bandmaster said. "But you'll have to let us have the place."

"Just a minute," begged the painter, his brushes still in his hand.

"I'm sorry, but we have to start now."

"Very well. You can start. You won't be in my way."

"Yes, but you are in our way. If your canvas was smaller——"

"Oh, the devil! You're a nuisance. I was here first, wasn't I? What are you going to play?"

"Donizetti."

"I don't like Donizetti. Don't you think a picture of mine is as good as any opera by that musical lacemaker?"

"That's not the question."

"It most certainly is!"

"Sir, in spite of our respect for foreigners in general, and for art in particular——"

The police were sent for as well as the fire brigade, while all Florian's, Quadri's, Lavena's, the employees from Jesurum's, Griffon's, Salviati's and Asta's, not to mention the entire crowd in the Piazza and the neighbouring alleys, argued the case furiously.

"The devil with them!" exclaimed the painter.

He was gently but firmly ousted.

"Don't worry about your picture," one of the firemen said to him, as he took down the painter's easel. "We helped to move Veronese."

"Never heard of him," snapped Van Dongen.

At the police-station, where Zorzi, Warnod and I went to bail him out, we found that, according to custom, they had slit his trousers. He returned to the hotel practically bare-legged, but quite unembarrassed.

In less than no time after Van Dongen got back to Paris he sold all the paintings he had done in Venice to Bernheim-Jeune. And they were re-sold almost immediately at such high prices that the artist resolved from then on to sell direct to individual purchasers. On the strength of the money, he rented a luxurious studio in the rue Juliette-Lambert.

★ ★ ★ ★ ★

He had previously lived in the Villa Saïd, where "all Paris", including Anatole France, used to flock to see him. Van Dongen had done a portrait of the author of *The Red Lily* that was so realistic, and made him look so senile, that it caused a scandal. When the work was sold for two hundred thousand francs at an auction, someone exclaimed:

"Two hundred thousand francs for that garbage!"

"That's not very kind to Anatole France," remarked Van Dongen, who was sitting next to me.

"What did your model say when he saw the portrait?"

"Why, he liked it. I think he is the only one who has, though—up till now, at least. . . ."

Many of Van Dongen's clever remarks are well known; but the following examples are typical:

"I never go to art museums: they ruin your 'eye'. After all, they are only cemeteries of dead painting. I love life—and the life of today."

"Why do I paint by artificial light instead of by daylight, like other painters? Because other painters have never realised that most of the time people see pictures in houses by artificial light. In my painting, the values don't change. Of course, in the past it was difficult to paint by candle or gas light, or even by ordinary electric light. But take these modern projectors, for instance. . . ."

Yet Van Dongen often paints out of doors, even in full sunlight. I came upon him one day on the Croisette at Cannes, where he was catching the effect of the tanned legs and white dresses of the passing women against the light blue air and the grey asphalt.

"You see," he said, "our profession is like the whore's. Matisse works from his windows in Nice, and I go street-walking in Cannes."

★ ★ ★ ★ ★

The rue Juliette-Lambert . . . a regular Veronese scene: two or three studios one above the other, separated by railings and little balconies that were almost terraces. And in each studio there were silver divans, as big as a lawn, where the prettiest women in Paris or Europe or America clustered when he gave his parties, a strange phantasmagoria of silks, bare shoulders and thighs; dozens of shapely legs showing through filmy dresses, and charming faces set off by coloured wigs, which seemed to be sown with diamonds and other precious stones.

All the smart set came, from Boni de Castellane, in his ageing splendour, to the Maharajah of Kapurthala; from the various Goulds and Rothschilds to the artist's latest models—in short, the upper-crust from all over the world could be found there, gazing at their portraits on the walls as though they had been hanged in effigy.

Cécile Sorel and Maurice Rostand were the chief attractions, when the master of the house did not have some Hindu priestess or the whole Russian Ballet on hand, as a special novelty.

"Can you tell me why they all come here?" Van Dongen once asked me, during one of his fantastic gatherings. "Personally I'm bored, and I can hardly wait till they all clear out. Let's go for a walk and a smoke."

He led the way downstairs. As usual, he had on his overalls. As we reached the street, a big, shiny car drew up before the door. A gentleman in evening clothes got out, followed by two ladies decked out in diamonds.

"Is this Van Dongen's house?" the visitor asked.

"I think so," replied the artist.

As the party started towards the entrance, Van Dongen said to the gentleman, who evidently didn't know him:

"What about my tip, sir?"

It was on this same evening that Henri de Rothschild confided to me:

"I should like to buy that big canvas of his, *Baigneuse*—the one that was reproduced on the cover of your book on Deauville; but, as I am a Rothschild, he would ask me a higher price than he would anyone else."

"I've heard that he wants two hundred thousand francs for it," I said.

"Would you be willing to approach him about it, and say that one of your friends would give him a hundred and twenty-five thousand this very moment?"

Before I had time to answer, Van Dongen, who had overheard our conversation, came up and said:

"No. The price is two hundred thousand. It won't be any more expensive for you."

One evening Van Dongen was giving a special exhibition of his portraits. This time there was neither entertainment nor refreshments, and the people who had waited around till one in the morning for champagne and fancy cakes began to depart, disgruntled and hungry, to cheer themselves up in the neighbouring bistros.

The next day I wrote a rather unfortunate account of the occasion which embroiled Van Dongen with half Paris. I described the actual reception in twenty lines, and then went on with a two-column article which began as follows:

"As soon as the bores had gone, the guests whom the host really wanted to remain assembled in the banquet-room . . ." And I described an imaginary scene, with a Gargantuan buffet-supper on the edge of a swimming-pool, and twenty completely nude bathing-beauties, illumined by coloured flood-lights, disporting themselves in the water. For dessert, I said, a life-size statue of Cécile Sorel in pistachio ice-cream was brought in for Van Dongen to decapitate with one stroke of a scimitar. Then lots were drawn for the breasts, the throat, etc., and I don't know what tit-bit from a certain part of the body fell to a notorious pervert.

The story took years to die. In fact, a decade later a Japanese newspaper published some "sketches" of the imaginary swimming-pool. People were always asking Van Dongen to show it to them. And each time he would put them off with,

"Oh, not just now. My *dog's* bathing in it."

That same evening Boni de Castellane, looking at a life-study of one of the Guy sisters, turned to a young journalist and asked:

"You know them, don't you? Which sister is this one?"

The young man went up to the picture, shaded his eyes with his hand, and, after a rapid glance at the subject's anatomy, said,

"It's Edmonde."

"Thank you, sir," said a Government Minister, an intimate of the actress's, who was standing behind us.

When Fayard, the publisher, together with Henri Duvernois, started the *Œuvres Libres*, in each issue of which thirty pages were allotted to the work of six authors, I asked him why he did not include thirty pages of drawings.

Fayard was the most progressive and enterprising of men, and he always welcomed new ideas.

"Whom shall we begin with?" he asked. "What about your friend Van Dongen, for instance?"

A week later I took Fayard round to the rue Juliette-Lambert. Van Dongen was most affable. But he asked such high prices that, with the best will in the world, the publisher was unable to meet them. So, to ease an awkward situation, I interrupted the discussion and suggested that Van Dongen should show us the pictures in his dining-room, which was kept closed during his parties. As a rule, he received only a few intimates of the house there. It was a huge room hung with large canvases representing, in all their nudity, Eve's original sin and Adam's fall.

"With pleasure," assented Van Dongen. "Will you come this way?"

There was a handsome flight of stairs leading to the dining-room, but instead of taking it, the artist made us go up by a little oak staircase, which was used chiefly to reach the bedrooms. The next time I saw him I said,

"Why didn't you let our friend go up by the main stairs?"

"Just an idea I had."

"What was it?"

"Well, do you remember those little corkscrew stairs we had to climb when we used to go and see publishers twenty years ago? We would have to wait for hours with our portfolios under our arms, and, at the end of it, we were lucky if we were able to sell a full-page drawing for sixteen francs, or a quarter-page one for four. Now it's my turn. And I made him go up by the back stairs even though he did offer me six thousand francs a drawing this time."

"But it wasn't Fayard [1] in the old days," I protested.

[1] Fayard was known to be such a "decent" publisher that whenever he drew up a contract with an author he would always say to him before-

"No matter. It was a publisher."

Incidentally, Fayard was the first to enjoy the joke on himself.

* * * * *

Sentimental reasons were the cause of Van Dongen's leaving his place in the rue Juliette-Lambert, and he went to live in Garches, near Versailles, where he bought *Bagatelle*, a little villa surrounded by a rose-garden, which was presided over by a stone statue of a mutilated Bacchus.

The artist removed his large dining-room panels to his new establishment, as well as his long, black marble table and—his imaginary swimming-pool. And he kept open house there for all his friends and clientèle every Sunday.

The war came, and then the Liberation. Van Dongen returned to Paris, and just before his retrospective exhibition at the Charpentier Galleries (which once more dazzled everyone and confirmed the almost unanimous acclaim of the critics), he took a studio in the rue de Courcelles. When I went to see him there, his first words were:

"A studio! It's odd, but this is the first time I've ever had a real studio."

His Delft-blue eyes shone as brightly as did his little red nose, and a smile spread over his lips in the midst of his rough, white beard.

"And I want you to know," he continued, "that I'm really *working* here, with my son, my pipe, my stove and my wife for company."

"Why do you make your figures like caricatures?" asked someone who was present. "That man you're doing has a regular horse's face."

"Because I go so often to the races, I suppose," replied the artist.

After the other had gone, Van Dongen turned to me and said in disgust:

"Like caricatures! Rembrandt and Hogarth were both accused of caricaturing people. What an 'accusation'! I paint what I see, and I don't see things or people as you do, or as that man does, or

hand, "Will you read this over, and then sign it?" and the author had such confidence in him that he would reply, "No, I'll sign first, and read it afterwards."

as others do. Each one sees people, things, colours in his own way. The important thing is that I should see clearly, and that my painting should exactly reflect *my* vision, and not yours, or his, or anyone else's. Then the painting will be true. A hundred men do not see the same woman in the same way. So why expect painters to? Caricatures? One day I heard you ask Sem how he arrived at such a synthesis of ugliness, and he answered, 'By trying to make them beautiful'. But I don't try to make the subject either beautiful or ugly, but to portray it exactly, just as my eyes see it. Here are my last two portraits. I made the one of Berry-Wall more 'elaborate' because he gives the impression of being a fastidious man. I rather scamped the actor Berry because he's a casual type. So much for the expression of personality. As a painter, I amused myself with these crude blues and the messes—well-chosen, all the same—that I put on my palette."

"And what about this?" I said.

I had just caught sight of a canvas I had never seen before, of an old man sitting in an armchair which several ladies, wearing only chemises, pink stockings with garters and high-heeled shoes, were bearing aloft through the clouds.

"That's a portrait of my father ascending to Heaven. I did it that way because he was so fond of his pipe and his red armchair. Why did I show angels wearing modern shoes? Because I wanted to portray them in the style of the period, just as the fifteenth-century painters represented angels dressed in the clothes of their time. Does that shock you? Well, you'll see that in a couple of hundred years people will find it perfectly natural."

* * * * *

I have run across Van Dongen at Deauville, at Cannes and many other places besides, in the company of his son and his pretty wife, who is a Breton. And he is always the same, always paradoxical. On one occasion he signed the register at the Casino as being a "painter-contractor"; on another, he tried to convince the art-dealer Georges Wildenstein that Ingres "drew badly":

"Yes," he said, "he's good on detail. Each finger he draws is perfect. But the whole is not in harmony. Picasso is the greater draughtsman."

MARIE LAURENCIN

Rodin named her "Fauvette" because she, too, was born to painting in the Fauve group. She was a grey-and-rose Fauvette, like her water-colours, like her canvases, her little girls with their winged gestures, her Amazons, her nymphs, her does: "an artist always paints self-portraits, in spite of himself!"

I first got to know her at the Closerie des Lilas, where she used to come and talk with the poets whose work appeared in *Plume* and *Soirées de Paris*. And each of them would recite in a purring tone the verses Moréas had composed for her. They are worth repeating for their charming, lyrical quality:

If she but laughs,
Marie Laurencin,
Gold encircles
Her lovely
Eyes . . .

Actually, the first time I met her was in Guillaume Apollinaire's study, at the time when the poet was living in the rue Léonie, now called the rue Henner. When I say I met her, it would be more accurate to say that I literally ran into her; and that day her eyes were not encircled with gold, but with fire.

"Yes," she told me afterwards, "Guillaume was afraid that I had come to bother him about something, so he made you stay on purpose. I even saw him make a sign to you. And as you were one of his best friends. . . . Oh, those were difficult times. I was twenty-five; he, twenty-seven. Those poets were all 'hard', in their way, even with each other. Picasso was not very nice to him."

"But I've heard Picasso defend his memory very fiercely," I said. "I remember a luncheon in Rome, where he got up and exclaimed, 'I forbid anyone to say anything against Apollinaire. You can say what you like about anyone else, but no one is going to criticise Apollinaire in front of me!'."

"Yes, my dear M.G.M., but in those days they were young. I met Guillaume through Sagot, the publisher, and it was Picasso who called me to the poet's attention by saying to him one day, 'I have met your fiancée'. Then Apollinaire lent me a book by

Marie Laurencin : Self-portrait

Thomas Hardy and another by Sacher Masoch. I went back to see him to get other books, which I took to my mother, with whom I was living at the time. . . . But it was Braque who really 'discovered' me, if I may use the expression. I had left a little portrait of myself in pink, white and black in the cloak-room at the art class where I was studying, and the next day it was gone. Braque had taken it to the Moulin de la Galette to show it to his painter friends, who all said, 'Why, she has talent!' When he returned the picture (which is now in a friend's home in England), he said:

" 'Little Laurencin [that's what he called me], you have real talent. You must keep it up; and come to see us, too. . . .'

"And the first thing I knew, I, who considered myself worthless as a painter, found myself the centre of attention: praised, encouraged and launched. Gertrude Stein bought one of my canvases for fifty francs—'to make fun of myself', so she said; but the truth is that she did not want to appear to have made a mistake, in case it turned out later that. . . . How afraid people are of making mistakes! Even Apollinaire was. To take one example: when the Douanier Rousseau brought him the picture he had done, entitled *Apollinaire and his Muse* (the Muse being myself), which has since become famous, Apollinaire turned to me after he had gone, and said,

" 'If I find that here tomorrow, you will have to take it down to the cellar.'

" 'Now, listen, Guillaume,' I said; 'you've got three mantelpieces in this house, and you can certainly put the picture on one of them.'

" 'No,' he replied, 'I could never do any work with that in front of me.'

"In the end, he sold *us* for three thousand francs to Paul Rosenberg, who bought several others, for about the same price, from Georges Courteline."

"Life separated us," went on Marie, "although we always remained friends. But there you are: I am the last free woman. That is to say, I have never done what I did not want to do. You see this portrait? It's my mother. I'm named Laurencin after her. She was very pretty—Norman, with a dash of Creole blood, which explains many things in my character, and in the freedom of my work. Of course, I have had a contract with a big art-dealer from

1913 to 1940. Now I have a new one with another big dealer. In my painting, just as in my life, I never do anything I don't want to do."

And with that Marie Laurencin, whose hair fluttered about her forehead and whose eyes were like sharp thorns on either side of her straight nose, began gently brushing in a grey background round one of her favourite subjects: an Amazon with delicate skin and light, airy gestures.

"Do you always use such a little brush?"

"Always. And by little touches, even what seem to be wide, flat areas. Look at it closely. Let the imitators do what they will: I couldn't copy my own work myself! Yet I use as few tones as possible, and only those that I can really bring out: white, crimson lake, cobalt blue, emerald green, ivory black, yellow ochre—the simplest colours. No chemical mixtures, so the paint will stay fresh till the end of time. In that way their lovely tones will last, and one creates shapes and colours around one that are pleasing. On the mantelpiece of my flat in the Champ de Mars I had a lovely boat, with big sails, and when I fell to day-dreaming it would carry me away to far-off places under wonderful skies. Between the sky and the pictures it forms, what beautiful dreams one can create! . . . Ah, well . . . Yesterday I went to see Louise Hervieu, that remarkable artist who did the illustrations for Baudelaire. I found her racked with pain by her illness, like a tortured tree. I wonder what has become of so many other women painters? Do you remember Marval?"

MARVAL

Dear Jacqueline! She lived in that old building on the Quai St. Michel, which had all those tortuous staircases, with Matisse, Marquet and Flandrin for neighbours. She always liked to work at the window, behind curtains of embroidered tulle.

"They give the place a 'Sunday' look, don't they?" she said in her little flute-like voice, as she stroked the curtains, which she so often reproduced in her flower-pieces, and even in the large panels she did for the foyer of the Champs Elysées Theatre.

Dear, huge, grotesque and tender—yes, really tender—creature! Her hair, a tuft of red hemp, like a doll's, hung over a white pierrette's face; and what greedy little red lips and kind eyes she had!

"Oh, he didn't bring me any chocolates!" she would sometimes say petulantly.

Her rooms were full of canvases, stretching-frames, dilapidated chairs, ribbons, empty boxes of sweets. I used to look in on her every now and then.

"No, I haven't got a thing for you. Oh, he wants to take something away with him again? Very well, then. Here, I'll sell you this, for the price of the frame."

"No, Marval. No!"

"Oh, when you scold me, you don't call me Jacqueline any more. I think my name is so pretty. I only put it on the canvases I really like. The others I just sign 'Marval', like a man. Here, I want to show you something."

She disappeared, and soon came back with a roll of twenty canvases, which she spread out on the floor. And out of them sprang bunches of iris, nodding poppies, roses as pale as those in her cheeks, and foxgloves which looked as though they might burst into flame like fireworks. And then there were the panels of children playing "ring-a-ring-a-roses", which were to be placed near the frescoes by Bourdelle, Vuillard and Bonnard in the Champs Elysées Theatre.

"Yes, I'll sell you this one for the price of the frame. But it's for you only, and not for a lady-friend. However, if it would make you both happy—— But you must come and see me together, and bring me some chocolates or fondants."

Poor Marval! We all knew she was poor, but not that she was in dire want. One day a friend of mine and I did go to see her, taking her a huge box of chocolates. We were so pleased with ourselves, thinking how delighted she would be with the gift. But as we started up the stairs, the concierge came running out and stopped us.

"Where are you going?" she demanded.

"To see Madame Marval."

"She has died, Monsieur, at the hospital."

And there was dainty Hélène Perdriat, with her black fringe, her cat-like eyes and that lithe Spanish figure swathed in black silk: Hélène Perdriat, convent-educated, who painted mischievous little girls and the Iles de Paris; oh, those balls in the rue Vavin, those soirées at Van Dongen's, at Poiret's. First she withdrew to her château de la Vaillette, where the peasants nicknamed her the

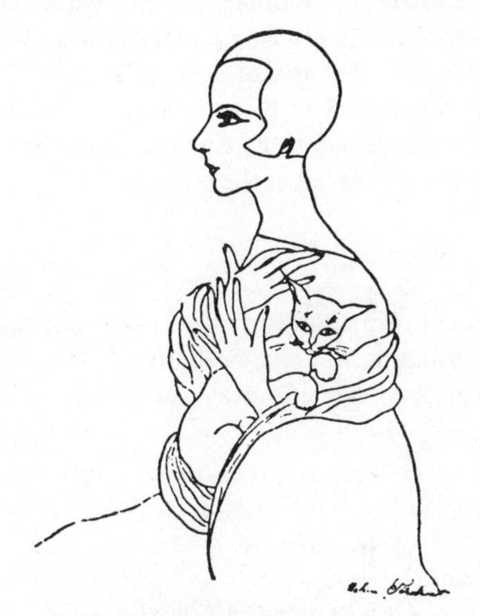

Hélène Perdriat : Self-portrait

"cat-fairy" because of the eighty-odd cats she took in and looked after. Then she adopted two orphans and, nothing daunted, married a blind doctor. . . .

There was Valentine Prax, a Walkyrie, whose canvases were so harsh they might have been painted on storm-tossed ships; wild Chériane, who married Léon-Paul Fargue; Crissay, the violinist who painted violins; Charlotte Gardelle and Halika, two princesses of the Orient; Geneviève Gallibert, who painted Paris, Morocco and Greece and was the first artist to take her brushes up in an aeroplane; Hélène Marre, who painted such spirited portraits; Jeanne Gil-Marcheix, who took her easel to Patagonia; Valentine Laroche, who took hers to the Pole; Hermine David, the psychic wife of tragic Pascin; Charmy, with her feminine brutality, her daring compositions of bees, birds and roses. There was also crazy Wassileff, who made dolls; a good sort, she was: a combination of Russian bohemian and Paris gamine. I recall sweet Louise Millet, who looked like a lady in a Mme. Vigée-Lebrun portrait;

Charlotte Brand, who wrote to me from a concentration camp in the Midi: "We're up to our middles in mud, but the Pyrenees are so beautiful"; Tamara de Lempika, the Hungarian countess, who avoided the pretty-pretty in society portraits; and Madeleine Luca, who did so many lively pictures of little girls. And Ghera; Guillemette Morand; Suzanne Tourte, so vital and tall; Anne Français who was always experimenting; finally, Jacqueline Zay, whose enormous *Liberty* was placed at the entrance of the San Francisco Exhibition.

* * * * *

And Marie Laurencin, sung by poets—was she not a poet too?

"Here's something new," she wrote me. "They are two different men. I am not carried away by what I have written. Nevertheless——"

PORTRAITS

Tu n'as jamais été séduit
par une belle journée
Mais quelquefois
Tu humais l'air
et t'acheminais
sans parler
En foulant la terre
de tes pieds longs et minces

Nous avions des chiens
Ils nous suivaient
Tu n'aimais pas l'obscurité
et depuis, seule
Je me suis trouvée sans lumière
Je ne t'ai jamais vu en colère
O regret

Pourquoi serions-nous des fâchés
Lorsque tu montes l'escalier
En grondant

Toute la place pour ta voix
Je me sens si légère
Que plus tu avances
Plus je flotte avec plaisir
Tu es un homme.

HENRI ROUSSEAU

My acquaintance with Henri Rousseau was very slight. Apollinaire and the Cubists regarded him as a profound modern primitive; but they also admired him because he was a painter who really "painted" at a time when, according to some, the Impressionists were no longer doing so.

But I had met the Douanier long before he had been "sanctified" by all these.

It was a year or two before 1900, when I saw a man of modest appearance, with a big moustache and large, anxious eyes, come one day to call on my father. He had a picture he wanted to sell him, a *View of Maisons-Alfort*, and it was signed "Henri Rousseau" in a large hand. I remember hearing him say:

"It's a view of Maisons-Alfort. Don't you feel you're really there? Look how well that boat is done."

My father bought the picture, and it was hung in my room. One day it disappeared, and I have never seen it since. Later on, I had occasion to meet Rousseau in the company of Apollinaire, and he was as serious as a judge. He greeted me; but, naturally, he did not know that I had been the one for whom my father bought his *Maisons-Alfort* picture.

COURTELINE'S DOUANIER ROUSSEAU PICTURES

I used to go to see Courteline sometimes at Saint-Mandé, where he lived in an apartment in which one room was reserved for what he called his "Chamber of Horrors". Juven's magazine *Rire* had actually printed reproductions of its contents, and among them were two canvases by the Douanier Rousseau.

"I set up this museum as a record of our times, for I wanted to show to what lengths human stupidity can go," Courteline declared.

Poor man, he had just had a leg amputated. When I went to see him the next time, he was, as usual, blustering and grumpy, but philosophic.

"Have you still got your Rousseaus?" I asked him.

Ensconced in his armchair, Courteline shrugged his shoulders.

"I sold them," he confessed. "A gentleman came to see me one day and asked if he could visit my museum. 'Certainly,' I said; and I showed him round. 'Would you sell me those pictures?' he asked. 'You're joking,' I said. 'For the small sum you would give me—because you couldn't give me much for them—it wouldn't be worth spoiling a collection which shows to what lengths——' 'I'll give you ten thousand francs for them,' said my visitor. I thought he was making fun of me, and I opened the door to show him out. But the fellow pulled a roll of notes out of his pocket. 'No. I won't allow you to,' I said. 'Even if you are as stupid as the man who perpetrated that rubbish, I am not going to take advantage of you.' 'You wouldn't be taking advantage of me. Quite the contrary!' the fellow kept insisting. And now it turns out that I'm the one who's stupid. I shouldn't have done it, it seems. At any rate, to call his bluff, I told him I would accept. And what did he do but count out the money then and there and put it in my hand? 'I'm sorry,' he said, 'but I've only got seven thousand francs with me;

but if you'll trust me——' 'Sir,' I replied, 'anyone who is mad enough to buy such stuff, and fool enough to pay such a price, would certainly be ass enough to go through with the bargain. Here are your horrors, and many thanks for your money.' But the best part of it is that he sent me the remaining three thousand francs the same evening. And, better still, it turns out that those daubs were worth even more!"

And, highly amused, Courteline stamped on the floor with his one leg.

The Six Sides of the Cube

PICASSO

PICASSO: A MYTHOLOGICAL, cosmic monster who, like all great innovators, arouses the most violent hatred in those who do not understand him, and an almost hysterical adulation in his admirers. The first to abolish academic forms, constantly reacting against himself, he appeared in the firmament of painting, and of all the other arts, like a comet which puts the other stars to rout, even those which should have been following their own paths, such as Stravinsky, who seems to have been troubled about what his ex-collaborator would do next.

I saw him arrive in Paris around 1900, when he was quite young and slender. An Andalusian from Malaga, the son of the Director of the School of Fine Arts in Barcelona, he descended on Montmartre and began to "paint what he saw", as he expressed it.

"In those days one saw things in a terribly Lautrec way," he said. "And because I used a Conté pencil, like Steinlen, and tackled the same subjects, people sometimes claimed that I was influenced by Lautrec and Steinlen. What a paradox!"

Picasso looked much the same then as he does now. First a pipe, at the end of which is a little fellow with a lock of black hair over one eye, an eye even blacker than the hair, full of mockery and fire, and a small, sensuous mouth. His sturdy neck is enveloped in a polo-neck sweater; and a watch-chain is fastened to the buttonhole of his jacket. On top, he wears an incredibly old brown raincoat, almost as old as the hat which is perched on his head at the same angle as the first day he put it on.

"Some people ask me why I paint pipes, guitars and packets of tobacco, and why these objects keep reappearing in the canvases of the painters of today. If Chardin, for instance, painted onions and peaches, it is because Chardin painted in the country, and near his kitchen; and onions and peaches were, naturally, familiar objects to him. What could be more familiar to most painters in Montmartre or Montparnasse nowadays than their pipes, their tobacco, a guitar hung on the wall over a divan, or a siphon on a café-table?"

* * * * *

On the evening of that celebrated day in 1907, after the private view of the *Demoiselles d'Avignon*, the Negro canvas which was the starting-point of a new period destined to have such a profound influence on young painters,[1] I was sitting with Apollinaire on the terrace of the Café des Deux Magots. He was explaining to me how he composed his poems.

"Say, for example, that we want to write an *Impression of Saint-Germain-des-Prés*," he said. "Here we are, sitting in this café; so we'll begin:

Assis à la terrasse
Il y a non loin de nous
Un prêtre au nez rouge
Couleur
Il lit un journal dont l'angle frôle le siphon
Un cycliste manque d'être écrasé
Par un omnibus à bande verte
Un vert de chemin de fer

[1] "Were you yourself directly influenced by Negro art, as people have often claimed?" I asked Picasso later.

"No. Definitely not," the painter answered. "But the discovery of their sculpture coincided, at the time, with the kind of thing we were searching for. And we all bought some of the sculpture, and for only a few francs! You've seen some of it at my house, as well as at Apollinaire's."

"*Chemin de fer* makes me think of the *Ceinture* Line, and of my different travels; so I write:

Chemin de fer de ceinture
Bourgeois, artistes
Sur la même banquette tachée de suie
Arbres et maisons de la banlieue
Barrière

"And suddenly I see La Gandara going by, and I write about him thus:

La Gandara qui passe
Il est fier comme un hidalgo
J'aime mieux son port de tête
Que sa peinture
Bien qu'elle soit honorable
Il achète un journal au kiosque et paie
D'un geste
Distingué

"I separate the word 'distinguished' from the rest because his gesture, you see, is detached."

Il n'ira pas chez Lipp
En face
Malgré la bonne bière
Et rentre chez lui
D'un pas choisi
Mais voici venir
Mieux sous les arbres
Voici Picasso
Avenir . . .

And along came Picasso, and sat down with us.

"It's hot," said Apollinaire.

"It's fine," replied Picasso, who is a sensible optimist.

No, we talked of neither painting nor philosophy.

Bergson once told me that one day, when he was out walking with Berthelot, they chanced to meet Renan.

"Of course I was all attention," he said. "But the two famous thinkers did not talk of the eternal verities, but of the various means of transport which they could take to go home."

And the same with kings. I was talking once with the Swedish sovereign at Cannes, when the King of Denmark came along. Their Majesties talked of nothing but their relatives' health, and one advised the other to try a hot water-bottle on his stomach, and to recommend it to the rest of the Royal Family.

That night Picasso, Apollinaire and I went to the circus together. None of us had brought a sketch-book; but Picasso's mind was busy. A young poet, René Fauchois, who was sitting opposite us, pointed to the circus-ring, and traced an imaginary circle in the air with his finger.

Then Picasso made an almost prophetic gesture.

"No," he said. And he, in turn, drew a circus-ring in the air, only he made it square.

* * * * *

One day in 1917, on the very day, in fact, that I was demobilised, I received an envelope containing a heavy key. The explanation was not forthcoming until, two days later, I had a letter from my friend Sergei Diaghilev, the amazing impresario of the Russian Ballet. It was, I learned, the key of Picasso's studio in the rue Victor Hugo at Montrouge. The artist was in Rome with Diaghilev, and both had written to ask if I would go to the studio, choose twenty or so of Picasso's canvases and bring them to Rome, where they were planning to put on an exhibition.

I went out to Montrouge at once, and showed the key and the letter to the caretaker.

"All right," he said. "It's there, in the garden."

A dog came up to me, sniffed, and wagged its tail.

I went to the studio, and, on opening the door, was struck immediately by the bare walls. But on the floor were thirty or forty rows of canvases, with twenty to twenty-five canvases in each row. And what canvases! Some were of his "Lautrec" period, some of his "rose" period, some of the "blue" period, as well as a number of his first analytical compositions.

"I hope the Customs Officers won't mistake them for maps of military areas," Diaghilev had said in his letter.

I made a selection, then closed the place up again.

"I'm taking these," I told the caretaker as I went out.

"All right. All right," he said again, without even bothering to look at what I was carrying.

Two days later I left for Italy.

In Rome, Diaghilev was living in the Palazzo Theodori, a large, square house of white marble, in the Renaissance style, situated in the Piazza Colonna. I was shown up a wide flight of stairs to the third floor, and, after passing through several high-ceilinged marble anterooms, I reached the dining-room, where there was a long table set for twelve people, with beautiful Italian china on heavy lace napery, countless bottles of various wines, and a great many heavy crystal glasses.

A large folding-door, ornamented with mouldings and paintings, led to the drawing-room, which was huge, and lit by four large, high windows looking out on to the fountains and noisy traffic of the Piazza. The domed ceiling was supported by double columns. The walls were superbly hung with tapestries. But scattered over chairs, stools, and even the piano was an unbelievable hotch-potch of lengths of muslin, silks and other materials, boxes, baskets, dancing-slippers, sketches for costumes, frames, tacked-up dresses, music-scores and dolls.

A number of people—princes and telephone operators, tradesmen and dilettanti—were sitting wherever they could find a space.

I examined a number of drawings which had been pinned on the walls between the tapestries. Some of them were of nudes, impeccably drawn; others were dancers in ballet skirts, with strangely voluminous arms and legs, pudgy fingers and bulging eyes, of a frightening realism despite the purity of line.

"What surprising Degas!" I murmured.

"Degas!" exclaimed a voice behind me. "When did you ever see any Degas like those? If you want to know, Monsieur Degas would not have been worthy to lace the boots of the artist who drew those."

I turned round. It was Diaghilev.

"Who is the artist, then?" I asked, in bewilderment.

"Here he is now."

And I saw Picasso enter the room—the same Picasso, just as I had always seen him at the Rotonde and in Montmartre, with his lock of hair over one eye, wearing a shirt made of synthetic fabric

instead of the customary sweater, the ring of his watch-chain as usual in the button-hole of his jacket.

"Yes. At present I am drawing like Ingres," he said in his Spanish accent, as he shook hands.

"Is the other genius here?" inquired Diaghilev. "Then let's sit down to lunch."

The "other genius" was Stravinsky. As I have discussed elsewhere [1] the latter's opinions on the subject of music, Rome, Wagner, Debussy, etc., here I shall keep strictly to Picasso.

I told him how surprised and delighted I was by his drawings of the ballet-girls. I tried to get him to talk about Ingres, whom some of Picasso's disciples considered the real revolutionary.

"But what about the cube?" asked a lady who was sitting at the end of the table.

Picasso threw her a black look.

"Well, what about the cube?"

"If you give up the cube, what are people going to say——?"

"Oh," cried Picasso, "do you suppose I paint for the habitués of the Rotonde? If that's what you think, you can think again. Now that I have imitators, I am going to——"

"Imitators?"

"Call them disciples, if you like. But I don't give a damn about them. They don't interest me. It is only the Masters who count: those who create. And they don't turn round when someone pisses on their heels," he added in a lower tone to Diaghilev and me. Then abruptly he said to me,

"What do you think of Raphael?"

"I take your view that Raphael is a Carpaccio set free. With one light bound he escaped from geometry, from the 'school', from the birth-pangs in which Michelangelo had brought him forth. He exists serenely on a plane of his own."

"There's no parallel in music," said Stravinsky. "Beethoven wasn't able to escape from Bach. He remained German, and lacked spontaneity. We still have to place Mozart and the earlier Italian musicians above everyone else because they are spontaneous—they correspond to the primitives in painting. Spontaneity is the only verity in art. I'm still working away, but I am spontaneous only in my subconscious."

[1] In *Les Montparnos* and *Cinquante Ans de Gloires Théâtrales.*

A significant remark, when one considers that surrealism had not yet been invented.

"Yes, but a Master must free himself from his instinct," declared Picasso, "and break the chain of rules, even at the risk of his life. I like to lose myself in Michelangelo, as I would in the majesty of a mountain landscape."

Someone passed him a photo of one of the figures in the Sistine Chapel.

"Ah!" he said, placing his finger on the toe of the youth and following the graceful outline. "What a feeling of pleasure I get when I go over this line. . . . But Raphael is the sky itself: what serenity in his line; what mastery! It wasn't Leonardo who invented aviation; it was Raphael!"

I can still see Picasso's stubby thumb on the photo, and I have never been able to look at the figures in the Sistine since then without feeling as though he were with me, and lovingly tracing with that thumb of his, from toe to hip and from hip to shoulder, the living, tormented lines of those characters in eternal converse with the gods.

Referring to Leonardo's *Saint John*, Picasso observed,

"Yes, Leonardo promises you Heaven with that raised finger; but Raphael gives it to you."

I helped Picasso hang his canvases for the exhibition.

"Did you see my dog at Montrouge?" he asked as we worked.

"Yes; he was quite friendly."

"What, he wasn't tied up? He didn't go for you? He usually bites everybody. He must have sensed that you were a friend."

"On the other hand, all the windows were open in your studio," I said, "and anyone could have got in and helped themselves to your canvases."

"I hope you took a dozen or so for yourself."

"A dozen! Why, I didn't even take one, Pablo."

"But you should have done. Why didn't you? You should have, you know."

Picasso had already begun work on *Parade* for the Russian Ballet. He was planning to do something very special, for instead of a Persian stage-set in the *Scheherazade* style, or a *Spectre de la Rose*, in the Munich manner, which the fashionable audience expected, he was going to throw a Cubist setting at their heads for the first time.

And what a première *Parade* had at the Châtelet Theatre, halfway through the First World War, and at the most critical time! Even so, the huge auditorium was packed to bursting, and with a turbulent audience, out to make trouble. Diaghilev and I had distributed tickets all over Montparnasse, which was in a state of nervous expectation. All the painters came, and stood about in their sweaters and working clothes, pushing their way among the fashionable ladies in the boxes. There were the most extraordinary combinations of people, some of the most picturesque of them in the Director's box, presided over by Missia Edwards, in black-and-white satin, and with Picasso wearing his customary jockey's-cap and garnet-red pullover. In the box where I was there were half a dozen painters from the "Cubist" cafés, and among them the melancholy "Noix-de-Coco", Modigliani's fiancée, Mlle. Hébuterne; the Citron Sisters, Hélène Perdriat, Lagar, Ortiz de Zarate, two actresses from the Comédie Française; and, in the next box, Maurice Rostand!

"What's *he* doing here?" demanded one of the Citron Sisters. "Just wait: I'll fix him." And, turning to the young man, she said, "Is it true, Monsieur, that you're a homo?"

But M. Rostand gave her back as good as he got.

"Mademoiselle," he replied, "in your presence I should imagine I was at most a lesbian."

The orchestra, which included a few typewriters among the instruments, attacked the opening measures of Erik Satie's score, stark by way of reaction against the nouveau-riche in art. Immediately a storm of whistling broke out, followed by frenzied applause and yells.

"Mauricette annoys me," cried a woman painter. "He shouldn't be here. There's only one way of disgusting him," she said to a young artist next to her. "Let's make love." And she began to undress.

Then people in some of the other boxes began fighting each other as the curtain rose.

Picasso had got permission from Diaghilev, despite the latter's artistic principles, to use as back-drop a simple curtain, dazzlingly white, lit by spot-lights. In this way the costumes of the dancers, dressed as Chinese, Jugglers, "Hommes-Maisons" (Managers), etc., were heightened in colour. The "Little American Girl" that Picasso and Cocteau had created was so true to life, even though the artists had never set foot in America, that when I was in New York twenty-five years later I saw her type time and again on Fifth Avenue.

There was such almost erotic excitement in the rhythm of the music, in the lighting, in the dancing, that those spectators who were not fighting or shouting "Bravo!" were performing like the couple in my box.

Out in the corridor M. Marcel Boulenger and the editor of *Le Matin* were exchanging cards for a duel.

When the final curtain fell on this triumphal scene, a young poet shouted,

"This is the end of the 'Battle of Hernani'!" [1]

* * * * *

Shortly afterwards, in Paris, a great event occurred in the private life of the artist. He was still connected with the Russian Ballet, for he was fascinated by that magnificent movement, which had brought him, Matisse and Derain, along with Cubism, to the stage of the Paris Opéra. And there he formed an attachment.

Diaghilev was preparing to put on the ballet *Pulcinella*, and Picasso, once more defying all the rules of décor and perspective, had "broken up" the stage by arranging a scene with a house in the middle-ground—something that had not been done in the theatre since Palladio's day.

While working on this project, he became very much interested in a young dancer who went by the picturesque name of Kokholova.

"Be careful," Diaghilev warned him. "A Russian always intends marriage."

"You're joking," replied Picasso.

"You watch out," Bakst told him.

[1] An allusion to a similar riot that had taken place years before at the première of the first romantic drama, Victor Hugo's *Hernani*. [*Trans. note.*]

Soon afterwards Picasso became engaged to her. The most paradoxical part about the affair was that the young lady's mother came to Diaghilev, very upset, and said:

Picasso by Bakst

"A painter . . . Is painting a respectable profession?"
"At least as respectable as dancing," answered the impresario.
"But can he earn a living?"

The years passed. One of Picasso's drawings, from a caseful of his works which he had sold in his Montmartre days for one hundred francs, went for twenty-five thousand.

Then came the exhibition of his still-lifes: a new "manner", resulting in a new success, which was as striking as it was complete, because the pictures had a freshness and originality of composition such as had never been seen before.

Paul Rosenberg followed Picasso's work with feverish interest. Each time he went up to the artist's apartment he would find a new masterpiece. One morning he was shown a large still-life of grapes, apricots and peaches.

"It's admirable," he said. "I'll take it, of course."

The next day Rosenberg went to look at the finished canvas. But Picasso had taken the fruit out of the dish and used their warm colours to paint the surrounding surface, leaving only one piece of fruit as a reminder. The day after that the canvas was once more entirely repainted.

He exhibited forty of the series, almost all of which were snapped up during the first week.

"Those canvases will have a few more brothers and sisters, I hope," Rosenberg said, enthusiastically.

"Certainly not," declared Picasso. "You mustn't expect me to repeat myself. My past doesn't interest me. I would rather copy others than copy myself. In that way I should at least be giving them something new. I love discovering things. . . ."

There is all of Picasso in that phrase.

* * * * *

For Picasso, the most important thing is always to find a new idiom in which to express his art. But he does not like to talk about it. Whenever a young painter comes to him, and wants to tell him about his theories of art, Picasso stops him and advises him to "say it with brushes and paints".

He doesn't care much about painting from nature. He is more interested in creating form. One day he said to us:

"I had engaged a certain model. After a short time I let her go. I don't like prisons."

On another occasion he told Rosenberg.

"Did you know I made a fortune today?"

"Oh? What have you been painting?"

"Oh, not in that way. I sold my 'mandolin rights'. I'm not going to paint them any more. I'm leaving that to others. . . ."

Another time his art-dealer came to see a canvas on which Picasso had been working for several weeks.

"Where is it?" asked Rosenberg.

Picasso smiled.

"I'm rich," he said. "I've just liquidated a hundred thousand francs."

Sometimes the artist, like the poet Gasquet, seems to be saying, "I don't give a damn". But, like Gasquet with his poems, Picasso is ready to give his last breath in his struggle with a canvas.

* * * * *

To mention another episode in his life, Picasso has a son, Paulo, whom he loves dearly. One night when Paulo was a child, he suddenly fell gravely ill. There was no telephone in the house.

It is curious how sometimes the most advanced, the most "contemporary", artists have unexpected prejudices against modern inventions and the simplest practical conveniences. How many painters of his time, I wonder, were impressed by a remark made by crusty old Degas: "Ha-ha! Forain has had a telephone installed in his house, and when it rings he actually goes and answers it."

But Picasso had no telephone. In desperation, his wife had to go to a neighbour's and telephone for an ambulance to take the child to hospital. The next morning Dr. Grosset, the well-known surgeon, operated on little Paulo, and saved his life. And when the doctor refused to charge any fee for his services, Picasso sent him one of his finest canvases: a portrait of a young boy dressed as Pierrot. Soon afterwards he had a telephone installed in his apartment. He does not like using it: but he looks on it, in its niche, as a sort of idol, to which he can always appeal in an emergency.

He has other whims, too. One day a certain painter in Montparnasse came to see me with one of Picasso's canvases. He wanted only a modest price for it, but he insisted on my getting Picasso to verify it. I took it to the latter, who gave one look at it, and said crossly,

"It's a fake."

"But I'm sure it's a genuine Picasso," my visitor protested to me the following day. "Here's another one. Doesn't that strike you as genuine too?"

"It certainly does."

But when I showed it to Picasso, he glanced at it even more cursorily and said,

"It's a fake."

By now I began to have some doubts myself. So I took one of my own Picassos down from the wall, and carried it to the rue de la Boétie for the artist to pass judgement. And again he stated flatly,

"It's a fake."

That was too much, and I exclaimed,

"But I saw you do this canvas myself!"

He gave a slight shrug.

"Oh, well," he said, with a smile, "I sometimes do fake Picassos myself."

However, when he heard the story of the poor painter who had brought me his Picasso to sell, he said,

"We'll buy his picture for four times what he's asked for it."

Picasso's generosity is in fact legendary. I hardly dare name the sums of money he donated for Spanish children in the 1930's during the Spanish Civil War.

Incidentally, he was then engaged on his *Guernica*, depicting a dying horse with a steel tongue, crushing a pregnant mother, whose fist clenches a lamp that is about to set fire to a house.

At the end of the annual ceremony in memory of Guillaume Apollinaire, which Picasso never missed, a Futurist academician, who had written things about Spain which had annoyed the artist, came forward to shake hands with him. Picasso clicked his heels together, drew himself up as if he were standing at attention, and said,

"You forget, sir, that we are at war. . . ."

Into his tragic fresco *Guernica* Picasso poured all his artist's blood, his whole Spanish soul.

He worked on it in his new studio in the rue des Grands-Augustins, on the second floor of an old building, which housed the Bailiffs' Union. To avoid being disturbed there, he had put a spiked barrier across the first step of the stairs leading to his place, so that it was impossible to ring his bell when the gate was closed.

Everything was orderly and austere in the studio: there were no ornaments on the walls, no curtains in front of the high windows.

For paints, Picasso used anything and everything, even furniture paint. For a palette he used whatever was handy—pieces of wood, cardboard, or the wall, or even the window-pane, on which he could gauge the transparency or opacity or luminosity of his brush-strokes. He worked every hour of the day and night. And what an experience it was to watch him work!

He had trained flood-lights on the huge canvas, in front of which he ran dancing up and down, rushing at it and darting away again. As I had occasion to see him in action, I jotted down the following notes on the spot:

"He seems to knead the handle of his brush in his short fist, sight his prey and take aim like a picador preparing to lance a bull. Or rather, the picador becomes himself the bull. His black eyes dilate; his nostrils distend; his legs tremble. He gathers himself to rush upon his work. But, no: he only caresses it. Then he flies into a rage. He rubs out what he has just done; destroys it. For had he not prepared it all beforehand in his mind's eye, as carefully as possible, face by face, expression by expression, plane by plane, volume by volume, colour by colour, as a general plans a battle? Even so, in the midst of the fight he wavers, and suddenly changes his plan. Then Picasso dashes forward, slashing out almost everything he has achieved, and begins again, more fiercely, more expressively, more boldly, more sentiently than ever. It is truly a battle, and in the course of it he will fertilise his mistress, the canvas, and fashion her as he wants her, more beautiful still. It is a mating of animals and a spiritual love; it is a carnage and the tenderest embrace. It is almost as if, in his ardour, he breaks the back of his beloved, while she drinks from his lips an intoxicating wine, a wine of life, of reality and of transfiguration.

"Broken and exhausted, he halts, then flings himself once more into the battle.

"Sometimes he works quickly, his hand trying to keep pace with his lightning thoughts. At others he paints slowly, almost coldly, diligently.

"My eyes do not leave him while he paints—for the tenth time, in his desire to make it more expressive, more convulsive—that clenched hand, with the sword falling from the wounded fingers . . .

"How joyously he paints these figures on the shore of a cerulean sea! His face is filled with light like the sky; his eye gleams with the malice of a pagan god. He smiles as he composes his detailed pencil-sketches with such care. But once more his brows contract.

Like a Japanese, he would chastise himself for a wrong line. Furiously he wipes out this or that piece of work, which has cost him so much effort, as a child kicks over a sand-castle.

"And when he takes up his etching-needle, it is a dagger in the Spaniard's hand, with which he scores the flesh."

The next morning he goes and looks over the previous day's work, his hands in his pockets and a smile in his eyes. He examines this or that detail. He stands back from the canvas; takes it in as a whole; glances at his brushes. All at once he picks up one of them, and the battle is on again: eventually he will win.

* * * * *

1954. Vallauris. From Golfe-Juan the road winds up through a rocky ravine interspersed with little cascades and groves of olive trees. Long before reaching the village, one encounters red and yellow signs saying: "Visit the fifteen pottery-works on the Fournas road to the right". To which one is tempted to reply: "And the eighty-five others in the town as well". There are other signboards displaying the pleasant names of various artisans who make pottery and majolica. At the end of the main street is a little square, in front of the town hall, where Picasso's *Man With a Lamb* can be seen on its pedestal.

"The Villa La Galloise? Oh, yes. Monsieur Picasso's place. The first street on the right, then go straight on up between the factories and the open country."

Although it is only half-past nine in the morning, a dozen cars are already parked at the foot of the villa's rose-garden, as if hitched on to each other along the steep road. Nearby a number of people are seated or walking about, talking in several languages, smoking, waiting for a door or a window to open in the villa. It is a regular siege. No doubt the pilgrims in Tibet wait about in the same way in front of the Dalai-Lama's palace.

Paulo, the painter's eldest son, drives up on a motor-bike, and comes over to greet me. He leads the way through the tangled garden blazing with roses.

"There's a good deal of grass," he says, apologetically. "Papa didn't want it cut, so he bought a couple of donkeys to keep it down for him instead."

We go upstairs, pass through a hall, and enter Picasso's own room. The painter is seated on a large brass bed, getting dressed, and he puts on his socks, his working-slacks and a sweater. No aesthetics here; no playing the bourgeois or the "artist", either. He rises to his feet and shakes hands.

"It's been a long time since we saw each other!" he exclaims.

I am struck by his appearance. The Picasso before me is entirely new to me. He no longer has his lock of hair over one eye. And the face below the almost shaved head (a veritable Dalai-Lama) is terra-cotta colour; his eyes, those famous flashing eyes of his, eclipse everything about him; and his smile puts us at our ease.

"This is Or de Fugères, the Curator of the Antibes Museum, whom you already know," he says. "And may I present the painter Pignon, and his wife; and Paulo—but you've known him since he was born. And this gentleman, here, has come to ask me to verify a canvas."

The walls are whitewashed. Over the mantelpiece hang two small, unframed portraits by the Douanier Rousseau. From the windows can be seen the slopes of the surrounding hills and several chimneys of nearby pottery-works.

"They are putting up a sort of cement building over there," Picasso informs us. "But we'll get used to it. Ugly? That depends on how you look at it."

As it is Sunday, all the young men in town are playing bowls in the Place des Ecoles. The artist takes us out to his studio, or, rather, to his studios. Paulo brings a long Hispano out of the garage. Picasso puts on a checked cap, like the one Renoir used to wear.

"You see, I'm still faithful to it."

"The same jockey-cap that helped you to win so many Grands Prix!"

Taking a round-about way, we arrive at the Fournas road, and find ourselves in front of half-a-dozen sheds (part of a former perfume factory), where his chief artisans, Suzanne and Georges Ramié, are waiting for us. In the first shed there is a remarkably fine metal cast of a *Venus* lying on the ground, ready for the arms and legs to be soldered on. Piled on various tables, on benches, on shelves and on the ground are hundreds of objects of all kinds and descriptions: cigarette-boxes ornamented with the skulls of twenty different animals; a couple of hundred pieces of pottery, which look as though they had been recently dug up out of the soil of Crete; faces made out of wire, wood or cardboard; screws and bicycle-chains; paint-pots lined up like regiments; coloured mouldings for experiments with new forms; rails, alembics, scales, gyroscopes and other articles scattered about the red-and-black earthen floor.

We make our way through this phantasmagoria to a second shed, and on to a third and fourth, to wind up in an even more bewildering one. It is like Ali-Baba's caves. We feel as though we had come in search of treasure at the bottom of the ocean, or in the Caribbean sea, or some prehistoric cavern. For there, under all these old tiles covering the unfaced walls, are literally millions of francs worth of canvases, most of them unfinished. Among them are some thirty large panels representing the head of a young, Botticelli-like English girl, her hair done in a horse's tail.

"If the Greeks had worn chignons like that, would their statues have been any the less splendid? That's a young girl who has been living out here recently. I've taken a model for the first time in my life, and I am really using her. She posed for this."

"Directly? Did she pose while you actually painted those large canvases?"

"Yes—instead of making studies on bits of paper. But I've done a hundred or so sketches of her as well."

And there they were, in fact: bundles of papers, sketches that had been carefully worked on, cross-hatched, shaded, modelled and modified so that the final versions were reduced to just a few simple lines.

"I'm beginning to 'get' it, I think," says the artist. "Paulo, will you open this door?"

Another shed, and twenty more canvases of the same head in profile, with hair drawn tight towards the back, some of them on the ground, some on the walls, some on easels, some on chairs.

"They look like a sculptor's drawings."

"As a matter of fact, I do want to use them for sculpture. What interests me most is to find exactly the right place for the hair and the face, in space, as well as for the chair on which the model is sitting. But I've got to try a few more canvases for it. There are some others in the next shed."

I look at them all, my eyes going from one picture to another, and I examine each one closely, first a profile, then a three-quarters view of the charming head, and so on, all done with a few long brush-strokes. Throughout the series the neck gradually becomes longer and narrower, but in such a way that, although it attains to three or four times its natural proportions, it seems normal in the geometry of the lines traced like a flight of birds, which cross and re-cross each other, and remain fixed.

Again the Protean monster has changed his form, and again found what the older generation called a "new manner"; and each time he has achieved something bolder, freer, more original and definitive, and with complete mastery!

M. Tériade, the editor of the art review *Verve*, who is one of our party, is overcome with admiration.

"Monsieur Picasso, you are the greatest draughtsman the world has ever known!" he exclaims. "And from what have you not delivered us!"

Picasso pays no attention, but searches through his canvases and puts aside half a dozen, which are still wet and rather stark in execution.

"Yes," he repeats, "I think I have almost 'got' it."

"Are you going to add another colour to those large, almost geometrical spaces, with their arabesques?"

"Um—an arabesque is a dance; a dance——"

"Do you intend to keep only the greys?"

His greys are so delicate and so light that, by contrast, the model's eyes look blue.

"Colour?" he queries. "I don't know. Yes and no. Perhaps. As you put salt in soup. Probably a little yellow and a very little green, which will give the face a slightly rose tint. But colour interests me less at the present time than 'gravity' or 'density'."

"Gravity is the balancing factor of density."

"Yes, it's like oil and vinegar. . . . Well, who knows? Perhaps some day painting will be done with oil and vinegar. But where's the dog? Tanger? He's run off to the café. It's noon already. Let's go and have an apéritif or a glass of Vittel water."

We go out to a little café along the road, where the terrace is filled with tables covered with red-and-yellow check cloths. As we sit down Picasso says:

"Yesterday Gauguin's son was here with me; and Oscar Wilde's son the day before. He resembles his father, only he looks older."

"And what about that musician you were so severe with?"

"I wasn't severe with him. He writes operettas and was silly enough to say to me, 'You know, I was meant to write grand operas.' 'No, you weren't,' I said. 'If you'd been meant to write grand operas, they'd have come out of your guts. Do whatever you do well: that's the most important thing.' It's like that other fellow who used to disparage Bouguereau. But Bouguereau painted quite well. I shouldn't say that to everybody because 'everybody' would interpret it differently from the way we do. . . . Well, it's half-past twelve. I must go to lunch and get back to work. I think that after I've worked out a dozen or so more canvases really well, I'll get what I'm after. I like that white area I leave behind the face. That's Space."

"And wrestling with Space has something titanic about it that fascinates you."

His dark eyes glow even more than usual. He gets up and shakes hands all round.

"Paulo!"

Paulo is already at the wheel of the Hispano, and he takes his father off into the mountains, into that clear light which strikes directly on the painter's forehead, the kind of light he uses with such serenity.

GEORGES BRAQUE

Who invented Cubism—Braque or Picasso?

If you ask them, Braque will say,

"Picasso."

And Picasso will always say,

"Braque."

For though they are of such different temperaments—one a punctual French bourgeois, the other impetuous, scattering his ideas and works like jewels to the four winds—they nevertheless have a deep admiration and affection for each other. As Picasso once said of his friend,

"Braque never sings off-key."

The time is 1910; the place, Braque's studio in Montmartre, with a violin, a mandolin, a pipe-rack and several Negro masks hanging on the wall. There are canvases everywhere. On the table stands a saucepan, on the floor a water-jug. For water, Braque is obliged to go down seven flights and fetch it up himself. But what is that for a painter who has tramped, knapsack on his back, up and down the country, visiting all the places Cézanne painted, in order to steep himself in them and "do them over again", "breaking up the volumes just as the Master of Aix had broken up the light".

He works like a jobber all day long, from six in the morning till eight at night. He is interested in nothing but painting. Unless he is in front of his easel and subject, he feels he is wasting precious time. I can still see him, in those days of the Russian Ballet, sitting restlessly on the terrace of a café in Monte Carlo, along with Georges Auric and the famous impresario.[1] He dressed conventionally, and even wore a derby. As he gazed out over the sea—which he loves, though he prefers the coast of Normandy to the South of France—Braque explained his theories of art to us.

"First, I get an idea. Then begins the great adventure, which comes into being under my brush. An idea for a picture is like a cradle [he meant the framework where a ship rests while it is being built], which is taken away when the boat is finished. The picture is completed when the idea has disappeared."

"Have you worked with Picasso?"

"Yes, we have worked together—principally at Sorgues, near Avignon, in 1912, under a broiling sun.

"The walls of the houses there formed large planes, grey in the light—the whole thing was nothing but a series of angles. It was then that I realised that light, or colour, destroys form. When I was in the Camouflage Service during the War, I tried out my theory with a toy cannon, using browns and greens. Horizon-blue was quickly discarded, and camouflage has been done in brown and green ever since."

He told us much more, and then went on,

"As I said to Apollinaire, painting is getting closer and closer to poetry, now that photography has freed it from the need to tell a

[1] Diaghilev had asked Braque to do the settings and costumes for Molière's *Les Fâcheux*, for which Auric composed the music.

story. Like music, painting must have its own means of expression."

Braque now works in the rue du Douanier, in a studio which was designed for him by Perret, the architect of the Champs Elysées Theatre. It is a wide, airy place with plenty of space, and the light filters through vellum blinds. There are divans here and there, and long wooden tables, on which are neatly ranged his

brushes, tools, paint-pots and other equipment. At the back is a large old-rose screen, whose colour serves not only as a control but also as a contrast and a point of departure.

Robust, slow and composed in his movements, the artist converses quietly. He wears sports shoes and a cap. One senses a great surge of strength in him, like a locomotive that can do eighty miles an hour, and only goes ten.

He walks over to one of his canvases and caresses it with his hand. The look he gives it is both deliberate and shrewd, and behind it there is a little gleam of light. He props up the frame, a frame which throws the picture forward.

"In the old days we used Renaissance frames," he says, "chiefly because of the lines of recession; and the 'groove' of the frame helped the illusion. But I've discarded the lines of recession, which are almost always false. A picture should make you want to live 'inside' it. I want the beholder to enter into my picture, and to feel as if the frame were behind him. . . . Oh, I didn't exactly originate that conception. Trouillebert said to Corot one day, 'Where's that tree you're putting into your landscape?' And Corot replied, 'Behind me'."

JUAN GRIS

What delightful recollections we all have of that charming fellow, who was so modest and bashful, his friends say, that he would never allow anyone to see him naked, not even his wife. He raised Cubism to an aristocratic level, "starting from the abstract to arrive at reality", a reality of pure and almost musical quality. If he accepted the Cubist discipline with the conviction that "here is a new language in which to paint the world", he did so as a poet no less than as a painter.

"Give me a branch to perch on," he said to the sculptor Jacques Lipschitz, "and I will sing like a bird on it."

And he elaborated his views in this way:

"I know that in the beginning Cubism was an analytical experiment which had no more to do with Painting than the description of a problem in physics has to do with Physics. But it was rounded out by technical experiments, and analysis has, in consequence, become synthesis by analogy with the subject-matter. With the result that Cubism will eventually cease to be an æsthetic movement and become an element of painting." [1]

These opinions may be forgiven those who were so ardently searching for a new truth, and above all those, like Juan Gris, who did not stop at intellectual innovations, believing that "a painting should last longer than a school, even though it temporarily belongs to that school".

Theories pose the problem; the solution is the work itself.

* * * * *

It is little known, perhaps, that Gris was one of Paul Iribe's

[1] Cf. Claude Roger Marx.

first associates, when, as a poor young man, he had to work on one of that designer's publications.

Diaghilev engaged him to do a ballet, a commission which freed him for a time from the poverty which none of us had even suspected.

One of the best things he created is lost to posterity. Gris had asked me to come and look at it before anyone else, and this is what it was:

When the Printemps store in Paris was being rebuilt, the poet Jean Valmy-Baysse, a friend of the owner's, suggested that Juan Gris should be asked to do the decorations for the opening ceremony. Gris accepted, but only on condition that he was allowed a free hand. The architect, Wybo, gave his consent.

Gris hung from the arches a series of long, banner-like bands of silk, ranging from the palest of greys to the darkest blues, placed close enough to hide the framework of the glass roof, yet far enough apart to allow the light to bring out the harmonies of colour. He covered the balustrade of the stairs in the same manner; while on the ground floor he set up great screens of the same shades some of them soaring high into the air. The whole effect made one of the largest and most beautiful so-called Cubist pictures I have ever seen.

★ ★ ★ ★ ★

Hayden and Marcoussis were the first real interpreters of Cubism. Every time I met Marcoussis, he would say to me:

"Do you think I shall be forgotten? I am very unhappy about it. I have spent my whole life trying to add my humble stone to the edifice."

Hayden, for his part, persevered for a long time in the Cubist idiom. His melancholy took quite a different line.

"I hope I shan't succumb under the weight of the cube," he said. "Yet what a fine death that would be! Heroic? Perhaps. But a fine death nevertheless . . ."

The works of the two painters have a prominent place in the Paris Musée d'Art Moderne.

LÉGER THE TUBIST

Among all the painters who were Constructors, Reconstructors, Constructivists and Cubists—that is to say, Juan Gris, Hayden, Marcoussis, Maria Blanchard, Jacques Villon, Gleizes, Metzinger, Herbin, Severini, Duchamp, Survage, La Fresnaye—the name of Fernand Léger is certainly one of the most outstanding.

He was another Norman, with square shoulders, light eyes, a large nose firmly planted in a heavy face and an air of knowing exactly where he wanted to go.

When you entered his Montparnasse studio (which was not far from the one that Whistler once had), you might think at first that you had got into a workshop by mistake. The whole place was a clutter of dynamos, gears and wheels of every description. But Léger would come out in his overalls from behind his turbines, cylinders and pumps, and, running his hand over the polished steel of a connecting-rod, would say,

"Don't you think they're beautiful?"

"They are your 'models'?"

"Yes, but I interpret them. I don't copy."

The walls were covered with canvases. He had been the first to interpret the human form in terms of the machine and find the appropriate style for the age; and with his massive volumes, which he painted without any concession to photographic realism, he reacted more violently than any other painter against the Impressionist theories, and even against the flat, single-toned areas favoured by the Fauves. In his picture *The City*, he captured, like Cézanne, the effect of depth solely through colour and without depending on perspective.

"Invent," he said, as he stood on his ladder, brushing in his wide areas of pure tones. "Invent forms as the Chaldeans did, and the Romans and the Gothic artists. But don't copy."

We sometimes went to the cinema together, especially in the rue de la Gaîté, the street which the Goncourts, Lorrain, Lautrec, Burne-Jones and de Feure had all been so fond of. Léger was enthusiastic about the cinema, which showed him new forms that even photography had not revealed to him.

"Look at that hand on the wall, on that white ground," he would say. "No painter has ever depicted it in just that way."

One night after we had gone to see a film, Léger seemed to be lost in thought. When we got back to his studio, he took out a large sheet of paper and began drawing on it. After a few minutes, he said:

"I've made a discovery. What is important now is not the subject, but the *object.*"

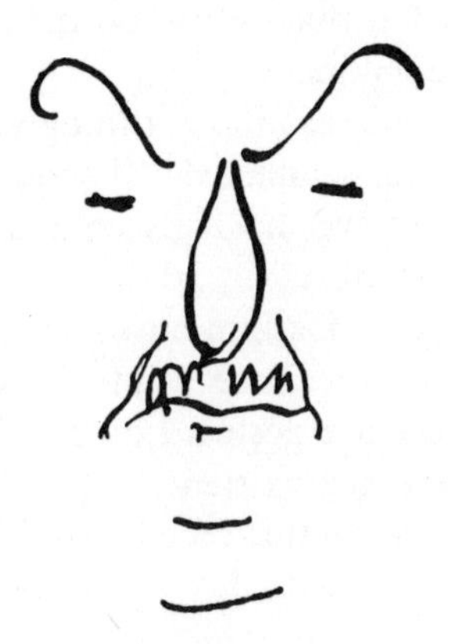

And thus he invented the "Religion of the Object", which was to play such an important part in the development of the new-born Cubist movement, as well as in the various trends of the Ecole de Paris.

It was at this time that, as a reaction against both the stippling technique of the Impressionists and the large, violently coloured surfaces of the Fauvists, the younger generation of artists turned to construction and, in accordance with Cézanne's doctrine, demonstrated that everything in Nature should be "treated as a cylinder, a sphere or a cone; that it should all be put in perspective —i.e., that each side of an object, of a plane, should converge on a central point".

Others chose the cube, the polyhedron and the pyramid. Being fascinated by the poetry of machinery, Léger began by expressing his ideas in tube forms, which prompted the art critic, Louis Vauxcelles, to nickname him "Léger the Tubist". It was, of course, only a play on words, for Vauxcelles really considered him one of the most powerful painters of his time.

Léger anticipated several of his friends by using pure, intense colours at a time when the first Cubists and Analysts were still composing their pictures in grey or brown only, some of them rebelling against the "*nouveau richissisme*" by tolerating only insipid colours, and subjects taken from the most banal aspects of daily life.

Moreover, Léger invented the "poetry of the bolt", the nut and the bolt, as opposed to that of the rose. And, in spite of the advent of neo-plasticism, he felt that he was on the right track, and continued to follow his own line.

"We are used to seeing too much through the medium of conventional drawings," he maintained. "I should like to meet someone who paints without ever having seen a drawing in his life: he could teach us a few things!"

One of his art-dealers took him on a trip to Rome, and I wondered what effect the experience would have on Léger. I soon found out, for I received a postcard of the Dome of St. Peter's from him, and on it he had written:

"It is beautiful; very beautiful; too beautiful. Beauti-beauti-ful. Bee-u-ti-ful!"

★ ★ ★ ★ ★

On his return to Paris, I happened to be talking to him one day about Picasso, and Léger remarked:

"He belongs to another order. I am of Romance origin, but I paint in a pure French tradition, and my art tends to prolong and add to that tradition. Picasso, yes. Yes. But two mouths and three eyes—that's 'Spanish torture'. Of course, there are Goya and El Greco. But they're of another lineage; they have another conception. . . ."

★ ★ ★ ★ ★

Léger had, moreover, interpreted landscapes and objects by the use of large planes, to which he gave not only plastic and pictorial value but also the particular significance which haunted him and which was to replace the futile arrangements of subjects that had been done over and over again. Not only had he introduced absolutely pure tones without any mixture of colours, but he inscribed each work within a geometric form, thus launching a new style of decorative art, which he hoped might spread to poster art and even to road-signs.

But he wanted especially to create new forms.

"Yes," he said, "to invent forms, but not to copy nature, even on the plane of Michelangelo. To draw well the vein of a hand is an old story now; it has become a form of illustration. Painting or literature that does not reflect its epoch is not healthy art. It produces a Maurice Rostand. In order to make people aware of what is happening in the world today, in Asia, on the high seas, in the air, you must have painting that is intense and violent, in a state of war, and not stuff that is all frills and futility. And you must find a new form for this dynamic conception; otherwise, it will be unimportant."

We were talking together at the time in his studio in New York, which looked out on the gardens of the Public Library. All round us were skyscrapers, the multi-coloured lights of their countless electric signs incessantly flashing a host of fantastic patterns, even though it was full daylight. Léger had his usual collection of motors, boilers, gears, piston-rods and fly-wheels of polished steel, from which he drew his inspiration, the model in each case serving as a stimulus, but not as an object to be copied photographically.

And it struck me as somehow paradoxical to see this man of ancient Norman descent, with his furrowed brow and red hair, in such an environment, and dressed in the same sort of green sweater and workman's trousers he was accustomed to wearing in Montparnasse.

"One must invent," he repeated. "The Cubists were inventors, just as the Gothic artists and Assyrians were. One must invent, not reconstitute. Invent with intensity, and on a scale appropriate to the country where one is and the period one lives in. Intensity is one of the chief aims. You attack a wall, you destroy it, you put life in its place. It is my ambition to do a fresco a mile long as the backcloth for an airfield, with landscapes and people propelled along as they are in actual life, by their muscles, their cars, their planes, and even by interplanetary rockets—all to be executed in harmonious and dynamic forms in a planned equilibrium, as willed by the painter, the Master! . . ."

AMEDÉE OZENFANT

Ozenfant has a face and a figure somewhat like his name: an O for a head; a Z for a nose; an F for a body. He is at present directing a school of design in New York. But he lived for a long time in Paris, where he founded another kind of school, that of "Purism", as well as any number of reviews. And it was the Purist movement which produced the architect Jeanneret, who became the architect Jeanneret-Le Corbusier and then simply the architect Le Corbusier—the man who, at every stage of his career, dreamed of a geometric urbanism which could only result in a nightmare—the nightmare of standardisation, of uniformity, of denial of fantasy; in short, utilitarian life, life without surprises.

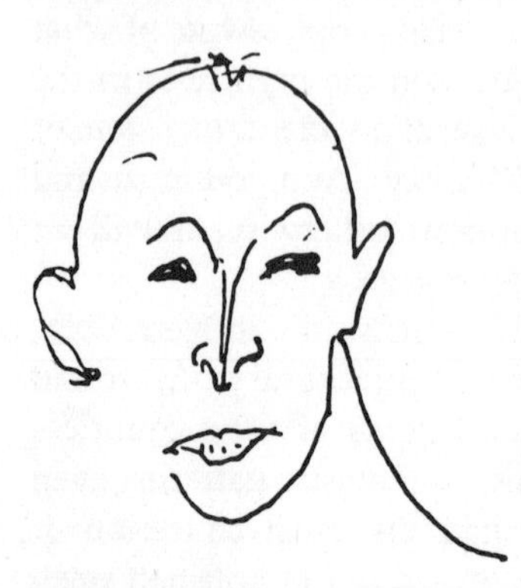

These reviews were very advanced, extremely interesting and highly critical. One of their specialities was to compare different civilizations at various times and places in history, illustrating their comparisons with numerous picturesque photographs. Names like Kong-Fu-Zu and Einstein collided like blinding flashes of lightning in a storm that threatened to annihilate the universe beneath a ton of words.

And yet how many original ideas there were to be found in the general welter of nonsense; how many important truths were brought to light. To cite one example, Ozenfant was probably the first to denounce the stylistic clichés used by some of the avant-garde painters, just as the latter had denounced similar clichés among the academicians. He would even have called them "Picassoids", if Picasso, with his customary astuteness, had not already disowned them. In fact, I have already quoted that painter's remark to the effect that "I have just sold off my collection of mandolins; I'm leaving them for others now".

Mandolins, siphons, tobacco-pouches, Harlequins, etc., had all become commonplace adjuncts of the new school, just as scenes of everyday life, pictures which "told a story", historical battles and the naked body had been adjuncts of the Salon painters.

Trained in the La Tour School, at St. Quentin, which the famous pastel artist had bequeathed to his native town "for the artistic education of the People", Ozenfant continued his studies with the Dominicans at Arcachon, going with them to Spain, to San Sebastian, where they established their centre at Monte Igualdo. From there he went to London, then to Seattle, and then on again to near Vancouver, which, he said, was "a place taken from the Indians only eighty years ago, and now with a population of six hundred thousand and avenues twenty-five miles long".

He eventually moved to New York, where he has remained ever since; and it was in his studio in 20th Street that he explained to me, with remarkable conciseness, his ideas on the subject of art.

"The human being has an inherent need for some forms, and not for others. To achieve these imperative forms is great art. Take, for instance, this pebble in the shape of a flattened sphere: doesn't it give you a feeling of satisfaction? As a peasant woman said to me, quite simply, 'It is beautiful'. And here is a spiral sea-shell, the lines of which resemble the eternal and perfect curve of the breast. Doesn't it give you a feeling of joy? Well, then, a work of art, in its parts and as a whole, should be, if not exactly in the image of such forms, at least suggestive of them, and therefore of that kind of pleasure, and therefore of art itself. Here are still other sea-shells and pebbles, which have natural designs and irregularities on them. They are amusing, like baroque or rock-work. They are not eternal, like Greek or Egyptian art. This pebble, which is perfect in form, nature has taken centuries to polish. Similarly, a perfect work of art that we achieve has been inherent within us for generations. This pebble, this shell, are both part of the cosmos; that is to say, they are in the atom, just as they are in the spiral nebulae, whose smallest star may often be a thousand million times greater in volume than our universe. I search far in the two dimensions of time and space and I end up with this design, for example. It none the less exists in its own right."

Ozenfant pointed to a piece of white paper on the wall, on which he had drawn a *Maternity* in a profusion of lines, lines which were pleasing not only as a whole but also in detail. The uninitiated might have seen in it only an ape-like head, without hair, with arms attached to the body like wooden beams, and the fingers growing out of the stump, like branches from a willow-tree. And yet no one could have denied that these lines produced an unconscious sense of well-being. A modern technician would have exclaimed that Ozenfant had gone beyond the earth-bound, and escaped into the metaphysical, universal and eternal world.

The artist smiled as he said to me,

"If I am wrong, the proper place for that picture is the dustbin; if not, it is eternal."

GROMAIRE

His studio is like his work: neat and bright. It has beautiful furniture in it, with modern cupboards harmonising perfectly with

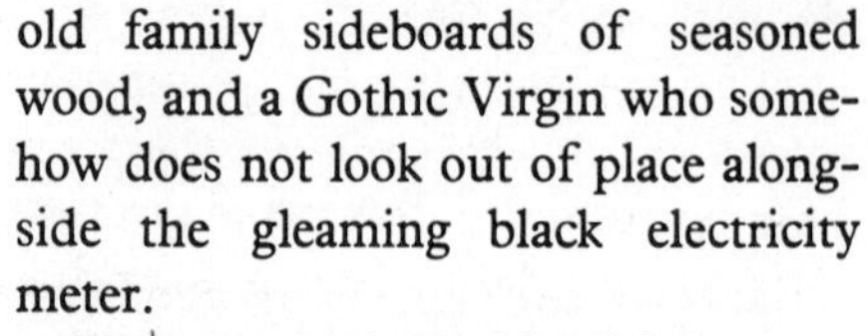

old family sideboards of seasoned wood, and a Gothic Virgin who somehow does not look out of place alongside the gleaming black electricity meter.

"I can't stand disorder," he says.

A man of the North, he has a straight figure and a well-shaped blond head, with a high and shining forehead.

Lying on several tables are small pieces of paper with exact, carefully-done drawings on them, placed side by side somewhat as Bonnard arranged his squares of colour.

"Ah, Bonnard!" says Gromaire. "What mysterious alchemy: yet so rich, so remarkably rich! It is too bad that the younger generation can't understand his work any more. They talk to us about the abstract! But their abstract is only the contemplation of themselves. The abstract is part of painting, but only a part. Because it has no weight except when in full contact with the concrete; otherwise it can never amount to more than an enlargement of small decorative motifs. But there's always been abstract painting, from Ucello down to modern times; down to Matisse, if you like. Some dig down and find it in places where others have seen nothing. Take, for example, the Poussin which was in the Exhibition of Masterpieces at San Paolo: a sort of cortège of dances; and what a composition! I have never seen such a marvellous piece of 'clockwork'. Compared to it, what are abstract pictures today? Lhote has written that Poussin used the Golden Section,[1] even in the smallest details. Pooh! The Golden Section, for me, at any rate, is a useful check; not a starting-point. Cubism didn't teach me very much. But it did Matisse. And what sincerity, what intensity he achieved, after so much labour! How did I acquire my personality? I had nothing to do with it. I interpret according to my vision, just as Van Gogh—whose 'motifs' from nature I've studied—interpreted, and to what degree, you can't imagine! The rest is only fashion. And the æsthetic aspects soon disappear, to the advantage of both the depth of the work and the intensity of the temperament."

CONCERNING JACQUES VILLON

I always heard the Cubist painters speak of Jacques Villon with a deep, almost mystical, respect.

After all, Jacques Villon belonged to our early years, to the period of Jules Roques' *Courrier Français*, of Boutigny's *Cocorico*, of the little *Chat Noir* and all that group: the smiling and grumpy Willette, who was both an anarchist and a believer, a revolutionary and a conformist; Widhopf; and Steinlen, with his little "frivolous" hat, and his cape.

There were the parties in his studio in the rue Caulaincourt, with the sculptor Villon-Duchamp, Crotti, Gleizes, Metzinger, Suzanne and the madcap Marcel Duchamp, the reverse of a painter's painter, who was like a breath of fresh air. Now he is in America, where he still manages to be that extreme of paradoxes: a painter who does not paint.

From drawing Villon moved to engraving, and from the rue Caulaincourt to a little house at Puteaux, hidden away in a mass of foliage. By way of recreation, the group would go on Monday to see Gleizes, who was continually busy with his theories in his

[1] Method for attaining the ideal harmony in art. It is "the division of a magnitude in which the smaller portion is to the larger as the larger portion is to the whole". It originated with Euclid, but its aesthetic value was only developed by the nineteenth-century German Zeising. [*Translator's note.*]

house in Courbevoie; on Tuesday we were all with Paul Fort at the Closerie des Lilas, which was to become the link between the Latin Quarter and the future Montparnasse Quarter. On Sunday we played *Courses* at Villon's, betting on toy lead horses. We had as much fun as any band of youngsters.

La Fresnaye turned up one Fourteenth of July with his large canvas *The Drinkers* on top of a cab, wearing a boater stuck with little tricolour flags.

If La Fresnaye brought out the essential elements of Cubism, and its feeling of sensitivity, it was Jacques Villon who was to reveal its innermost subtleties.

"Cubism acted on me like a tonic," said Villon, "although I did not remain a Cubist any more than Picasso did, or any of the others. . . . But at that crucial moment in Painting it seemed to us, it seemed to me, that to copy a subject for the sake of the subject was becoming *useless*. Cubism was moving towards creation, towards a new vision and a more intense realisation of objects. When I discussed the matter with Sagot, who had brought out my engravings, all he said was:

" 'I am too old to bother with theories. Go and see my brother Clovis: you'll feel more at home with him.'

"Similarly, as regards abstract art, I would say: 'I, Jacques Villon, am too old to go in for Abstraction; or, to be more precise, the Abstract.' It certainly has a side to it that is really important; but it also gives more of an opportunity for cheating! I don't believe we can yet dispense with the Abstract in painting, although many painters like Estève and Bazaine, for whom I have the greatest respect, are becoming less and less abstract."

* * * * *

When he is talking, Jacques Villon's finely lined face, over which a light seems to play, grows more subtle still. Yes, the word "subtle" is the most appropriate in describing not only his physiognomy, but also his work.

Let us listen to him as he discourses in his studio, while his wife, sitting nearby, nods her approval.

"My kind of Cubism is not entirely orthodox. But the essential thing for me was to find the right means, without concerning myself with the ultimate purpose, if there were any, by following what

Bergson called 'the line of intention'. On the other hand, the painter is also a musician, a pianist, his right hand playing the melody, or line, while the left elaborates the line, surrounding and supporting it, just as in this canvas, for instance, which depicts an aeroplane. For I always start out from a visible, intelligible base. Here you see the 'line of intention', the point of view I have decided on, and the harmonies. Now, these large triangles of colour round about are the zones dividing the canvas, which is arranged like a pyramid: a dark tone here; a light one there; then two medium tones. I always use that arrangement. Then I start on the details, using countless little overlapping pyramids as focus-points for the eye—an old theory of Leonardo's.

"The resulting rhythm has become more vibrant, especially since the latest discoveries, from those of Chevreul to O. N. Rood, whose chromatic Circle I find very useful as a base. It is very good, with its 'triads' of the 'finest harmonies'. But there are even simpler methods. Take this blue background, where I have increased the intensity of the blue as a contrast to the yellow foreground: between these two colours I have to create a whole accordion-like range of tones, with various focal points. And I must blend in the harmonies, which influence each other. It is like working with the spectrum, with a prism, and it pleases me very much, especially when I discover a yellow tone, for example, which, superimposed on the blue, turns it white—not pure white, of course; a slightly grey white, but white, nevertheless. It is what I call the interdependence of values. I have been seeking for twenty or thirty years, and little by little I am reaching my goal; and that's the important thing. . . ."

His is the life work of an alchemist, the results of which give, even to the uninitiated and uncomprehending, a feeling of visual satisfaction by their perfection and grace.

A LESSON BY ANDRÉ LHOTE

André Lhote's books on art—*Traité du Paysage*, *Traité de la Figure*, *Peinture d'Abord*, etc.—have been translated into many languages, and his pictures are hung in art galleries all over the world. For he is one of the greatest, one of the most subtle and above all one of the most lucid theorists of Painting.

He is "modern" in the most advanced sense of the word, but he constantly refers back to the Old Masters, especially the Primitives. The names of a great French painter, Poussin, and a great Italian, Piero della Francesca, frequently recur in his writings, when he is explaining the Golden Section, or Composition by Colour.

He has many disciples and pupils in France and abroad; and there are few of the younger modern masters who would think of denying that they had learned a great deal from him.

I have often stood in front of one of André Lhote's pictures and recalled what he has written about art, even though he may insist that his teaching and his pictures are quite separate (whereas, for instance, a Metzinger or a Gleizes will invariably put his theories into practice in his paintings as those theories evolve).

But so far as Lhote's teaching is concerned, there is not an exhibition or a salon where you will not come across canvases which show his influence. All too often, unfortunately, they follow blindly one of his principles, namely: "Light splits up objects into fragments, sometimes incomprehensible fragments, and the problem is to arrange them in a logical pattern."

In vain he repeats at each of his lessons:

"Compose your pictures rationally, lean on someone stronger than yourself—Jacques Villon, or some other authority—but in the final analysis follow your animal nature."

For Lhote is careful not to talk about taste, and still less about "good taste".

As for Lhote's lessons, I attended many a session of "correction" in his spacious studio in the rue d'Odessa, behind the Gare Montparnasse. The big room was full of sketches for various pictures, such as his *L'Escale* and *Fourteenth of July*, now in the Palais de New York and the Petit Palais.

I remember one typical occasion. On the couch the model keeps her pose while Lhote's pupils (among them two old American ladies, a Negro and two young men with beards) gather round the master. One of the group presents his work for criticism and guidance. With his eye-shade on his forehead, Lhote examines the inevitable arrangement of yellow, ochre and lemon areas in the picture, and then asks.

"Who splashed the egg-yolk on this canvas?"

"I did, Master."

"Yellow is a dangerous colour, especially when it is as intense as this."

"But, Master, didn't Gauguin say——?"

"Gauguin initiated a partial return to the purity of the Primitives, but his disciple, Matisse, went further. If you had looked more closely at the work of those two master-colourists, you would have seen that they compensated for each violent colour with a neutral tone, and their violent colours harmonise. Hand me your palette. . . . Of course you must 'interpret' objects, but it is best not to lose sight of them entirely, if you want to avoid turning out a confused mess. There. You see, by putting grey-green next to your egg-yellow, you will get a less aggressive effect. And don't be afraid to change from brush to pencil from time to time. The brush is often blind, so to speak; but the pencil is always intelligent, for is simplifies the relations between the different parts of the picture, being concerned only with the linear rhythm, which is always necessary where plastic coloured orchestration is involved. And the pencil discovers the plastic symbol, which will summarise the complex object you are looking at, and which you will never succeed in reproducing exactly, any more than I could."

"Yes, Master."

In the study made by the young girl with the innocent eyes, the model is little more than a jumble of lines, which are well enough drawn, but——

Lhote gives a start when he sees it, and, adjusting his eye-shade, says:

"The general effect of this picture is slightly academic, so that the green of the hair jars absurdly, since the model's hair is blonde. Oh, yes, I know you are going to tell me about the 'colour equivalents' of Gauguin and Matisse and Picasso; but they should at least harmonise. Your green is as out of place in your canvas as an Impressionist colour would be in a portrait by Rembrandt. You high-light the leg by giving it a second outline in a light shade. It is monotonous; moreover, the light on an arm or leg never follows the contour exactly because of the transverse muscles. You must make the stronger values play their proper role of architectural support. Who's next?"

"Master, I find that the Byzantines took the same liberties in their art as the moderns do."

"Yes, but that is no reason why you should draw a Byzantine face literally. If the model's nose is a little long, you can, if you wish, accentuate the feature to the point of eccentricity; but at the same time you must include its specific elements. Otherwise, it will become just a piece of tiresome geometry. And how many shadows you have! You must be as careful about putting in too many shadows as about putting in too many violent tones. And you should balance the bright colours with grey, white and black—just as in this study."

"I wanted to make it very brilliant."

"But your picture is lacking in concentration, young man; it is too scattered. Look at all those brush-strokes, all those arrows flying out towards the sides of the canvas. Where do they lead? There: 'close' the circle around the centre, as you would around a navel; give your vortex a centre, if it's movement you're after."

As he talks, Lhote retouches the different pictures and shows how they can be improved. He surrounds the "egg-yolk" with grey, which takes on a lilac tone; he breaks up a high-light which has been badly indicated; brings out objects by placing them on a neutral ground; balances one mass with another; puts the different planes back in their proper place. And in a few minutes, in a few seconds, even, what was before "tiresome geometry" has become luminous composition, forms in space, imaginary but convincing. With the necessary clarity and balance, each little study turns into a picture that pleases the eye, and lives up to the "imperatives" of modern painting, which is a "summary of the techniques of all periods".

"Be as daring as you like, and interpret as you will, but only on condition that what you create implies reality, and can stand the critical test of professionals. . . . But it's one o'clock, and I've been here since early morning. You can get dressed, Mademoiselle."

"Did I do well as a model?" she asks.

"You are the nicest model I have ever had."

The model, whose little girl has been playing nearby, gets off the stand and stretches herself. After posing for so many hours she has a reddish crease across her abdomen. She apologises, saying,

"I'm unfolding myself again."

She smiles. The little girl hands her her sweater, dress and shoes.

The students all put their work aside and become very animated. One girl evidently intends to work a little more before she goes to lunch. A young man puts his canvas in the corner. A young woman plans to take hers home; but it is certain that she will be careful not to admit that it has been "corrected". Lhote takes off his eye-shade, wraps his scarf around his neck, and goes off to his private studio in the rue Boulard, where he will presently take up his own palette and work on a canvas he has begun, until the following week, when the class is to meet again.

André Lhote : Self-portrait

From the Snows of Moscow to the Bright Lights of the Russian Ballet

BAKST · JUSSEAUME

SOME TIME BEFORE André Breton's surrealist "revolution"—which was far more than a revolution in subject-matter alone—two painters had emerged who styled themselves Irrealists, namely, Chagall and Chirico.

Chagall was a pupil of Bakst's, the great designer of the Russian Ballet, and it was at the latter's studio in the Boulevard Malesherbes that I met him for the first time; and Modigliani, also.

When Diaghilev descended on Paris with his Russian Ballet, that "Cossack charge which so proudly swept away Munich art", with its cressets, its funeral urns, its stylised roses and garlands, Bakst may be said to have been its standard-bearer. For he and Fokine were chiefly responsible for the success of *Scheherazade*, and they paid a tribute to the art they had vanquished by creating out of its ruins the enchanting *L'Invitation à la Valse*, which, as *Le Spectre de la Rose*, was danced by Karsavina and Nijinsky. And those who marvelled at the famous dancer's amazing leap at the end of Jean-Louis Vaudoyer's ballet never suspected that it was Bakst who had conceived the idea of such a spectacular surprise.

"You see," the painter said, as he showed me the maquettes he had done for the piece, "throughout the entire ballet I shall have the dancer, dressed in red, perform against a white background. And at the final moment he will leap through a window with green lighting behind it. That one instant will suffice to give the audience a sudden and tremendous visual thrill just by the simple and unexpected contrast of complementary colours."

And if the truth were told, the success of Nijinsky's celebrated "leap" was due much more to that effect than to his grace and extraordinary agility—a fact which neither his successors nor Fokine's have ever been able to appreciate. I have seen many

Spectres since, dressed in pale rose, performing against a grey décor, with the window in the background inadequately lighted. And when one rather naïve dancer went so far as to resort to the artifice of a spring-board, he was astonished to find that he did not produce the same staggering effect as Nijinsky, although he had jumped twice as high. Nor has any ballerina since thought of throwing a coloured shawl over her shoulders to cover her white dress, as Karsavina did, thereby creating a most vivid effect, which also gave "visual satisfaction" by its contrast with the white of the setting.

But it was only when, after Rimsky-Korsakov's prelude, the curtain rose on the harem scene in *Scheherazade* that Paris was really bowled over and left gasping with admiration. The audience shouted in wild applause. Never before had such dazzling display of colour burst forth from behind the footlights of any stage.

The young sultan-king of India and Persia
Sparkles like a jewel, reclining upon his cushions
At the foot of three red columns
Holding up the three enamel ceilings
From which hang enormous lanterns.

Three dancing-girls
Crouching face to face at the end of the blue rug
In the rays of the sun
Twist their arms, scattering saffron . . .

The two hundred favourites of the fabulous palace
Raise their lithe bodies on their undulating arms
And presently, in their aramanthine and pistachio trousers,
Festooned with pearls and jasper,
They all rush out from their bowers,
Their painted toe-nails
Peeping from their silken Turkish slippers.

And the Negroes! Blue Negroes and black ones, captured along with the elephants and sultanas; the golden Negro: Nijinsky!

He has a child's eyes and a beast's mouth.
Rings tinkle on his ankles . . .

Dwarfs place on their heads
Great trays of fruit overflowing like the gardens of heaven
Beneath the stamping tread of girls bearing amphorae.
The thick rug, bleeding with crushed roses,
Palpitates;
And the petals flutter about their feet.

For Bakst always stressed the importance of stage accessories.

"Have you ever noticed that I always have the head-dresses made three or four times the ordinary size? I do the same for the trays, the fruit and the costumes; and even the details of the sets, such as lanterns, screens, and so on."

No doubt the reader will recall the Holy Shroud which he used later in d'Annunzio's *The Martyrdom of Saint Sebastian*, so superbly interpreted by Mme. Ida Rubinstein.

For the scene in the Port of Famagusta in *Pisanelle*, Bakst, in collaboration with the Russian producer, Wsevolod Meyerhold, had worked out the following: the back of the stage was filled with several hundred people costumed in the most brilliant colours, without one white note, and moving against a background of red gauze. Almost everyone knows the value of white in a picture. Suddenly, in front of the glowing enamel setting of Famagusta, there appeared a white horse, caparisoned in white and ridden by a white knight with a long white cloak and standard. The effect was miraculous.

"You see," Bakst said, "in the foreground I arranged several groups of lords, dressed in costumes ranging from dark red to light orange. At the Beaux Arts we were forbidden to combine 'related' colours of that kind. I did it, nevertheless, and it was a great success."

In the same way, when Tchaikovsky's *Sleeping Beauty* was given in London, in the hunting scene he used only the natural forest colours—even for the costumes, which ranged from the lightest of greens to an almost reddish brown.

It was a fundamental principle with the Russian Ballet always to have the stage-sets and costumes done by the same artist, a custom which was not then current in France. And it was one of Bakst's principles to group the characters in the ballet in such a way as to form areas of colour and planned values, moving about against the setting in accordance with the colours of the sets themselves. Sometimes he would make a whole group of dancers perform beneath a coloured canopy.

He was very careful about having everything as authentic as possible. As he told me while he was working on the settings for Verhaeren's *Helen of Sparta*:

"I'm going to surprise everyone by dressing the characters just as they were in the days of 'red' Greece.[1] You don't imagine they would do *Oedipus Rex* at the Comédie-Française in costumes dating from the time of Pericles, a difference of three centuries?"

* * * * *

A vivid personality, he had red hair like Poil de Carotte, a prominent forehead and bright, shrewd eyes with wrinkled lids, which gave him a sceptical look behind his glasses. He always liked to do everything himself, attending to the smallest detail, from the ear-rings to the shoelaces, and the supports for the stage-sets to the making of the wigs.

Here he is, for instance, in the workrooms where the scenery is being made. He doesn't bother to take off his hat or coat or gloves. He looks over the work first as a whole, and then in detail. Suddenly he bursts out,

"What's this?"

"But, *Maître* . . ."

[1] In the early centuries of their history the Greeks wore clothing dyed in red ochre.

"What I drew was an eagle. You've made it a chicken. Here. Hand me that brush."

"But, *Maître*, no eagle has such a large beak."

"That's the very reason why I've done it that way. An eagle is all beak, eyes and claws—a terrifying sight. The body itself follows quite naturally, with feathers bristling like spears." Then, turning to another of his assistants, he asks,

"And you: what are you doing now?"

"Why, *Maître*, I'm cleaning up the lines."

"Cleaning up the lines! Don't you realise that it is the fuzziness that gives life to a line, and relates it to the background? Otherwise it would look like the eyebrows of these women who listen to beauty-specialists and commit the crime of making the lines exactly 'even', as they call it. And so, instead of a lovely flame which kindles admiring glances, they produce a lifeless thing, and make the pupil look like a boot-button or a chicken's eye. It is the same with this eagle. . . . Now we'll go along to the costumier's."

There we have another session. They bring him samples of silks and braids to decide on.

"Not so fast there, please. I must see how this goes with the décor."

"It's beautiful, *Maître*."

"Beautiful! When you buy a cravat, do you choose it because of the way it looks in the show-case; or do you hold it up to your shirt to see how well they match? And isn't a costume against a setting far more important?"

For Bakst had made experiments of which the costumier had no inkling. For example, he had had the dancers rehearse in short, white smocks, and he had noted down, in the order of their entrance on stage, the names of the characters and groups so as to be able to grade his costume-effects. Then, before the costumes were finished, he made the actors walk along in front of the décor, with the different materials pinned on them.

"Take care not to leave the maquettes lying around," he warned them as he departed. He knew only too well what use was made of any that were picked up.

On one occasion a noted couturière had bought from him a design for a costume that was never executed. Imagine the painter's surprise, therefore, when he went to America some time later and discovered that the costume had been divided by the enterprising dressmaker into separate parts, and sold to the trade piece by piece; in consequence, Bakst belts, Bakst collars, Bakst lapels, clasps, etc., were turning up everywhere.

Of the actress, Mme. Ida Rubinstein, with whom he collaborated on several productions, he had this to say:

"When she came towards me and I saw her long, ungainly body, and the face which was almost that of an ascetic, I said to myself, 'This dancer should have a saint's robe like those in a Primitive painting'; and for the second piece in which she played I thought, 'I must design a suit of armour that will make her look like a large, disjointed, stylised insect'. And she was a success both times. Then, against my advice, she insisted on trying to dance on her toes. She managed it, but they gave her a costume so ill-suited to her build that she looked like a giraffe adorned with ostrich-plumes. A painter is very important to an actress or a dancer; and when they try to do things by themselves, that's what happens."

* * * * *

In London one painting of Bakst's was greatly admired. It was the remarkable *Fall of Babylon* which he had exhibited at the Salon des Indépendants in Paris. James de Rothschild, among others, had commissioned him to do some frescoes that he wanted executed in the fifteenth-century style, after the manner of Gozzoli, and portraying his entire family and ancestors! Bakst worked on the project for six years.

He had very keen powers of observation. I remember sitting next to him at a dinner given in London by the Marchioness of Ripon. During the evening a storm came up, and Bakst leaned over to me and said:

"My fr'en'," (he had a slight defect in pronunciation, which caused him to twist his mouth in an odd way) "if the lightning should strike this gathering, it would wipe out not only the most brilliant minds in England [Shaw, George Moore, Henry Arthur Jones and Nijinsky were among those present], but also the owners of more than a third of the wealth of the British Empire. I want you to notice something amusing. Opposite you is the Duchess of Westminster, who owns a whole district of London—you might say almost all of London because it is the wealthiest. Ten minutes ago she dropped her most beautiful pearl, the pear-shaped pearl which hangs from her necklace. She is tormented by her entirely natural desire to recover it, and at the same time by her fear that her agitation will be remarked by all the ladies, who have noticed her dilemma, and are watching her and enjoying her discomfiture."

When the dinner was over, Bakst nudged my elbow. The Duchess had got up and, turning to the flunkey who had drawn back her chair, was saying in the most casual tone possible,

"Pick up that pearl . . ."

★ ★ ★ ★ ★

When Diaghilev, his boyhood friend and schoolmate, seemed disposed to desert him for Picasso, Derain, Matisse, and the rest of those who followed after, Bakst fell prey to such neurasthenia that it almost finished him. I was alarmed, for the Russian Ballet had already claimed one victim: the painter Jusseaume.

Jusseaume had been commissioned by Albert Carré to do the scenery for the latter's production of *Louise* at the Opéra Comique and he had also executed a number of settings for Antoine.[1] He had departed from the tradition of the admirable Bertin,[2] and adopted the idea of using vertical planes to obtain certain effects of perspective.

He was a handsome, well-built man; and he affected a Rembrandt hat and a Van Dyck moustache.

"It was Antoine, you know, who took me to Spain and Italy to get material for my work. I was delighted, of course, for I had a wonderful trip with that extraordinary man for company. But when all's said and done, everything looks much the same everywhere. Put a palm-tree on a set, give it orange lighting, and you've got Africa. Or you can put a log-cabin on the same set, use a whitish-green light for the sky, and you've got Norway. And so on."

True, he was being humorous. But when the Russian Ballet

[1] Antoine (1858–1943) founded the Théâtre Libre and the Théâtre Antoine in Paris. He directed the Odéon Theatre and the theatre movement of his generation. He discovered the chief French playwrights of his day, and put on productions of Shakespeare, notably *Julius Caesar* and *King Lear*, as well as plays by Ibsen, Sudermann, and other foreign dramatists.

[2] A well-known designer of classic stage-settings.

came along it was too much for him. At first he tried to keep his end up and would say defiantly:

"Humph! Your Russians—nothing but violence. A punch isn't difficult. Just watch me: I'll give 'em a punch."

But when I ran into him some time afterwards, he seemed utterly crushed.

"Yes," he admitted, "I thought violence was easy; but it is just the opposite. The colours are much more difficult to harmonise. Take Corot, for example, who has been imitated so much. Well, his imitators have never risked doing any 'Italian' Corots. The Ville d'Avray ones are another matter: naturally, a simple *frottis* [1] is easier to do. But delivering a punch is something else again. If you miss, you break your jaw against a wall. I'm afraid I've broken my jaw."

Some time later, I learned that he had hanged himself above one of his décors in his studio in the rue Vicq d'Azir.

* * * * *

But Bakst, fortunately, did not hang himself. I saw something of him again in Cannes. As we were lunching together one day in the Winter Casino, near the yacht harbour, he said to me:

"Whatever you do, don't talk to me about the Russian Ballet. Look at Poiret at that table over there. He's another who owes me a great deal, and he knows it."

When Poiret had finished his lunch, he got up and politely came over to speak to Bakst, whom he addressed as "*cher Maître*". The artist, like a good Russian, was rather solemn, as he had once been towards a young woman who, taking her cue from another lady who was rumpling the cravat of Barbey d'Aurevilly, was becoming too familiar with him. "Don't forget, my dear," he had said to her, "that I am a member of the Academy."

Nevertheless, when we were alone again, he said:

"What do you think of the trick that swine Diaghilev played on me? And so far as distortion is concerned, I was doing that ten years before Picasso."

Could it be that he saw only the accidental, and not the significant, in what Picasso had contributed to the history of painting?

[1] A light coat of paint, applied by rubbing the canvas delicately with the brush.

And yet Bakst had been one of the first to collect Douanier Rousseaus, and among them the well-known *Football Players*. He appreciated Negro art; and he had been the first to talk to me not only about Chagall and Modigliani, but also about Charlie Chaplin, who was then timidly beginning his career in the cinema.

"You'll see," he prophesied. "He is a great, a very great actor."

Diaghilev and Bakst eventually became reconciled, and the result was the ballet *The Good Humoured Ladies*, with music by Scarlatti.

"I've made a distorted setting for it, as though the stage were one of these glass paper-weights, with the puppet-like characters dancing inside, with long hands that look as though they were made of wood."

But Massine, who did the choreography, was unable to carry out exactly the idea Bakst had in mind; for this reason the painter was obliged to revise his set, and he designed in his own style a charming little Venetian village piazza, with a campanile and Longhi characters which he interpreted in his own style.

* * * * *

In Paris Bakst lived in an apartment at 112 Boulevard des Malesherbes, near the Place Malesherbes. His studio, office and drawing-room were all contained in one large, rectangular room, which was kept scrupulously clean and neat, with decorated cupboards and filing-cabinets which almost had an American air. There were also a life-size bronze reproduction of Donatello's *David*, Chinese porcelain vases and a variety of cactus-plants.

"My fr'en', look how heavy and voluptuous I was able to make the breasts of that odalisque; just look at the tips. . . . Just smell them. Isn't the whole of the Orient there? They smell of roses and musk and sweat—yes, sweat, too. Just smell them. . . ."

By going down a few steps you came to the "sanctuary", in the form of a little sitting-room where Bakst had hung his *Football Players*, which did not seem at all out of place alongside the Primitives he had bought in Spain. Next to the "sanctuary" was a mysterious room, which I was never invited to enter, although I was probably the most intimate French friend Bakst had. In fact, he never allowed me to leave without first calling the maid.

"Louise, is the door closed properly?"

"Yes, Monsieur."

"Is it tightly closed?"

"Yes, Monsieur."

"Good." Then, turning to me, he would say, "Goodbye, my fr'en'. Come back and see me soon."

But when Bakst died——

He must have planned the ceremony carefully in advance. The catafalque had been set up in the middle of the studio, and on each landing was stationed a beadle in full regalia: in fact, the whole get-up of plumed hat, gold-braided coat and halberd looked as if Bakst had specially designed it for this occasion. But the door of the mysterious chamber, whose secret the artist had jealously guarded for so many years, was wide open, and through it could be seen a sort of store-room filled with a clutter of canvases, stretching-frames, paint-pots and rags. And that was all! Everyone present filed by the room, between the beadles, without, apparently, noticing it. I tried to close the door, but Louise prevented me.

I left the funeral with several friends among whom was Jean Cocteau, who remarked,

"Now Diaghilev will be able to take down those bananas in *Scheherazade* and get Matisse to do some new scenery for it."

However, that was something Diaghilev did not do.

* * * * *

JOSÉ-MARIA SERT

José-Maria Sert, the latter-day Renaissance artist from Catalonia, who painted huge panels and ceilings in black and gold in New York and Paris, Lisbon and London, and even in the League of Nations building at Geneva, always believed that "a décor should be a picture". The Waldorf Hotel in New York has its "Sert Room", and the Rockefeller Center its regiments of elephants, Chinese landscapes, whole Chicagos aflame on lakes of ice—all giving the same effect of balance and illusion that one finds in the frescoes of Michelangelo. But, first and foremost, Sert was Spanish, and the flamboyant mastery and extravagance of his ceiling decorations would have made Tiepolo's head spin.

He married first Missia Edwards, the presiding genius of the *Revue Blanche* and the Russian Ballet; and afterwards Princess Divani, who was killed in a car accident.

As a commentary on Sert's particular kind of art, I recall the sardonic remark Forain once made about an enormous canvas the Spanish artist had executed for the apse of a chapel. As Forain was standing looking at the vast numbers of fat-cheeked, full-breasted, wide-hipped, big-bottomed angels, a friend who was with him asked:

"But how will they ever be able to ship the thing? Will they roll it up, or fold it; or will it have to be cut up into pieces?"

"No," Forain had replied, acidly. "It can be deflated."

But Sert's retort to Forain is less well known, for later on, when he happened to meet the latter, who pretended not to see him, the Spaniard exclaimed,

"So, Monsieur, you've been deflated, too?"

NATHALIE GONTCHAROVA

There must still be a few people who can recall the first performance of Rimsky-Korsakov's *Coq d'Or* at the Paris Opéra in 1913.

Diaghilev had commissioned Mlle. Nathalie Gontcharova to do the sets. He and I went together to meet her at the station. While we waited for the train to arrive, Diaghilev talked to me at some length about Cubism in Russia.

"It descended on the icon-painters like a rain of ortolans on a population of bean-eaters. Most of them took it up with a frenzy that soon sent them into paroxysms. And the whole crowd who had, until then, been calm and rational, suddenly turned into demons. Twenty different schools sprang up in less than a month. Futurism and Cubism were soon considered as antiquity, pre-history. In three days the most advanced painters became academic. Mototism ousted Automototism, which, in turn, was outdistanced by Trepidism and Vibrism. Those gave way to Planism, Serenism, Exacerbism, Omnism and Neism. People organised exhibitions in palaces and garrets. Duchesses climbed up to attics to see Neo-airist pictures by the light of candles stuck on the floor. And even the great landowners began taking lessons at home in Meta-chromism. I won't try to give you the Russian names of all the different schools, but I can assure you that even the most insignificant artists were ready to die for their faith.

"The best-known of the advanced painters is Nathalie Gontcharova. She recently gave an exhibition of seven hundred canvases representing 'light', and she included several panels whose total surface area was at least forty yards. As she had only a small studio to work in, she did them in sections from memory, and only saw the picture as a whole when it was assembled for the exhibition. Now she has all St. Petersburg and Moscow running after her. But what will interest you especially about her is that she herself is imitated as well as her work. She starged a vogue for night-gowns in black and white, and blue and orange. But that's nothing compared to some of her other absurdities. She began painting flowers on her face, and it wasn't long before both the nobility and the bohemian set were going out sleigh-riding with horses, houses, elephants and I don't know what daubed on their cheeks, necks and foreheads. When I asked her one day why she smeared her face with ultramarine, she replied that it helped to 'soften the features'. Then she explained that the elephants, carriages, orchards, etc., she decorated her forehead with were a 'make-up more psychological than naturalistic'. I'm not exaggerating. In Moscow you can run across women any day with whole collections of daggers and pearls painted on their faces, instead of veils."

After listening to his description, I was more anxious than ever to meet such an extraordinary woman. The train finally drew in to the station, and I saw a sort of Bécassine, dressed in black, descend the steps of the carriage. She had a round forehead, a round nose, round cheeks, mouth and chin. But she was a Bécassine with the bearing of a princess, and then and there she curtsied on the platform, as if she were being presented at Court.

I don't believe any spectacle has ever given such an impression of splendour as did the first performance of *Coq d'Or*. For the backdrop Mlle. Gontcharova had designed a fantastic multiple Kremlin, painted in ochre, gold and red. And on either side of the stage she had erected two red grandstands, which were filled with three hundred singers from the Moscow Opera, all dressed in red.

That performance marked for us the beginning of the renaissance of Russian stage-design, the painter Larionov subsequently bringing with him the generation which was to succeed that of Bakst.

The Reality of the Unrealists

CHAGALL

"CHAGALL IS MY favourite pupil," Bakst once told me. "And I like him especially because, after he has had a lesson from me, he takes his pastels and brushes and does something entirely different from what I do, and that indicates a complete personality, and a temperament and sensibility such as I have rarely known."

The next day I saw a being almost like Shakespeare's Ariel come into Bakst's studio, walking as if on a cloud. He had eyes as bright as the sky, and hair that seemed to lift his slender body into the air. His name was Marc Chagall.

He came originally from Vitebsk, in White Russia. His father was a poor cooper's assistant, who earned the equivalent of a hundred francs a month to support his whole family.

"For days on end, his hands petrified with cold, he would lift and carry round huge barrels of salt-herring," Chagall told me. "My mother, who died at forty-five, was very pretty—a grave and smiling sort of beauty. One day she came into my room while I was drawing pictures in my school copy-book. Although she was illiterate, she said to me, 'You have talent'. It is true that she also said, 'Perhaps you will be a photographer. That would be better.' "

Chagall showed us a canvas he had just finished: it was of a house that seemed to have sprung out of a bouquet of flowers, while up above there was a Russian woman holding a book. Her head was turned the wrong way, and looked as though it were floating off over the roof. On the ground a child with a donkey's head was playing the violin.

But everything about the scene was so harmonious, and painted in such delightful colours, that I was not in the least shocked by it; and I was quite ready to follow Bakst's advice. He had said,

"You mustn't ask him about anything, and don't look surprised; let him do things as he feels them, because he feels things beautifully, and in just the right way."

As I talked to him, Chagall explained that he felt it would serve no purpose to be a poet if he could not create beings according to his dreams and fantasy, or if he had to turn himself into a photographer, as his mother had hoped he would do.

"In Russia, and elsewhere in Europe, I have lived only in gardens," he said. "I wanted only to glimpse the world from my window through beautiful trees and clouds; and to create unreality. . . ."

And so he portrays an engaged couple marrying in a bouquet of roses, and surrounded by candles as tall as oak trees, and animals that seem to have come out of all his midsummer, or mid-winter, night's dreams: a sort of Chagallian mythology, which no one can borrow from him because he himself has borrowed from no one. But he is a painter first and foremost, and his painting is, therefore, more important than the subjects he depicts, however startling they may be. Although he came to Paris in the full flower of the Cubist explosion, nevertheless he was not drawn into that artistic movement (which came at its own logical time); this was because the young Russian's personality had already been set by his early environment. It is not so easy to tear one's childhood impressions out of one's soul, even out of the soul of an artist. Indeed, this sensitive, almost feverish man was to be haunted all his life by the memory of the little alleyways of his native quarter, of the close-packed houses and the jumble of streets, through which there wandered goats with an almost human expression in their eyes, chickens of all colours, and roosters with brilliant plumage; where huge hands suddenly slammed shut the blinds, and pedlars strayed like phantoms, carrying on their backs the burden of all their miseries; where young girls in white dresses appeared like fairies among the spring foliage, their braided hair tied with ribbons—"the plastic song of things", as he called it.

Chagall was, no doubt unconsciously, the first to rebel against the new dogmas. And the Surrealists later on thought that they should win his support for their revolution. But the painter was wary of any such association. He told me so emphatically in Paris, and again afterwards in his New York studio which, with its mullioned windows and waxed floors, made one think of Rembrandt's old house in Amsterdam.

"I know," he said, "that people often label me one of the fathers of Surrealism. No. Call me an 'Unrealist' or a 'Supernaturalist', if you like. In 1911, Apollinaire and Cendrars referred to me as super-real, a word which I much prefer. . . . Impressionism and Cubism are still realism. Literature, no. My pictures don't tell a 'story'; they have neither a beginning nor an end. I am an artisan, and more even than the dream aspect of my work, I love the quality of my métier. After that simple statement, I must add a rider. Once I've mastered my métier, then, and then only, can I give the greater part of myself, as I want to do, to the dream aspect. And if the landscape I am painting does not satisfy me completely, I add what I want to it. That is my right as a creator—on condition, of course, that the picture, while being idealistic, remains plastic. It is the interplay of contrasts that unifies the whole. That's quite logical. They say that madmen are logical. I agree, on condition that the finished product holds together, and is beautiful. The real truth is that I am perhaps not sociable; that is to say, I cannot accept—in painting, at least—all the usual laws. . . ."

* * * * *

Chagall had just lost his wife, the poetess Bella, whom he had so often painted, draped in white veils and surrounded by roses, wax candles and angels. He fought his grief by working harder than ever. I happened to visit him one day as he was painting some flowers.

"I like artists who are fond of flowers," he told me. "People don't realise how difficult it is to paint them; to divine the fairy-like and supernatural quality they have about them. It's curious, isn't it, how few of the great painters of the past ever painted flowers. Rembrandt did one, pinned to the breast of his wife Sophia, and some shy roses on the hat of his *Flora*. . . ."

We went to lunch in a cafeteria, where we were joined by his daughter Ida, who is also a painter. Chagall hadn't much liking for what is known in America as "society". He always dressed in a velvet jacket, left his shirt more or less open at the neck, and let the wind ruffle his hair. And he kept very much to himself.

During the meal we continued to discuss painting. Chagall was distressed because he had left a great many of his canvases in Paris during the War, just as in 1914 he had been obliged to leave a hundred and fifty of them in Germany, after the exhibition organised there by Apollinaire for the group known as *Der Sturm*. In the same way, he had had to leave many of his murals, including *The Dybbuk*, in Moscow.

When I learned that Chagall was going to redesign the *décors* for *L'Oiseau de Feu*, I said to him,

"What, you're going to change Fokine's sets?"

"You'll see," was all he said.

And I did indeed see. I saw a first act entirely in blue, ranging from the palest cerulean blue to the deepest ultramarine, with a red rooster in the moon. The second act ran the gamut of reds; while the third was done in shades of orange, so that the total effect was of a multitude of blazing suns, eclipsing or illuminating one another.

"You were right!" I told Chagall enthusiastically, after the première.

"Ah, if we could only see Paris again!" was his melancholy reply.

* * * * *

"If we could only see Paris again!"

As soon as it was possible for him to return there after the War, he fell upon it like a starving man on a loaf of bread. He literally caressed its old stones; buried his face in the leaves of the trees in Montmartre, where he lived with his daughter Ida; and walked till he was ready to drop along all those familiar streets, each one of them filled with memories.

He even went back to Venice, where I ran into him at the Tintoretto Exhibition.

"You know," he said frankly, "I don't care much for Tintoretto, apart from some of his work in the Scuola di San Rocco."

"I could see that," I said. "You even made a face at his *Susanna*, from the Vienna Collection."

"Yes."

In vain I remonstrated with him, and pointed out how much freedom the old Venetian master had introduced. Chagall stubbornly shook his head, then burst out with,

"It's botched. And it's been damaged by time. Other painters foresaw the effects of time. Tintoretto's work is botched even in its composition. In some cases you can hardly make it out because of the lack of contrasts."

"Whom do you like best, Chagall?"

"The Egyptians, the Assyrians, the Greeks; Cimabue, because he is so Byzantine; Paolo Ucello, Masaccio. . . ."

"In short, all those claimed by the Cubists?"

"Exactly. Then Giorgione, El Greco, Rembrandt, Daumier, Seurat."

"Cézanne?"

"I 'feel' Cézanne. But he is too important. You can criticise all other painters, but not him. I am afraid of Cézanne. I even tremble when I pronounce his name. His is great art, achieved, it seems, by a paradox. I like the Rouault of the 1905–1907, period. He, too, is paradoxical and erratic in his methods.

Michelangelo I envy. My ambition is to go back to mural painting. Raphael? He is too beautiful for me. I haven't got beyond Piero della Francesca or Masaccio."

"And what about the Spaniards?"

Chagall answered by asking me,

"What do you think of Velasquez and Goya?"

"When I entered the Velasquez Room in the Prado for the first time," I said, "his pictures, as a whole, struck me as being cold. Perhaps it was because I had heard so much about that collection. I was ready to be bowled over, just as one is on first entering the Sistine Chapel."

"And Goya?"

"When I went into the smaller, more intimate, room on the right, and saw the first Goyas, I was really happy, jubilant. But then I returned to the Velasquez Room—and I stayed there."

"Well," said Chagall, "I prefer Goya. It is true that Rembrandt and El Greco touch me more deeply; but Goya fascinates me. Velasquez' *The Blind* is wonderful, of course; but the subject is purely academic. No one has done better than that—except Raphael, perhaps, with his incredible techniques. But what Velasquez can you put alongside Goya's *Mayas*? Not one. And not even Manet can approach his portraits!"

"Whom do you like among the present-day painters?"

"Oh, I'm all for order. Yes, even though I'm more than anything else a dreamer, I'm all for order: for Fernand Léger; and for all those who are trying to express something new: Masson, Ozenfant, Ernst, Mondriaan, Berman, Yves Tanguy, Matta. . . ."

* * * * *

The sculptor Lipschitz and the painters Bonnard, Rouault, Fernand Léger, Lurçat and Chagall were all commissioned to design the interior of the church at Assy in the Savoy. And so it turned out that an atheist, several Cubists and two Jews portrayed traditional Christian scenes; and the Church, in opening her arms to these artists without asking anything of them except their work, did something that was highly significant. No less significant on their part was the willingness of these artists to accept the commission.

Yet, after all, in the canvases of Chagall, who is essentially a painter of Old Testament subjects, we have often seen the Crucifixion, and Rabbis going towards Christ, holding out their *torahs* towards the Cross, whose shadow no longer seems to hang over them. And it is, perhaps, through a man like Chagall, who is a friend, almost a disciple, of Jacques Maritain's, that Jewish priests now look upon Jesus as a sufferer like themselves.

"Have they not also suffered Christ's Passion for years; for centuries?"

* * * * *

Not far from the Matisse Chapel, and only a few miles from *Les Collettes* at Cagnes, where Renoir spent his last years, Chagall now lives in a beautiful old house, surrounded by a big garden. Through the trees he watches for the unreal characters he sets down on paper, canvas or stone; and for the Provençal peasants, the lovely firm-breasted girls carrying flowers, and the familiar animals—all radiant from the sun, just as his first models were lit by the snows of his native land, which he still remembers with wondering eyes.

But his eyes are colder now. And he has cut his hair, the hair that might have been an angel's, which gives him something of the severe look of a monk. Even so, whenever I have occasion to talk to him again about Tintoretto, he clasps his hands, and exclaims:

"Did I say that? Did I really say that?"

GIORGIO DE CHIRICO

Venice; and the rose-coloured terrace atop the Hotel Danieli. Across the Canal the little island of San Giorgio lies in a milky patch of sea, its campanile pointing like a finger towards the moonlit sky. The view extends from the Church of the Salute, which resembles nothing so much as a splendid piece of jewellery, to the distant light of the Lido, winking along the Adriatic.

The restaurant itself dominates the dark, pointed roofs from which Casanova made his famous escape, and the grey cupolas of Saint Mark's, casting their round shadows over the carving of the Bridge of Sighs, with its red-tiled roof.

Just as in America people in evening-clothes dine at lamp-lit tables high up in the warm skies of Miami, or above the canyons that run in parallel lines across New York, so here, high above Venice, the dining-room is equally modern, and the head waiters, in the clothes that head waiters wear the world over, perform their duties like dancers in a ballet.

One of them leads the way among the tables. All at once I am brought up short by a strangely familiar face. Can it be——? Yes. It is Giorgio de Chirico, looking like Bonnat's *Renan*, with his hands on his knees, his head hunched down between his shoulders. He has the same Olympian eyes, a curling lip, and a lock of white hair falling over his wide forehead.

Giorgio de Chirico! Along with Chagall, he was one of the immediate forerunners of Surrealism.

In *The Dream* the Douanier Rousseau made use of an ordinary, everyday object when he painted a red couch with a naked woman lying asleep on it in the middle of the jungle, surrounded by monkeys and tigers. Similarly, Giorgio de Chirico, the Italian artist, who was born in Greece in 1888, conceived the idea of "ennobling" household articles, such as clothes-hangers, wardrobes, rocking-chairs, etc., by putting them in Greek or Roman or Florentine settings, his argument being that we can think of Hellas perfectly well with all those objects around us; and, furthermore, in Hellas itself people lived in daily contact with them. By so doing he related the poetic dream to our everyday reality and brutally made us aware of the close link between them. This reasoning eventually led him to represent human beings as puppets of his own devising, which he placed between compasses and square rules in beautiful landscapes whose perspectives were sometimes fantastic. The time came, however, when, moving more towards tradition, he replaced his brooms with trophies of war, and his puppets with prancing horses, snorting along the Mediterranean sea-shore and browsing on laurel leaves among the ruins of an ancient temple.

One day his dealer burst into his studio, exclaiming:

"Monsieur de Chirico! your horses have been a tremendous success! I beg of you to paint stablefuls of them, squadrons of them, stud-farms, pampafuls!"

De Chirico calmly put down his palette and brushes, turned his canvas round, and said haughtily,

"I am not a painter of horses."

He frowned, and looked so angry that the dealer fled from his studio, his temple. Then he became self-absorbed and meditative; presently he returned to Italy, to Rome. For several years he worked in silence in his studio in the Piazza di Spagna, looking out over the towers of the Church of the Trinità del Monte, which figures so often in the novels of Gabriele d'Annunzio. Suddenly he became infuriated by the Venice Biennale, even though his earlier works, his puppets, his geometrical designs and prancing horses, had had very favourable treatment.

"Take those canvases down," he raged. "Most of them are false anyway. Modern art is nothing but rubbish, impotence and the merchandise of dealers!"

His next step was to rent an immense palazzo in Venice between San Moïse and the Piazzetta and, in competition with the Biennale, to hang there forty of his canvases, all as richly framed as the Tintorettos in the Scuola di San Rocco. Then he made his exhibition known to the public through lectures and with the assistance of the press and his disciples.

I went to it, of course. I could not help but admire the result of so much hard work, which was obviously sincere, prolific and a proof of stubborn faith. I looked with respect at his *Three Graces*, which was in the same kind of frame as Michelangelo's *Holy Family*; at his furious battle-scenes, executed in the style of Salvator Rosa; at his little still-lifes, whose rich pigment was like that of the old Flemish Masters; at his large nudes, which were reminiscent not only of Titian but also of Delacroix. For de Chirico used the *flochetage* method, so dear to the Romantic master, even though he still ribboned his compositions with the pale whites of his earlier manner. There were numerous self-portraits, too: the artist in seventeenth-century costume; the artist with his palette; the artist in modern dress; and—Heaven help us—in the nude as well! And on the other side he had put life-like portraits of his wife, a young and beautiful Russian, with an enigmatic smile.

* * * * *

"Modern painting is equivocal. Young? It is more than fifty years old, and for fifty years it has flouted all the rules and canons which have held good for centuries. It is based on lack of control.

It was not a revolution, but an involution. Instead of being painting, 'modern art' has become mere reasoning. 'Cerebral', 'sensitive', etc.—what does all that nonsense mean? In my opinion, modern painting is like a singer who, his voice gone, has turned into a blue-stocking: a make-shift."

"Even so, Chirico, there are some great painters today, don't you think?"

"*De* Chirico, please. There is a particle in front of my name. Hm. . . . Great painters? No. None—except Picasso, and to a lesser degree Derain, perhaps. . . ."

"Picasso, then?"

"Picasso is a sort of visionary, a great man, who really has something: he has shut himself up in a room and he alone has the key to it. He has a certain quality, but it is harmful. All the others since Courbet have invented a revolution out of necessity: they didn't really know anything. Decadence set in with Renoir's last period. But no paper would ever dare to print what I'm telling you. They've nearly all been bought off by the art-dealers, just as certain art-dealers are bought off by certain painters. The Surrealists wanted to include me in their group, just as they've included Leonardo da Vinci. But I'd have none of it. André Breton bribed the dealer Paul Guillaume, of all people—the same Paul Guillaume who proclaimed: 'Only those whom *I* choose have talent.' The art-dealers' combine—which did not exist from the age of rock-drawings and troglodytes to Courbet's death—has killed true painting."

"But what about yourself?"

"I am a painter, not a clown. And it makes me furious to see my work hung alongside the clowns in the Biennale."

"Nevertheless, you were one of the first of the avant-garde painters, weren't you?"

De Chirico avoided my question by calling the waiter and ordering another maraschino ice. Then, turning back to me, he said, "Now, Rubens, you see . . ."

Mme. de Chirico smiled. The violins struck up a lively tune. From down below rose the refrain of another canzonetta:

Non, "cara piccina, non"
Così non va. . . .

The Unreality of the Surrealists
or from
Lautréamont to a Tuppeny Leonardo

IT WAS THE poet André Breton who introduced Surrealism into painting. He wrote a manifesto which attracted into his orbit several painters (and poets) who, according to the formula of the first Impressionists, "were seeking something new". Surrealism introduced the subconscious into the compositions of the new painters, an event which gave rise to much serious research, even though—as with Cubism—a few charlatans mingled with the sincere artists. The latter, however, were not above doing a certain amount of drum-beating, which the most convinced of the Occultists had once indulged in, thereby adding to the confusion in the minds of the public: surprise exhibitions held in mysterious booths, like side-shows at a fair, etc. Then some of the artists were ostracised; others left the group of their own accord.

Even so the "revolution", which had already lasted for thirty years or more, brought to light much talent. It embraced such men as Van Bosch and Lautréamont, even Jarry and Albert Roussel. The last used to travel about in a hermetically-sealed car, and he covered the whole of the West Indies without casting a single glance at the landscape.

Many may remember Max Ernst and Kurt Seligman, who were accused of "projecting" their "interior mirror" or their "over-self" on to their canvases, using a sponge dipped in paint to get their tones, and achieving, it must be said, quite deep and moving nightmare impressions. More subtle was Tanguy, with his luminous bladders that looked like lanterns; and the Spaniard, Miro. There was a fine outburst of anger from the purists when Miro and Dali were asked to do the sets for the Russian Ballet's *Romeo and Juliet*; and an even louder uproar was created among the audience by Breton and Aragon. While Diaghilev exulted, Isola, the frightened director, called out the Republican Guard.

"Nothing like this ever happened when we put on *No, no, Nanette*," he said to me quite seriously.

* * * * *

I made Dali's acquaintance while I was in America. He has always been too much of an exhibitionist for my liking. He is a talented trickster, who has succeeded in impressing ingenuous New Yorkers with his Renaissance style paintings. I always think of him in connection with the quip Vauxcelles made about another talented imitator, named Sarluis, a much simpler artist, whom he called a "Twopenny Leonardo".

However, at the instance of several friends, I wrote a not too severe article on one of Dali's exhibitions. Later, we were introduced to each other, and my article was shown to Salvador. He proceeded to roll it into a ball which he pressed against his forehead, remaining thus for several minutes, as if in prayer. Eventually he said:

"I don't need to read it. The substance of what he has written penetrates my brain in this way, and I can spiritually drink in his sympathy or antipathy."

FROM NEW YORK'S BOHEMIA TO THAT OF SAINT-GERMAIN-DES-PRÉS

(by way of a Sophisticated Venice)

Hélion, Peggy and Pegeen: the names sound almost as if they had come out of a musical comedy by George Gershwin.

One night in 1951 Pegeen, the daughter of Peggy Guggenheim, the multi-millionaire, was discovered lying with her veins slashed in her black-marble bathroom in the Venier-Casati Palazzo on the Grand Canal in Venice. It was quite incredible. For little Pegeen had been in the best of spirits the night before, when, perfumed and smiling, her hair done in a horse's tail, she had appeared in Harry's—the bar which, with its white walls and severe lines contrasting so sharply with the Church of the Salute opposite, seems to be defying the aristocracy of Venice. Yet that same aristocracy crowds into it, fills it to bursting point, and brings with it whichever artists happen to be fashionable.

One such artist was Hélion, whom I met again in America, after he had made two sensational escapes: one from Germany, where he had been a prisoner-of-war; the other from Surrealism, which had been much more difficult.

I had gone with the Marquise de Charette to see him in his studio in New York, during the exhibition of his pictures, which were remarkable for their large luminous areas of colour.

Studio, did I say? It was a little box of a place in a bohemian district, with whitewashed windows, curtains in typical Greenwich Village style, a red brick floor, and a distinct air of shabbiness. Such studios were, in fact, more makeshift than the ones the late Montparnos used to inhabit. Hélion introduced us to his wife, who was small and bare-legged; she wore red bedroom slippers, and her hair hung loose like Ophelia's.

"You mustn't be taken in by all that," the Marquise had said to me afterwards. "It's considered very smart by up-to-date American artists, whenever they have visitors, to put the broom in the coal-scuttle and a saucepan on the piano. That boy has great talent; and he hasn't married a pauper, either. His wife, in fact, is Pegeen Guggenheim. Yes, he married—and very sensible of him, too, because she is exquisite—one of the richest heiresses in America, the daughter of Peggy Guggenheim."

* * * * *

I had already met the formidable and charming Peggy Guggenheim at an exhibition of paintings by a group of ultra-modern women artists in East 57th Street, which she had organised and financed. She stood near the door and loftily questioned the visitors as they went out.

"And what did you think of the paintings?"

"Er—I don't understand them very well, I'm afraid."

Peggy shrugged her shoulders disdainfully.

"Come back again in fifty years," she said. And to the next person, "And what did *you* think of them?"

"If you will pardon me for saying so, I think they're quite mad."

"It is you who are mad, if you don't understand art. Good afternoon."

When it came to my turn, I replied politely,

"It is all very nice."

"Nice?"

My answer seemed to take the wind out of her sails.

"But what do you *really* think of them?" she insisted.

"In Paris we got over making a fuss about such things a long time ago. They either end up in a museum or in the cemetery."

Peggy leaned back against the wall of the staircase.

"But—what is being done then, nowadays?"

"Well, Madame," I said, "as you are a Maecenas, it is up to you to find out." And I departed, thoroughly pleased with myself.

Since then, whenever Peggy and I meet, we embrace in all friendliness, and on my side without qualms, though I must say that on that first occasion I was seriously afraid she might take a bite out of my throat.

* * * * *

In Italy I met Peggy again, with Pegeen and Hélion. With her usual energy she had bought the palazzo where Casati had once given her famous Venetian balls, complete with leopards and gilded Negroes, while the riff-raff of the town went by with torches on the Canal—all of which would have been admirable material for Mlle. Léonor Fini, who would have fitted into the scene so well herself, with her Bérard eyes, feathers, and black veils.

In the Venier-Casati palazzo, which still echoed with the music of Stradella and Scarlatti, interpreted by Giorgio Levi, Peggy Guggenheim had installed a kind of garden-museum of Cubist sculpture, with painted trees of reinforced cement. There she housed her pet artists in rooms which had been entirely modernised, even to the lighting-fixtures, each of them with its black-marble bathroom. It was in one of these bathrooms that Pegeen had slit the veins of her wrists, for the noblest of reasons: namely, because of an argument about painting. Her husband, it seems, had accused her of painting "gingerbread" Surrealist figures. One wonders if, in revenge, she had taunted him with his umbrellas blown up to the size of trophies of war.

No matter. Pegeen's life was saved, and she went back to the Café Flore, where she was joined by the Modiglianesque Hélion. And Peggy, for her part, continued to play the Americanised lady-Doge, in her garden filled with glass flowers and plastic fountains wired for sound.

In the Teeming Jungle of Montparnasse

MODIGLIANI

BAKST, WHO HAD prophesied a great career for Chagall, said to me one afternoon as I was about to leave his studio:

"Don't go just yet. I'm expecting somebody who really is 'somebody'—the Italian painter and sculptor Modigliani, from Leghorn. He is doing my portrait. Here's a line-drawing he's done for it. Look at the care he has taken. All the features in my face are etched as if with a needle, and there's no retouching. I'm sure he must be poor; but he has the air of a *grand seigneur*. He really is 'somebody', I assure you."

I was working on a novel at the time—it was in 1919. I mention this because the chief character was none other than Modigliani, at least so far as the general facts of his turbulent life were concerned.

Ever since the last century Murger had set the style for the *Vie de Bohème*. But I had just discovered a new kind of bohemia, more liberal and infinitely wider in its significance, in the Montparnasse quarter, to which there flocked painters, sculptors and intellectuals from all over the world, bringing with them their own very individual ideas. All sorts and persuasions were to be seen in the cafés—even Trotsky and Lenin. The latter, who at one time considered taking a job as a model in the South of France,[1] spent night after night playing chess.

In this Montparnasse, so full of ferment, I sought a hero who would represent the quarter and the new bohemia, as well as the struggles and aspirations of its habitués.

I asked the advice of a number of people, and, as everyone said "Modigliani", I decided on him, changing his name to Modrulleau, and that of his mistress, who was known as "Noix-de-Coco", to "Haricot-Rouge".

And thus my "Montparnos" came into being. Such is the

[1] Bourdelle's son-in-law told me that Lenin gave up such a modest ambition because the Russian sadly realised that he was "too small".

power of the written word that even today some journalists, who have never bothered to read the book, and who want to evoke the so-called "heroic" period of Montparnasse, speak of "Haricot-Rouge" as if she were a real person.

Bakst was, therefore, going to introduce me to the living embodiment of the character I had in mind.

Presently, into the studio walked a tall, upright young man, who had the lithe, springy gait of an Indian from the Andes. He was wearing espadrilles and a tight-fitting sweater. And in his pale face, which was shadowed by a shock of thick hair, his eyes burned beneath their sharp, rugged brows. I learned afterwards that the intensity of his gaze, which seemed to be fixed on some distant object, was unfortunately due to the use of drugs.

Modigliani went through the formalities as quickly as possible, as if he were in feverish haste to set to work; the tea Bakst had prepared for him grew cold.

He applied the paint to the canvas slowly but firmly, all the muscles taut in his cheeks, jaw and hand. He replied briefly but courteously to our questions, but his whole attention was concentrated on what he was doing. Apart from his work, he showed no sign of interest in anything, except when Bakst talked to him about Utrillo. And when a visitor dropped in and asked him why Utrillo painted only gloomy subjects, Modigliani answered less in bitterness than in anger:

"You have to paint what you see. Give a painter some other place to live in than a slum. How shocked the collectors and art dealers are because we give them scenes of horrible suburbs, with trees twisted like salsify and blackened by soot and smoke; or else indoor subjects, where the dining-room is next to the lavatory! And since we are obliged to live like rag-pickers on the outskirts of town, we simply make a record of what we see. Every period has the painters and poets it deserves, as well as the subjects that go with the life they have to lead. In the days of the Renaissance, painters lived in palaces, wore velvet, and enjoyed the sunshine. But when you think of the squalor a painter like Utrillo lives in, and how many hospitals he has been in, from Picpus to Fontenay, you don't have to ask why he doesn't paint anything but walls covered with fly-specks, and leprous streets, and an endless series of railings!"

Modigliani : Self-portrait

Modigliani was very fond of Utrillo. Their first meeting had been quite picturesque, in its way. To begin with, as a token of their mutual admiration, they exchanged coats. Then one said to the other,

"You are the world's greatest painter."

"No. You are the world's greatest painter."

"I forbid you to contradict me."

"I forbid you to forbid me!"

"If you say that again, I'll hit you!"

"The world's greatest——"

Biff! Bang! And the fight started. They made it up in a nearby bistro. There they consumed a large number of bottles of wine, and exchanged coats several more times. Then they went out.

"You're the world's greatest painter, aren't you?"

"No. You are."

Biff! Bang! Wallop! And they were at it again, landing up in the gutter, where they went to sleep, and woke up at dawn to find that they had been robbed.

* * * * *

When I was in the United States a year or so ago, I saw in the Pennsylvania Museum some canvases of Modigliani's that had once passed through my hands. People over there are fond of telling you the price of things, and one of the attendants crudely informed me that each picture was worth sixty thousand dollars.

In the gardens of a big industrialist on the Riviera, I saw a number of admirable statues by Modigliani, and, among others, one that he had carved for his own tomb and that of his wife, who, according to the well-known story, threw herself out of the window on learning of his death.

* * * * *

In conclusion, I must relate an anecdote about the artist which, better than any comment, shows what a profound influence Modigliani had on others, even on the subconscious of some of his friends.

When I came to write the scene of my hero's death in my novel, some intuition prompted me to describe him as uttering with his last breath the one word "Rome".

Some time later I met the Basque painter Ortiz de Zarate, who had been with Modigliani in his last moments, and had, incidentally, inherited the latter's studio.

"Do you happen to remember what his last words were?" I asked him.

"Yes," he said. "He died in the Charity Hospital in the very same bed that Jarry had died in. And I heard him murmur feebly, '*Cara Italia!*' "

CHAÏM SOUTINE

"You do realise, don't you, that your book *Les Montparnos* is not to be taken seriously?" people had said to me, even in Montparnasse. "You talk about Soutine, for instance. He may seem picturesque hereabouts; but outside the quarter he is unknown, and will remain so."

Frankly, Soutine was not much of a celebrity in those days. His lean figure—his shadow, you might say, so timid was he—could often be seen lurking around the Dôme or the Rotonde cafés; but he would not have dared to enter even if he had had the ten sous which would have enabled him to spend the afternoon and evening, and even the entire night, there, in the company of the painters and poets who were just introducing the new Constructivist ideas to the world. He was already a stooping, round-shouldered individual, and he would stand about shivering, his

Soutine in the manner of Modigliani

hands in his pockets, hitching up his shabby coat. His shaggy head, with its unkempt hair, was hunched between his shoulders. His whole face was an unhealthy red, even to the tip of his nose; and he had fleshy lips, like those which had so disfigured Toulouse-Lautrec.

But in spite of his unprepossessing appearance, he had eyes of a surprising serenity: light blue, smiling, almost happy eyes, which, if they did not bring him success, at least secured him the feminine attentions which made his life happier. All the same, he painted women as he looked himself, twisted and grimacing; or else attenuated, like El Greco's figures, by a sort of deep and mystic suffering, and suspended in the midst of landscapes that were themselves deformed and sinister.

"He seems to use dish-cloths to paint on," a captious critic once remarked to me.

"Yes; but he sets fire to them!" I replied.

It was Zborowski who first "discovered" Soutine.

Zborowski was a Polish poet. He was a member of the *Groupe du 41ᵉ Degré*, which had started in the Academy of Tiflis, and spread throughout Russia and Europe, with a branch even in France. It seemed to be a Constructivist school of poetry, and had its extremists just as Cubism had in painting. And what extremists!

Kruchenik, the most important of the contemporary Russian poets, had invented what was called "zaoumian" or "pure spirit" poetry, that is, poetry which did not have to make sense, and was supposed to be sung for the sake of singing. It was also sometimes called "the poetry of sounds".

Kliebnikov had composed a *Treatise of Supreme Impropriety*, which was printed in Moscow by order of the Soviet Government for the purpose of undermining "bourgeois morality". The first sentences of the treatise were retrospective, and based on the edifying theme that "up to now the whole of Russia has been built out of dung".

By way of contrast, Sovour had written and published an ironic *Bourgeois Poetics*, based on the taste of "vulgar concierges".

Zborowski was the "nightingale" of the group. Though he railed against the poetry of old Poland, each of his poems nostalgically evoked his native land. He demolished whole cities, but rather in the manner of a jeweller, who might take a tiara apart, holding each precious stone up to the light to make it sparkle and seem more golden against the distant snows.

Soon, however, the group resumed their carping, and again cursed the past centuries, during which "hundreds of millions of men in Russia and throughout the world had suffered cold and hunger for the benefit of a small minority". Things were no better in 1920. Some of the poets were obliged to clean oil lamps on the railways, or carry ridiculous advertising placards along the boulevards in order to earn a crust of bread. The luckiest of them got a job grinding powders for chemicals; Zborowski himself was hired by an agency to address envelopes at the rate of three francs the five hundred, working by artificial light while summer called to him from out of doors.

In the evening, the poets used to foregather at the Café de la Rotonde in the company of painters as poverty-stricken as themselves. One artist, named Berline, was a taxi-driver by night, and in the daytime he painted when the spirit moved him.

Among all these people, perhaps the most poverty-stricken, yet the purest in heart, was Soutine.

Zborowski's comment on him was as follows:

"He is probably the most vigorous painter of our time, but the poor fellow doesn't suspect it. He emerged from the depths of Russia, and feels as though he is in the Seventh Heaven here in France, where at least he has the right to sit on a public bench if he wants to, without fear of being beaten by the police. I bought him a coat one day. He would have taken any coat the salesman offered him, for he had never worn anything but a Russian blouse. There was no point in picking and choosing: it was extraordinary enough to have a coat at all! He hated wearing a hat. Why, you wouldn't want to 'dress up like a Czar' every day, would you? When he arrived in Paris, Soutine was taken in by the sculptor Mietschaninov who, alarmed at the sorry state of his guest, put a little trough between their two beds and poured paraffin into it, as a protection against vermin.

"But just look at that canvas of Soutine's! Do you know how he does his painting? He goes off into the country and lives like a tramp in a sort of pigsty. He gets up at three in the morning, and walks twenty kilometres with his paints and canvas to find a site that pleases him, and at night returns to his sty to sleep, quite forgetting that he has had nothing to eat. When he gets back, he takes the canvas out of the frame, puts it on top of the one he did the day before, and goes to sleep beside it. Well, I paid him a monthly stipend"—for Zborowski had eventually taken to selling pictures, first to help out various friends, and then to make a modest living for himself—"for two years, without his giving me anything in return. When I finally went to stir him up about it, I found three hundred paintings piled one on top of the other in his wretched hole, which stank to heaven because he never opened the window for fear of 'damaging the canvases'. While I was out getting some food for him he set fire to them, giving as his excuse that he wasn't satisfied with them. However, I managed to save a few, but only after a knock-down fight with him. You're looking at some of them now—those pictures of meat. I must say that he paints meat well, especially when he's hungry. Have you ever noticed his terrible jaws? Well, he buys a piece of raw meat and fasts in front of it for two days before he starts to paint it. Look at that red: hasn't he put all his cannibal appetite into it? And that plain wooden table, laid for a meal with all the things he has never had himself. He even eats without a knife or fork, tearing the food apart with his teeth, and drinks water straight out of the bottle.

"Look at the meat in this picture: he spent two weeks painting it, and after that it was completely unfit to eat. Did even Rembrandt do that? No, I want to keep this one for myself. But if you like the other two, you can have them for forty francs."

"All right. I'll take them."

Zborowski was then living with his wife—a woman of very distinguished appearance whom Modigliani had often painted—in the rue Joseph-Bara, between the Boulevard Montparnasse and the Luxembourg Gardens, just below Kisling's modest lodgings. Kisling was another of his "finds". Zborowski's apartment consisted of two low-ceilinged rooms, cluttered with canvases by all the different painters he was trying to help. And out on a kind of balcony he kept several of Modigliani's sculptures, which, though exposed to the rain, dirt and smoke, he was eventually able to sell at a good price—most of them to M. Monteux, the industrialist.

I went home with Soutine's two canvases, and the next day I wrote a couple of articles on the painter in the hope of helping his cause. Then I talked to Paul Guillaume about him.

M. Guillaume was extremely cultivated and had an inquiring mind. He was probably the first to exhibit Negro sculpture, which such people as Picasso, Apollinaire and Baron Golubev were collecting in those days.

In his enthusiasm for the new painting, he had shown considerable enterprise at the very start of his career. A Swedish gentleman had bought thirty thousand francs' worth of pictures from him, which were to be sent to Sweden. But this was in the middle of the First World War. Nothing daunted, Paul Guillaume took passage with the canvases on a small cargo vessel, and succeeded in delivering them safely.

On his return to Paris, he opened his gallery in the rue de la

Boétie, where he gave a showing of Matisse's first large paintings, *The Piano* and *The Forest*, as well as some by Picasso and Derain, and a few Modiglianis.

"You ought to buy some Soutines," I told him.

"No. Not yet," he said. "But if you know of any Modiglianis. . . ."

One day I had the luck to come across a fine "Modi" and a Soutine in a photographer's shop, of all places. The Soutine was the little pastry-cook in his apron, with his ears sticking out. As I was standing there looking at the two canvases, the photographer said to me,

"They're for sale, if you'd like to buy them."

"I'll bring a buyer to see them," I said. "But only on one condition."

"Oh, I'll give you a commission," the fellow assured me.

"I didn't mean that," I replied, laughing. "My condition is that you won't sell the Modigliani without requiring the buyer to take the Soutine as well."

"Oh, I see," he said. "You're Monsieur Soutine, I suppose? All right. I agree."

An hour later Paul Guillaume and I walked out of the shop with the two canvases, which the photographer had let us have for three hundred francs.

"You're right: it's not bad at all," declared Guillaume, examining the Soutine. "It's stunning, in fact. And there's an extraordinary vehemence about the colour, just as there is about the character of the subject. Now, I'm going to do something that will please you," and, turning to his secretary, he said, "Mademoiselle, will you put this canvas in the window? We'll pick out a handsome frame for it."

I ought to mention that another prominent art dealer, Georges Bernheim, had already become interested in Soutine's work.

M. Bernheim was one of the most cultivated, honest and enterprising of men. It is impossible to guess how many painters are indebted to him for launching them. To give an idea of his character, I must relate one anecdote out of the many that have been told about him. It concerns a collector who was negotiating with him for a Cubist picture, but appeared not to be able to make up his mind. In all fairness, it should be said that the prospective customer was more interested in speculating, since the market was rising, than in buying for his personal pleasure.

"I am afraid," he said, "that my wife will scold me if I buy it. Would you be willing to take it back if she raises too much of a row?"

"Why, certainly, sir," replied Bernheim. "The cashier will give you a receipt for ten thousand francs, on the understanding that the sale is conditional."

The customer paid the money. But a week later he returned with the canvas.

"I'm sorry," he said; "but my wife just can't stand it."

"Very well," replied Bernheim; and, calling to the cashier, he said,

"Will you give this gentleman back his twelve thousand francs?"

On hearing this, the customer, an honest man, exclaimed,

"I beg your pardon, but I only paid ten thousand for the picture."

"I know," retorted Bernheim. "But since you were last here the painter's work has gone up in value. Cashier, will you kindly give the gentleman twelve thousand francs?"

"Oh, well, if that's the case," said the visitor, "I think I had better keep it," and he hurried out of the gallery with the parcel still under his arm.

It so happened that one day Georges Bernheim rang me up.

"Have you got any canvases by that painter Soutine you talked about in your last book?" he asked.

"Yes: two landscapes and a flower-piece."

"Would you let me see them?"

"Yes, certainly."

Bernheim arrived half an hour later, and, pushing his spectacles up on his forehead, examined the Soutines carefully.

"Will you sell them to me?"

"Well, no. Besides, how much could I sell them to you for? I bought them from Zborowski for only forty francs."

"I don't care. I'll give you three thousand francs for them."

"No. I'm sorry."

He thought I was trying to bargain for more.

"I'll give you six—ten—twelve—I'll give you thirteen thousand francs for them."

"Oh, no," I said to myself. "There's been a 'rise' in the value of Soutine's work." (But, quite unknowingly, I had been the one who had caused the "rise".)

"Stop!" I said. "You can have the two landscapes, but I want to keep the flower-piece."

"Good. Here's twenty thousand francs. And if you have any others, you know . . ."

I went round at once to see Paul Guillaume. He, too, had sold the Soutine I had persuaded him to buy. This is what had happened.

A gentleman came into his shop, and asked,

"How much is that canvas?"

"Twenty-five thousand francs," Guillaume had replied at random. At the time, he might not have given more than five hundred for it himself.

"I'll take it," said the stranger.

"Very well, sir. My secretary will take your name and address."

"Here is my card. And I will take anything else you have by that painter."

Guillaume glanced at the card. The gentleman was none other than the well-known Dr. Barnes, the inventor of "Argyrol" and founder of the Barnes Foundation at Merion, Pennsylvania. As it turned out, Guillaume was shortly afterwards to become his European agent.

Guillaume and I then went up and down Montparnasse, trying to find more Soutines. When I next saw Zborowski, I said to him:

"Put ten of your Soutines under your bed [where he kept most of his valuable canvases], and go to Paul Guillaume with the rest of them. He'll take them in a flash."

"But why not all of them?"

"Do as I tell you, and you'll thank me for it afterwards."

"Oh, all right, then."

"What about the 'Beef' picture?" Guillaume asked Zborowski. "The big skinned beef that Soutine kept in the house so long, while he was painting it, that all the neighbours in the rue Saint-

Gothard complained to the police because of the smell of decaying meat."

"I don't want to sell that canvas," the poet said.

They weren't on speaking terms after this incident.

Next time Dr. Barnes called at the gallery to see Paul Guillaume, the latter had some forty Soutines in his racks. But he doled them out one or two at a time to the collector, occasionally putting him off with:

"I haven't been able to find any more. I've been promised one for tomorrow, or the day after. Call in again, and maybe I'll have something for you."

One morning Zborowski blew into my house, his hair in disorder, his shirt open on his naked chest.

"Monsieur Georges-Michel!" he cried breathlessly. "Could you lend me twenty-five francs right away?"

"Why, certainly; and more, if you need it, Zbo. Anything the matter?"

"No. Quite the contrary. What's happened is that a well-known collector is coming to see me this evening. He can only come at night, and, as the gas has been cut off because I haven't paid my bill, I must settle it at once. I can't show my pictures by candle-light."

"Here you are, Zbo."

"Thanks so much. You have no idea what a favour you're doing me."

Two weeks later I had occasion to go to the *Bal des Petits Lits Blancs*, which was being held in the beautiful Théâtre des Champs-Elysées in the Avenue Montaigne, where I was then living. Among the many tables filled with fashionable society people I noticed one in particular, where it looked as though a private banquet was in progress. There were thirty people at least; and there were as many bottles of champagne on the table, and twice as many under it—a veritable Russian orgy. At one end of the table I perceived a sort of Alfred de Musset figure in evening-clothes, with glass raised high. On catching sight of me, de Musset put down his glass and hurried over to beg me to join in the festivities.

"Another bottle of champagne!" he called to the waiter. "Two bottles! A magnum!"

It was Zborowski.

"No, no, Zbo. Don't be so reckless."

"Here. Look," he said gaily. And half-opening his dinner-jacket, he drew out of his pocket an enormous roll of thousand-franc notes. "Sixty of 'em," he informed me. "And I've got a lot more. So you'll surely allow me——"

"He's mad," said Margouliès, who was standing near us. "Yesterday he ordered three hundred francs' worth of soup for his dog in the restaurant where he was eating."

It turned out that the collector, who had bought the ten canvases I had advised Zborowski to hold in reserve, was the wealthy Dr. Barnes again. I might add, in passing, that he had bought them by candle-light after all. For when I went to see Zborowski at his house a week later, not only did he not have a single thousand-franc note left, but he still hadn't paid his gas-bill.

In all fairness, it should be stated that Soutine received his share of the windfall. His pockets well filled with money, he went down to Cagnes, in the South of France, and rented a villa there. Every now and then he would telephone to Nice, which is about six miles away, and order a taxi to come out for him. Then he would go to the Hotel Negresco, or the Rhul, and ask for a manicurist. The taxi waited for him, took him back to Cagnes, and went back to Nice, the return journey paid for, needless to say. It wasn't long before he was calling the manicurist to come out to Cagnes. . . .

But Soutine was always highly critical of his own work, and used to destroy eight out of ten of his canvases. Once, when Bernheim acompanied me on a visit to the artist, he literally had to tear out of Soutine's hands a piece of one picture, which he then bought for twelve thousand francs. Soutine had simply taken the scissors and cut out the part that didn't please him!

He never drank anything but water. Whenever anyone offered him champagne, or even ordinary wine, he would refuse, saying, "No, thanks. I don't want to become corrupted." And his thick lips would break into a smile, and his expression grow more angelic—if I may use the word without irony.

Shortly before the Second World War, I chanced to run into Soutine in the Halles quarter of Paris.

"I want to buy a chicken," he told me, "but I don't know whether I can find what I'm looking for. I'd like one with a long neck and a bluish skin."

He pronounced the word "bluish" greedily, almost gluttonously.

"May I help choose it?" I asked.

The owner of the shop we went into was undoubtedly a decent sort. Soutine, as usual, was dressed like a tramp, and when he asked for a chicken the poulterer brought him a nice fat pullet.

"No. I want one like this," said Soutine, pointing to an emaciated-looking cockerel.

"No, no," the poultry-dealer answered. "I understand. But you needn't worry: I won't charge you any more for this one. I know what hard times are like. You take this one, and have a good meal."

"No," repeated Soutine, stubbornly. "I want the skinny one, with the long neck and flabby skin."

"No, no," insisted the tradesman again. "You just take one of these, and pay me what you can afford."

In vain I tried to explain to the good man that my friend only wanted the chicken to paint, not to eat. He raised his hands in despair. And, as Soutine departed with the chicken he wanted, the poulterer stared after him and shook his head. And no wonder. For Soutine had paid him with a thousand-franc note and told him to keep the change.

After we had left, I said,

"Soutine, you're mad!"

"Bah! What's money, anyway?"

"But the man's much richer than you are."

"What difference does that make?"

"It makes this difference: that if you're going to be so generous with your money, you'd do better to help someone who really needs it—a few of your fellow-artists, for instance."

Soutine stopped short and looked at me in surprise.

"Yes, you're right," he agreed. Then he unwrapped his chicken in the middle of the street, and remarked,

"I'm going to hang it up by the head on a nail, and in a couple of days it will be just about ripe."

The last time I saw Soutine was shortly before the Big Offensive.

As I had an errand near the Place Denfert-Rochereau, I thought I would drop in to see the painter in all his splendour, for I knew that he had bought himself a house in the neighbourhood. It was a quaint little place, two stories high; but inside the walls and the floors were bare. Near the stairs there was a camp-bed with a mattress on it.

"I won't ask you to go upstairs," said Soutine, "because there's nothing there, and besides, I've taken in a woman refugee."

"How's life going with you?" I inquired, not without a certain diffidence, for times were growing very difficult.

"Oh, I've still got twenty-three francs," he informed me. "And a cheque for"—he searched his pockets, and finally pulled out a slightly soiled piece of paper—"twenty-five thousand francs," he went on. "I got it for two small canvases."

"But you must go and cash it, Soutine," I said. "In a few days the banks may refuse——"

"Do you think so? I've had it three weeks already. But I've still got my twenty-three francs." And he thrust the crumpled cheque back into his pocket.

I was among those who helped to organise the last Soutine exhibition at the Venice Biennale. As a commentary on the effort that was made to ensure its success, it is worth mentioning that a million and a half francs were spent in bringing over from America thirteen canvases which Mrs. W—— had been kind enough to lend for the occasion.

Soutine was survived by a daughter who, it is said, barely manages to earn a living as a charwoman.

KREMEGNE

Soutine himself had a shadow, but a shadow which, in course of time, became highly coloured: the painter Kremegne. Perhaps it was because he was smaller and thinner than Soutine, and seemed more harassed by destiny, but the fact remains that Kremegne was the more timid of the two. He would trail along behind Soutine as they went up and down in front of the cafés which, though full of light and warmth and friends, their poverty made them too proud to enter. For I have never known two human beings who had more genuine dignity.

Kremegne's painting is well enough known in the art world today. Though less vehement than Soutine's, it is perhaps more tortured and less dramatic. Some people are inclined to criticise him for being too Russian, too "cerebral".

No matter. Kremegne was acquainted with art galleries all over the world. He used to sit with me in a little café, his elbows on the marble-top table, and his eyes would light up as he talked about the painters of the Renaissance.

"Ah, Raphael!" he would exclaim. "Everything Raphael did was divine: the smallest bit of canvas, a beggar's shoe, the perspective of a palace; every detail as well as the whole picture. And how his work lingers in one's memory."

"What delight Raphael must have had," I said, "in creating only beautiful things, just as Racine did. And his atmosphere——"

"Yes. His skies. We don't really know what their beauty consists of, or their lightness, or their living quality. They are so full of joy; they soar; they sing. They are all order and buoyancy and gladness and colour. A man feels transfigured by them; simply looking at a Raphael makes him feel both naked and a god."

"And Michelangelo, and Leonardo?"

"There's too much will-power in Michelangelo. He is all strength, but Raphael is grace. Michelangelo takes you by force. Raphael smiles and charms you. He is a believer; and at the same time he is a god, he is an angel. Leonardo is too intelligent to believe. He tries to make you believe. He imbues a lip or a glance with mystery, the mystery we want to pluck from art. Raphael is direct. With him, we believe the minute we see. He doesn't just promise you Heaven, as Leonardo does; he shows it to you, he gives it to you. Others are gracious; others are aiming at the celestial: Perugino, for instance. But they are not divine. Only Raphael has the gift of prophecy because he is the descendant of five generations. He is diverse, as Picasso is today. He is Perugino, Leonardo, Bartolomeo, all rolled into one, but in a higher, transfigured, form; for he infused them with the enchantment of divinity. Raphael alone is a god."

ZARRAGA

It is odd that so many painters, even the most diffident, talk about painting in mystical terms. Painters all over the world do it, and each one has his own ideas, which are often diametrically opposed to those held by other artists, even of the same generation. There was, for instance, the Mexican painter, Angel Zarraga, who was a great admirer of Renoir (whose portrait, incidentally, he painted). And yet his way of contrasting Raphael and Michelangelo was altogether different from that of Kremegne.

Zarraga, who had a pinched face but placid eyes, lived in the boulevard Arago. When he worked, he always wore a sort of Spanish robe with a hood, not out of any love for fancy dress but because he thought it more convenient, and also because he had brought the costume back from Spain.

He had been all over Europe, and had steeped himself in the Tintorettos in Venice, the only place, he maintained, "where it is possible to understand and interpret that great colourist". In Spain he had painted the walls of cathedrals, less for the glory of God than for the glory of El Greco, in whom he had discovered—along with several others—what Barrès had never even suspected: namely, the elements of Cubism or, at least, what used to be called Cubism.

Brought up on pictorial scholasticism, he never began a canvas without preparing it as if it were a geometrical problem in space, or even a problem in algebra or logarithms.

I ran into him one evening in Venice. We went out in a gondola together, and were taken along the great lagoon near San Marco. Across the way the beautiful façade of San Giorgio loomed white against the darkness; whereas the Doges' Palace, the Campanile, the Biblioteca, the great piazza were all drowned in the rosy glow of the new electric street lamps.

A number of other gondolas had gathered in groups around us so that their occupants could listen to the musicians who were playing a serenade in a *peotta* hung with lanterns.

"This is more like Van Dongen's Venice than Canaletto's," I remarked to Zarraga. "But it isn't so far removed from Guardi's."

"Yes, in the same way that Goya's Spain seems nearer to us—not in time but in appearance—than Velasquez' does. Yes, Venice on such a night as this wears a different robe of light, artificial though it may be, which those who paint her must strive to recapture."

"Yet what is eternal in Venice is its real light, and the proportions of the city. Canaletto realised that; whereas Guardi was more fascinated by the atmosphere of festivity, and a kind of pastoral intimacy that certain aspects of Venice suggest. But Canaletto is the whole of Venice."

"Yes, he has the last word."

Zarraga had been one of the first to explain to me that Cubism was undoubtedly helpful in preparing for the advent of a painter who, in combining in himself the efforts of the whole of his generation (just as Raphael had assimilated the art of his predecessors), would become the Raphael of tomorrow. And this theory had given me the idea for the underlying theme of the novel I was then preparing to write on the Cubist painters.

But this idea had evidently fermented further in Zarraga's mind, for presently he said to me, as our gondola rocked gently under the Venetian night:

"Whether or not Cubism was preparing the path for 'the one that is to come' was beside the point. Cubism was to be an end in itself. It died because it developed too fast, and also because no great Cubist appeared."

I mentioned a number of names to him, but he shook his head.

"You can't get very far with theories," he declared. "Lhote and

Metzinger simply dropped out of sight. Braque has stayed in a blind alley. And Picasso has simply jumped over the wall. So far as that goes, just look at his so-called Cubist paintings: nothing but surfaces. Obstinate as he is, Braque has remained well balanced, with infinite delicacy in his daring. He is solid. He is French. He is not saved just by Italianism and patching up. As for Picasso? Of course, I agree that there isn't a single painter in our generation who doesn't owe him something. A malicious critic once said that his pictures are done as a milliner makes a hat, which is 'saved' by adding a rosette here, a ribbon there, or else by snipping off something. They are none the less masterpieces, for being largely the result of intuition and luck."

"Well, don't you prefer—if not luck—at least spontaneity, the unconscious, the something which can't be acquired? For isn't it here, in this mystery, that genius, the spark of divinity, lies? That is what Raphael had."

"I prefer Michelangelo," said Zarraga. "Just as I like Delacroix better than Ingres, whom certain ignorant people compare, claiming that Ingres was the true revolutionary—because he pleases those who have knocked their heads against the sharp angles of Cubism and have come back to the smoothness of academism. Vigour and strength have nothing to do with grace. Grace can be imitated in one way or another, but not passion. Michelangelo and Delacroix have fought and won; theirs is the final achievement that admits of no going back. They are the closed door. But there is everything to discover in them. Raphael an angel? That pretty little angel was a minotaur who swallowed and assimilated everything from Phidias to Michelangelo. And yet Raphael, like Rembrandt and El Greco and Ingres, has left the door open for others. Michelangelo and Delacroix have dominated art—one for five centuries, and who knows how long the influence of the other will last? We can pass over the rest, taking from them in the process their flames and tinselled finery, correcting all their errors and drawing nourishment from them. Signorelli, Michelangelo (without whom Raphael would have been nothing), and, later, Delacroix, Courbet, Chassériau, Seurat . . . think what they would have accomplished with the tremendous discoveries of Cubism!"

MOÏSE KISLING

I first made Kisling's acquaintance by getting into a fight with him. And perhaps it was because of our row that I subsequently wrote *Les Montparnos*; poor Kisling will never see the film version, in which I gave him a prominent place in spite of our quarrels.

Apollinaire and Blaise Cendrars brought us together again.

It was at the time of what was called the "heroic" period in Montparnasse, when the Constructivist painters, or Cubists, were trying to establish their theories.

Kisling was not a Cubist. He pretended to know nothing about theories. But, having come to Paris from his native Poland, he happened to frequent the quarter inhabited by the great theorists.

One day when he was painting at Céret, along with Braque and Derain, one of them said to him,

"Kisling, why do you put windows inside that house instead of all round it?"

"Because they are in the house," he answered, quite logically.

No less logically, the other retorted:

"What difference does that make to you? The house isn't yours."

He painted violently, desperately, even, it has been said, with a certain vulgarity. And by way of self-defence, he once wryly declared,

"Painting is a battle; but in battle one does not always distinguish oneself."

During the First World War he enlisted in the army long before the Polish Legion had been formed, and he returned from the Front to fight a duel with one of his compatriots. The incident was famous in the annals of Montparnasse. Some said it was all a fake; others that it had been a dangerous encounter. For some of the smaller art journals had already begun to make jokes about Kisling. He lived in the rue Joseph-Bara, in the apartment above Zborowski's, who, as I have said, was such an admirer of Modigliani, Soutine, Kikoïne, Kremegne and others among the new painters.

It was quite a long room, and on its walls Kisling had pinned photos of various friends, together with newspaper articles and reproductions of the latest masterpieces. Under the skylight there was a big square table, which served as a palette, and around its edges were the bowls in which the artist kept his paints.

In the centre of the room was a dais on which many well-known people had posed, including Kiki, the famous model, who died shortly before Kisling, Colette and the former Mrs. Jefferson Cohn.

Kiki herself told me how she came to know Kisling, back in 1920.

"One day a newcomer appeared at the Rotonde," she said. "He was sunburned, wore his hair in a fringe, and had a disagreeable expression. I hardly dared look at him after I heard him say to the manager, 'Who's that new tart over there?'—that didn't help to endear him to me. I didn't say anything because he frightened me a little, with his red scarf, his hands in his pockets, and his way of staring at you. But a friend of mine who admired him said to me, 'That's Kisling. I'm going to introduce you to him.' After that, every time he saw me in a café he would shout out at me and call me all sorts of names. Of course, I know that the first words most foreigners learn in another language are always dirty ones. But I was furiously angry, and decided not to speak to him any more. It was a pity, because I rather liked him.

"Then he promised he wouldn't insult me any more. He gave me a contract for three months. But I'm a gloomy kind of model most of the time. So then he would start yelling his head off to make me laugh, or else he would make . . . well, rude noises; and we tried to out-do each other in that. That's the only thing that really makes me laugh. He was very nice to me after that. I would steal his soap and his toothpaste, and he never said a word. He was a terribly decent sort, a real pal. Zborowski would come up two or three times a morning to see how we were getting along . . . and also to take a good look at me. I've only known one other chap as amusing as Kisling, and that was Fujita, who would sometimes say to me in his funny little voice, 'Why your dirty feet?' That was because I used to walk round in my bare feet, and Fujita had forgotten to put rugs on the floor. Whenever he sold a picture I had posed for, he would slip me a few hundred franc notes. He would ask me to sing *Louise* for him, and I would imitate an orchestra, and bring out the flute part especially, which made him roar with laughter. 'It's a sc'eam!' he would say in his funny accent."

Kisling's talent, his odd way of dressing—for people liked a little fancy dress in Montparnasse—his pranks in smart society, into which he began to be invited, all helped to change the "Montparno" into an almost "Parisian" painter. Before long he was getting his clothes at the most fashionable shops, and even went so far as to wear white gloves. He was the talk of the town: "It's really not done to paint the eyes with shoe-polish," said some. "Not all women have jaundice, or a stiff neck," said others. But he was an artist and painted well, and he made a solid reputation for himself with his portraits of women with an air of Oriental melancholy. He was conscientious, even painstaking. He painted magnificent pictures of nudes, which were sought after both by collectors and by art-dealers, although his highly-coloured flower-pieces seemed somewhat stiff. On the other hand, when it came to some of his pictures of fish on a fishmonger's slab, few could surpass him, and that alone would have been enough to class him as a master.

As his first name was Moses, of which he was very proud, Kisling decided to leave France at the time of the German invasion in 1940. He was detained in Portugal, and it was always being rumoured that he had died there. But he eventually succeeded in getting to New York, where he rented a studio in Gramercy Park. At first, things were so difficult for him that he had to ask one of his compatriots, whom he had helped in Montparnasse, to come to his aid. His so-called friend, who had made a fortune selling pictures, was crass enough to boast afterwards of what he had done for Kisling. On learning of it the artist was furious, and, the next time they met, publicly reminded him of his Paris days, when the friend had to go round in down-at-heel shoes. And even then they weren't his own.

Almost at once a number of more tactful people came to Kisling's rescue, and he soon acquired a first-rate studio overlooking the Park, to which he invited the cream of New York society as well as some of his refugee friends. Commissions began to pour in. Kisling became the chairman of a committee for the relief of needy painters in Paris, and sent them money and painting materials. He made the mistake, however, of thinking in all sincerity that he should discriminate between those who did, and those who did not, deserve help, and the result was another falling-out between us, which lasted, unfortunately, until his death. But he had the courage to admit his mistake, and the work of the committee goes on to this day. For his part in the undertaking Kisling was awarded the rosette of the *Légion d'Honneur*.

When he returned to France, the painter retired to his home at Sanary, near Toulon; and it was there, after the triumphant exhibition of his work put on by Drouant-David, that he died, surrounded by his family and his two friends, André Salmon and Maguy.

It was, perhaps, characteristic that such a magnificent colourist as Kisling, who lived only for painting, should have gazed wistfully at the lovely view spread out before him, as he neared the end, and murmured:

"I love life so much. . . ."

FUJITA

Fujita was one of the most outstanding personalities in the great days of Montparnasse, and he became equally prominent at the fashionable sea-side resorts and in Paris salons. He always wore his hair Papuan-style, and sported earrings; and his shirts he made for himself out of the oddest materials, such as sacking, curtain material and corset fabrics.

When he arrived in Paris he rented, in the rue Delambre, near the Café du Dôme, an old stable which he transformed into a kind of Japanese studio.

He repainted the woodwork, beams and walls in light colours, put straw mats on the floor, and hung large red and white check curtains in the windows. From the ceiling he suspended a typical Japanese lantern; and in one corner of the room he kept little dishes of dried, slightly-sweetened fish, which he served to his guests on a low table, along with a magic green tea which was supposed to have rejuvenating properties. It was in this room that he gave shelter to the unhappy woman who had been living with Modigliani, and tried to comfort her the night before her tragic death.

It was here, too, that Fujita married his second wife, Fernande

Barrey, a talented woman-painter, whom he enjoyed dressing up like a Lautrec doll, with sky-blue stockings and a bow in her hair which was almost as large as herself.

At an Artists' Charity Ball organised by Gustave Kahn, Fujita made his appearance naked from his loins up and tattooed all over in blue. On his shoulders he carried a cage, in which sat Mme. Fujita, even more naked than her husband, except for the ribbon in her hair, while in her hand she held a sign reading, "Woman for Sale: S.G.D.G." [1]

Life eventually separated them—life, and another Japanese painter named Koyonaki, which means "Little Weeping Willow". It must be admitted that Fujita, who was a day-dreamer, was often far away from his wife, even when she was in his arms. . . .

When Sugu Horu Fujita found out what was going on, he made no protest. For since "Sugu-Horu" means "Heir of Peace", and "Fujita" "Field of Wistaria", he could hardly have been expected to fight a duel, even with flowers, with a rival called "Little Weeping Willow", especially in a foreign country.

Fujita, therefore, literally faded out of the picture, and left Fernande to the new Samurai. But he continued to dream and also occasionally to paint, and then one day he chanced to notice a young woman, with cheeks reddened by the sharp morning air, walking gracefully along the Avenue de Villiers, in Paris.

"*Youki!*" he called out to her.

"What's the matter with him?" said the girl.

"*Youki*," repeated Fujita.

"*Youki* yourself," she replied.

"In the language of the country I come from, *Youki* means 'Snow Rose'," Fujita informed her.

"That's rather nice."

"Well then, let's go and baptise *Youki*," suggested the artist.

They went into the first café they came to; then to a restaurant; and then, without further delay, they set off for the nearest registry office.

From that time on, Fujita and Youki were always together, usually in the company of Van Dongen, Vertès and Jean-Gabriel Domergue, either at Deauville, or the Lido, or the dress-rehearsals of all the latest plays.

[1] *Sans Garantie du Gouvernement.* [*Trans. note.*]

Fujita had many imitators. He had one at Deauville, for instance, where a poor Russian painter also wore his hair Papuan-style, put rings in his ears—and even in his nose—and walked on his hands, balancing his portfolio between his legs.

His "society" career did not prevent Fujita, lying naked on his mat, from painting portraits of himself with a lot of cats perched on his shoulders, or of Youki in the nude, or screens with gold backgrounds and huge panels in a beautiful ash-grey wash.

He made a great deal of money and he spent as much as he made. One fine day he was notified by the tax authorities that he would have to pay a fine of two hundred thousand francs just when he had barely enough to buy a case of vintage champagne, settle his laundry-bill and give Youki a new dress. He packed his bags: that is to say, he put a few brushes into a reed case, stuffed a shirt or two into his pockets, left all his pictures to Youki, turned her over to a Surrealist poet, and started off on a tour round the world.

He had left his "Memoirs" with me, and I recall one of the passages, which went like this:

> *My Departure:*
>
> *And the more I looked at myself, the older I seemed to grow.*
> *My last night was a night of frost:*
> *I spent it between a painting of a flower*
> *And my mirror;*
> *And the flower remained fresh.*
>
> "As I departed, I grasped tightly the rail of the boat. Already my native land was only a mirage in the distance. . . .
>
> "In the mirror I was amazed to discover that I had so many grey hairs. My face was beginning to look more and more like my father's.
>
> "But the flower remained fresh."

* * * * *

I used to see Fujita in Montparnasse and Deauville, in his studio, at the beach and at thé-dansants. I also saw him hard at work on a portrait—and what a portrait!—of the Comtesse de Noailles.

I happened to be at the Countess's house one day when Fujita was expected. As usual, she was sitting up in bed, the outline of

Fujita and Youki by Vertès

her figure faintly visible under the covers, ensconced among her pillows of creamy lawn. She was writing. For the celebrated poetess, like Mark Twain, rarely got up before dinner-time, as she liked to meditate and compose while reclining. She was not at all displeased by a little *hai-kai* verse I had brought her. It ran as follows:

The whole of summer entered her like a frenzied lover,
And she swooned in Alexandrine lines.

Unfortunately, it was winter, and the pale sun shone timidly through the double window. Mme. de Noailles was still writing away when Fujita was announced.

Many painters had tried, in the portraits they had done of her, to catch and record her flashing eyes, her determined nose, and those restless lips of hers, which seemed to perfume every word she uttered. Her shoulders were remarkably smooth and shapely. ("My shoulders are quite shapely, aren't they?" she would say.) And her slender hands with their child-like fingers: La Gandara, Jacques-Emile Blanche, Zuloaga, Forain, Hélène Dufau, Helleu, Zaslo had all painted them, and Rodin had modelled them with strength and tenderness.

But never had her secret nature, as revealed in her poems, been completely portrayed in any of these interpretations. Compared to them the model was as a living flame is to embers. Perhaps Fujita would be the mirror which would reflect her beauty in eternity?

For him, the poetess made a gracious and most unusual effort: she rose from her bed on the stroke of noon, arranged her dark hair, which fell, like the descending night, fan-wise to her waist, and put on a dress so sheer as to be almost intangible.

The artist was ushered in. He was always the same small figure, with his thatch of hair pressed down on his head like the straw roof of a Hottentot hut, the spectacles that made him look like an Oriental philosopher, and an impeccably white silk blouse. His appearance hadn't changed at all in the three years that had gone by since Tristan Derême had first introduced him to the Countess.

For three years he had worked on her portrait, at each session adding a touch here, a shadow there, as transparent as the vapour that rose from the golden tea he sipped as he worked.

But today was to be the final sitting, and Fujita was to sign the portrait for her.

As he entered, he crossed his hands over his breast, and bowed over the hand held out to him, with its fingers curved like those of Falconnet's *Graces*.

The poetess took her pose in front of the window; or rather, sitting upright, she began to quiver, to ripple like a wave, to move her whole delicate, magnificent being with a swaying motion of which she was perfectly conscious.

"Either I am dead," she said, "or I am dancing."

But Fujita, who was putting the final touches to his canvas, glanced out at the balcony and saw an enormous black-and-white rabbit munching away at a box of flowers.

"Ff! Ff! Ff!" (that was the kind of noise he made when he laughed). "Look at the rabbit eating violets!"

"Violets!" echoed the Countess, indignantly. "They're *agera-tum*, or *agerata*, I should say. They are much bluer than violets; and there are some pink begonias, too. . . . But aren't you going to paint any more?"

"I have finished."

Mme. de Noailles went over to inspect the tall glazed panel, and what she saw made her go into another kind of dance.

"You probably won't like the forehead, which I have made too low," said Fujita. "Or the eyes, which I have drawn out a bit; or the mouth, which doesn't really give your expression; or the hands, which look dead, compared with yours. Only the shoulder is exactly right: not even our snowy Fujiyama has been more subtly interpreted. . . . But I am pleased with the portrait, which will go to the Louvre. That is why, out of deference to you, I shall do no more work on it." And taking up his finest brush, he signed in Japanese, "Heir-of-Peace-Field-of-Wistaria".

Then he bowed to the Countess, and she returned his bow; for she had the greatest respect for the artist's convictions, and she admired him for his character and talent. No evil spirit had come between them, spouting fire and smoke, as in the old folktales.

Fujita went home to his studio to finish the portrait of another of his gods. And the poetess took up her pen, and went on with a poem:

Midi cligne des yeux dans l'or de ses rayons. . . .

* * * * *

During the Second World War, many stories were told about Fujita. When he returned to Paris, I went to see him in his new studio on the third floor of a modern building in the rue Campagne-Première. It consisted of a square room with white walls, on which were drying some twenty squares of canvas with their flake-white grounds laid on with a palette-knife.

"People think it's lacquer," the artist told me. "But it isn't: I simply give my white a good polish, and then cover it with transparent colours. Oh, you want to know what I did during the War? Yes, people said that the Japanese Government commissioned me to do a large painting of a flag-ship, with all the officers assembled on deck. My nicest friends say that I refused, on the grounds that I was not a 'military' painter. It is also said that I was put in prison because of my refusal. But the truth is that when I got to Japan they didn't ask me to do anything of the kind; or anything else, either. I took the very last boat going to Japan, and arrived there just in time for my father's birthday."

"Your father was still alive then? I remember your poem."

"Yes. I had the good fortune to see him on his last birthday, just a few days before his death. We celebrated his eighty-eighth birthday, which we call the 'rice age'. There were forty-five members of the family present, and we were all dressed in national costume. We gave him presents, swordfish and the symbolic baby-lobster, with a round back and long feelers, which signifies long life. . . ."

"This was in Tokyo?"

"Yes. While I was there, I kept thinking as much of Fouquet's painting and the School of Avignon as of Picasso, and I added a great deal of colour and shadow to the black and white I was using. Then, as a reaction against the violence of the times, I began doing very gentle subjects, childish ones, in fact. When the war came closer to us, we went out to the country and lived on a farm. My companions raised vegetables, and I grew flowers—chrysanthemums, roses, wistaria. . . ."

"Do you mind my asking you what effect the bombing of Hiroshima had on the people around you, and on you yourself?"

"Very little at first. The reaction must certainly have been greater in Europe. We didn't know then what the atom bomb was. We only learned its importance gradually. Besides, we never talked about the war except with reserve, with a certain discretion. Out on the farm we were isolated, anyway. You will hardly believe it when I tell you that I never saw any dead or wounded. . . . Now, this porcelain white of mine I get by using a palette knife on a simple canvas. If it is prepared right, it will never turn black, or even darken at all. And if you are careful to use pure colours, very transparent. . . ."

MAN RAY

I must relate an amusing, if paradoxical, anecdote about Man Ray, the photographer and friend of all the artists in Montparnasse.

One day I went to his studio. The walls were covered with hundreds of photographs of such disparate objects as pins, springs, screws, cubes, cones, cylinders, dummies, etc., for which he had used a variety of carefully chosen lighting-effects.

However, at the moment Man Ray was not working on photographs but on a painting in the most lovely colours.

"I suppose you have taken all these photos," I remarked, "so as to understand painting better?"

"No," he replied—and he was speaking truthfully—"I am painting in order to understand photography better."

The Past of the Futurists

SEVERINI · BALLA · DEPERO · MARINETTI

ONLY A VERY few art critics, such as Gustave Kahn, Geffroy, Roger Marx and Tabarant, lent their support to the Futurists at the time of the 1910 Exhibition. The Futurists were trying to introduce dynamism into painting or, to put it in simpler terms, movement. They did this not so much by suggestion as by mechanical means. Futurism was somewhat outside painting as such, and the practitioners of it owed a great deal to the Cubists. But the examples of work shown by several good painters, like Severini, were interesting. He was one of the high priests of the Golden Section, along with Princet, Gleizes, Metzinger and that great theorist of Painting, André Lhote. Severini's compositions are entirely French in their restraint.

In addition to Severini there were also Carra, Boccioni and Balla. The last-named returned involuntarily to the "static" method. I well remember the settings he designed in Rome for Stravinsky's ballet *Feu d'Artifice*. Although the painter had led us to expect a "velocity" of colours, you can imagine our surprise, when the curtain rose, to behold three brilliantly-coloured pyramids, which took up so much room on the stage that the dancers could hardly execute a single step. Even granting that a stage-designer should be allowed a certain amount of liberty, this was obviously self-defeating.

"As a painter, I had no one to account to but my painter-self," declared Balla egotistically. "I have no need of music. My work is sufficient to itself. After looking at it for a quarter of an hour in reverent silence, the audience is in ecstasies before the most beautiful ballet that has ever been danced."

Unfortunately for him, the audience allowed the painter to "go into ecstasies" all by himself.

Another eccentric with even more self-confidence was Depero; he nevertheless produced a number of interesting works. I once went to his studio in Rome. The one he had at the time was a sort of shed, with a multitude of cardboard disks of every size and colour hanging from the roof by strings. There must have been at least two thousand of them.

"Now, this," he explained, pointing to one, "is the disk of joy, and that one is light and that one dance; and the one over there is music. The smallest ones, my soul tells me, are all the human feelings and objects."

As a matter of fact the effect was quite agreeable, even though most of the disks looked rather mildewed and warped by the sun.

"I hold the view," he went on, "that everything should start from the sphere and return to it. Are not the world, the universe, the eye, all spheres? Thought itself, like all abstract and concrete things, is a sphere, like light and strength and joy."

Did not Rodin, and later Brancusi, express the same idea when they said that all volumes should derive from the egg, since it was from the egg that the universe and, subsequently, living beings evolved?

* * * * *

I also knew Marinetti, the forceful personality who had given Futurism its chief impetus. The first time I met him he said to me:

"You are with us, aren't you? Come and help us, and we will break down the doors of the Impossible, burn the cities and museums of the past, and pluck the stars to build the world of the future. The petrified blood of the slothful and the faint-hearted will serve us as a pedestal."

He published books of extraordinary intensity, which had a certain influence on poets as well as painters. Then during the Mussolini régime he became an academician. D'Annunzio, with whom Marinetti had been foolish enough to enter into controversy, nicknamed him, rather unjustly, "*il cretino fosforescente*" ("the phosphorescent cretin").

Picabia: Self-portrait

The Picaresques

PICABIA

I FIRST MET Francis Picabia at the time when he was trying to undermine Cubism and foreshadow Surrealism. His work took the form of a vertical black line a quarter of an inch wide and eighteen inches high; to one side the date 1879 (which had nothing to do with his birth); and above the vertical line, in capital letters, these words: THE CHILD CARBURETTOR, MY PORTRAIT, THE STATE OF MY SOUL—the whole on white paper in a tin frame.

This particular picture was hung, if I am not mistaken, in one of the rooms of the National Salon, round about 1902, at a time when that Salon, which today has the same official standing as the *Indépendants*, was considered "revolutionary".

I met Francis Picabia for the second time thirty years later, at Espeluche, in the Rhône Valley. I had stopped there for the night, and in the hotel where I was staying I encountered a local poet who offered to show me round. As we came out on to the main square, we were startled by a bright light, a good deal of smoke and the sound of shouting.

"A fire?" I asked my companion.

"No. Only a marriage."

We then made out a brazier burning on the pavement, and around it some twenty or thirty people, in wedding-clothes, dancing the farandole. From time to time a policeman or one of the shopkeepers would throw an old chair, a table leg or some rags on to the flames, while the dancers sang:

Et vive Diou
Et vive la mariée,
Ne cessera la farandoulle
Qu'avec la flamme foulle.
Ah! Flamboyeurs n'ayez pitié
Ni des fii, ni de la mariée,
Si ses jambes deviennent moulles
Le mari mieux les enrebottira . . .
Et vive Diou! . . .

"It's not so much a local custom as a Montélimar one," the poet explained; "but since the bride comes from there, they're celebrating as they do in her town. You're welcome to join in, if you like."

"What, and jig round till the fire burns out? Here come some more people with a whole wooden bedstead!"

"In the old days the one who held out to the last could claim the *droit de jambe* from the bride, if the fiancé made a mess of it. . . ."

I prudently went to bed.

At six o'clock next morning the fire was still burning and the merry-makers capering; so I went down and joined in the fun. I noticed that a heavy-set fellow with thick hair and bushy eyebrows, dressed like a sailor, was holding the bride by the arm. How long had he been dancing, I wondered? I asked where the groom was, and learned that he had passed out.

"Then you have the *droit de jambe,*" I said to the sailor, and told him about the local tradition.

"Well, how about it?" he asked the bride.

"No," she replied. "But I'll go for a ride with you in that fine car of yours."

"Why, certainly," said the sailor, and he led the way to a huge American car drawn up at the kerb nearby.

"Would you like to come too?" he asked me.

Of course I wanted to know how the adventure would turn out. The "sailor" threw a trench-coat over the bride's white dress, and she settled down on the seat in the back. He motioned me to take the seat next to him. Then, to the amazement of what was left of the wedding-party, he started the engine, and we drove twice round the square. Glancing over his shoulder, he discovered that the bride had gone to sleep; so he turned to me and said,

"Why not go on a bit further?" And he drove out of the town and took the road to Marseilles.

After we had passed Avignon and were well on the way to Arles, I felt that I ought to introduce myself.

"Oh, it's you," said the sailor. "Would you mind taking the wheel for a minute?" And reaching down to adjust his shoe, he introduced himself in his turn:

"My name is Picabia."

"The painter?"

"Some people say so."

We drove on for another thirty miles.

"If it wouldn't be too indiscreet," I said, "would you mind telling me when we ought to take the young lady back?"

"Oh, yes. You're quite right. There is something asleep back there. Well, I think the best place to lunch is Marseilles, don't you?"

The Old Port. The Restaurant de la Cascade on the quay. Street musicians singing "*Une de Paris*". Old Marie doing an Italian dance on the cobble-stones. Accordions groaning to the right and left of us, even out on the boats in front of us.

"Bring me some more bouillabaisse, with lots of shellfish and bread in it," the bride was saying in her strong Midi accent. "And for Monsieur a bottle of *Camp Romain*, the wine which makes you smile."

She was running the show. She sat opposite me, the trench-coat thrown over the back of her chair. She ate steadily, quite indifferent to the crowd of other diners or the onlookers around us. She ate, she drank, and she smiled, showing all her gleaming teeth.

"What will your husband think?"

"Eh—— You've got more curiosity than I have. I haven't given it a thought. Besides, I can't stand him."

"Why did you marry him, then?"

"I can't imagine. He's neither young nor handsome nor rich nor intelligent. I don't like his manners; I don't like the clothes he wears; and he eats his supper at six o'clock, puts all his food on the same plate, and only has a clean one for jam."

"Why did you marry him, then?"

"I can't imagine, I tell you. As I haven't asked myself the question, I haven't needed an answer. He kept insisting until I said 'yes', just to have a bit of peace. Anyway, it's right to get married, don't you think?"

"Why?"

"Because that's what people say, of course. Give five francs to that fellow who sang *Douleur d'Amour*, will you? He has such a beautiful voice."

The singer bowed.

"Yes, beautiful lady, I could have sung in the theatre, you know. But I would rather be free. Oh, I didn't mean to say that because you've just been married. . . . Thank you, gentlemen."

"I'm not the one who's been cuckolded," remarked Picabia.

"No one has yet," retorted the bride.

As soon as we got back to the car she went to sleep again.

"Well, it can't be helped," said Picabia.

And we set off on the road to Toulon. We didn't reach Cannes till evening, and we went straight to the port, where Picabia kept his yacht *l'Horizon*.

"Carry her carefully into the cabin," Picabia told the Russian sailor in charge of the boat. He and I then went off and spent the night at the Château de Mai, the house the artist owned nearby.

"She'll look pretty foolish tomorrow," said the painter as he wished me good-night.

But he was the one who looked foolish when he went on board next morning. For the Russian sailor and three other men were busily employed painting the masts, the railings and even the decks of *l'Horizon* a ghastly red.

"What's all this?" he demanded.

"Lady's orders."

"What lady?"

"The new lady Monsieur's just married."

At that moment she appeared, dressed in a captain's uniform which she had found among Picabia's belongings.

"I love red!" she told him. "I wanted to give you a nice surprise. And I've wired my husband to come and join us, poor man. I'm a respectable woman, you know."

The dinner we had that night was magnificent. The husband drank to the health of his host. But towards midnight he said goodbye to us, explaining that he had to catch a train home; and away he went, leaving his wife behind. Every time I visited Picabia after that I found her there, abusing the Russian sailor and tending the sheep she had installed in a pen on board. She had had the engines removed because, she said, they took up too much room; moreover, they were useless since *l'Horizon* never left the quay. She served tea to the artist's guests and entertained them with her theories on the Dadaist paintings of Picabia, based on notes she had asked me for as the price of not insulting me for two days.

"Why, it's quite simple," she would begin. "All the other painters paint what they see outside themselves. But Picabia paints what he sees inside himself. There are some critics like *him* [designating me] who try to make things complicated, and claim that Picabia is to painting what Jarry was to literature and what *Ubu Roi* was to the heroic theatre of Henri de Bornier; and that he has baffled the Cubists (who do more calculating than painting) by putting nothing but numbers on his canvases. Who really knows those gentlemen, after all? But I know *my* Picabia. Will you have a little more tea, Mademoiselle Lily Pons? It softens the voice, you know. Won't you tell us again that story about the Mexican Revolution, eh?"

The story she was referring to was really Picabia's, and he had probably got it from J.-G. Domergue.

"When I got to Mexico, three cannon-shots had just been fired to announce the start of the Revolution. There were no cars anywhere, so I had to take the tram—just as Victor Hugo and Degas had done in Paris."

"First class, I presume?" put in Mme. d'Escardot, a Picabia collector, who was listening to the tale.

"Yes, although the first and second-class passengers were all packed into the same compartment."

"How could you tell them apart?"

"The conductor made those who wore shoes pay the first-class fare and those with bare feet the second. As it happened, a good many of the latter were rich. But during the Revolution it was forbidden for people to wear new shoes, and since there was only one cobbler in the whole town——"

"He must have been kept pretty busy."

"Yes and no. I went to his shop, and found him smoking a cigar and staring at a mountain of shoes. He looked up at me and said, 'I haven't the courage to begin'."

* * * * *

When he wasn't on his boat, Picabia was usually to be found at the Château de Mai, situated on a hill near Mougins. It was surrounded by water and cemeteries.

"I didn't know you had such morbid tastes," I said to him, when I noticed the gloomy situation.

"Don't worry. Those are fake cemeteries."

"What do you mean, fake?"

"Just that. I've camouflaged those fields of mine so as to force down the price of the adjoining property, which I want to buy. . . . But, speaking of morbid stories, I must tell you about the magnificent ebony coffin with bronze handles that was sent to me the day I gave my last big luncheon-party here. When it came to the time for dessert, I asked my guests which of them had been responsible for the joke. And, do you know, they all turned pale, and told me that each of them had received a similar present that same morning? I didn't manage to clear up the mystery until a week later. It turned out that an undertaker friend of mine had sent us all 'samples' of his wares. And when I protested he said: 'Don't be annoyed. Business has been bad and my stock was going to be seized. So, in order to save as much of it as I could, I sent it to my friends.' "

Apart from the cemeteries, Picabia's château was charming. Everything was quite informal. Chickens wandered into the bedrooms without even knocking on the door. And how pleasant the bedrooms were! There was the sailor's room, the wild man's room, the room of the lady of 1840, and the children's room, which was adorned with Negro masks and suits of armour, and furnished with cannons, all the paraphernalia of witchcraft, and instruments of torture. Every night a mechanical ghost went the rounds, twitching the sheets and rattling chains.

"I designed it like that," the artist explained to me, "because I wanted to train the children from childhood to be quite fearless. When they get a bit older, I shall replace the ghost with a creditor waving an unpaid bill."

His studio was an immense shed, in which sixty or more canvases were under way at the same time: lovely Spanish women, with flowers for eyes; and charming rose-bushes, with human hands instead of leaves, each nail in the form of a snail reading a newspaper. . . . The whole effect was sparkling and delightful.

"Do you know, old man, that it's all painted with ordinary house-paint, the most durable kind you can get? I mix it with aviation fuel, and then varnish it with car polish, which never turns yellow and protects the picture. Now, let's go and have a look at my stable before lunch."

He took me to his garage, where ten Fords were lined up in the stalls.

"So you're selling cars now, are you?" I said.

"No. But I've found Fords so practical that I don't want any other kind. I bought ten of them at the same time to be on the safe side, and so that I wouldn't be tempted to get any other make. You can have ten Fords for the price of one Hispano. Wouldn't you rather have ten Fords than just one Hispano? Of course you would. . . ."

However, when I went to pay Picabia a visit on board his boat the following year, I found him on the quay, gazing rapturously at a huge Rolls-Royce; and his first words were,

"Isn't she a beauty?"

"Is she as good as a Ford?" I asked.

"Oh, shut up," he said. "I've just bought it. I got it for running about in, errands in town and so on. But I've got something better. I'll show you. . . ."

We climbed into the Rolls and sped off to the Château de Mai. As soon as we arrived, Picabia jumped out and ran to the staircase leading to the square tower.

"Where on earth are you going?"

"Come on!" he called back.

We came out on to a terrace, and there was a superb car, with enormous exhaust-pipes and bonnet, mounted on a steel bar with a vertical pivot, like the horses on old-fashioned merry-go-rounds.

"And do you know what she can do? A hundred and twenty-five miles an hour."

"I don't understand," I said.

"About the pivot? And the terrace? Why, it's all very simple. Watch."

He sat down at the wheel, and started going round at a dizzy pace.

"You see? I love speed, but I'm afraid of danger. So I thought up this little dodge."

"But what about the pleasures of motoring? The scenery?"

"Well, I've got the hills round Grasse on one side, and the sea and the islands off Cannes on the other; there are woods close by, and the plain just beyond. Where else would I find more beautiful scenery and such peace? Where else could I do a hundred and twenty-five miles an hour without the risk of skidding, or running into a telegraph pole, or colliding with some fool coming along on the wrong side of the road? You try it. Get in and see. It's like being on a boat; if you're not used to it your head starts spinning. Perhaps we'd better have lunch first. Let's get back to the port and go aboard the boat."

At that time Picabia had no less than three yachts, named respectively *l'Horizon I*, *l'Horizon II* and *l'Horizon III*.

"So you don't approve of my cars? Whenever anything goes wrong with one of them, I buy a new one. Do you like dessert? For lunch today I've ordered nothing but various kinds of dessert, served on palettes out of old paint-tubes. After all, old man, you're visiting a painter, you know. . . ."

My charming, eccentric friend eventually died in poverty, almost completely paralysed, and speechless. He could speak only with those flashing eyes of his—and in how tragic a language. . . .

JAMES ENSOR

In 1901, when I was still quite young, we had devoted one of the special numbers of *Plume* to the painter James Ensor. And on my first trip to Belgium I went to see him.

The well-known artist, with his fiery beard, ruddy lips and blue eyes, was then living in Ostend, in the funny little rue de Flandre, which, as it flows down to the beach, is a veritable flood of people, flags and little carts with fried potatoes.

To get to his apartment, which consisted of two high-ceilinged rooms with tall windows looking out on to the street, you had to pass through a shop where all sorts of trinkets made of shells and other souvenirs were sold. Ensor drew on these shells as much as on his Flemish background for his inspiration.

"When I go through the shop in the evening," he told me, "as I have had to do every day since my childhood, all those shell-like objects seem to me like curious little people. At first I used to amuse myself by adapting them for illustrations. It was, of necessity, only later that they transformed themselves into dream, into nightmare, figures."

The man himself resembled the crowds he used to draw, for he was astonishingly many-sided. At one moment, as he bent over his table, he looked like a little old man; the moment he straightened up he was a blond Don Quixote.

HENRY DE GROUX

I knew another Belgian, Henry de Groux, much better than I did Ensor. But he was just as phantom-like, if not more so. He often used to say, "It's not me; it's my ghost who's walking around. And that explains a good deal about my queer behaviour."

The "queer behaviour" deserves a special chapter to itself.

Henry de Groux, the son of Charles de Groux, was a pupil of Rops and Constantin Meunier; the painter of the famous *Christ aux Outrages*; the madman of Florence; the sham corpse of the Beaux Arts Salon episode; and the wandering ghost of the First World War.

Whenever I met him he was always the same, with his long poet's hair under his wide-brimmed charcoal-burner's hat; his dark brown overcoat, whose frayed ends had swept the dust of every city in Europe; and his sallow face, with its china-blue eyes and ferret-like nose. His appearance never changed in more than thirty years.

"Hi! De Groux!"

He would turn round, his eyes hardening at first beneath his flat, straggling locks, and then lighting up.

"I've seen your face somewhere!" he would exclaim, as if searching in his memory, despite the number of times he had stayed at my house, and all that had passed between us in former years. But suddenly he would add: "I was wondering, too, who could not only know me, but recognise me in this most extraordinary and woeful of all the places I have ever been in."

It was through Catulle Mendès that I had first made de Groux' acquaintance. I remember seeing them come into the Café Napolitain together, one evening back in 1901. His Lavallière cravat hanging loose, Mendès pushed his corpulent way among the tables, flicking at people with his light cane, while behind him trailed a sort of "stage" priest who affected a timid and modest air.

Calling as witnesses the waiters, the women at the adjoining tables—all of us, in fact, even the café mirrors—Mendès announced indignantly, in his burring voice:

"It's unheard of, absolutely unheard of! Tell them about it, de Groux. Do you know what someone has just done to him? It's unbelievable! De Groux has just spent two years of his life—two whole years!—painting a fresco in a gem of a church in the North: the Life of Christ and the Apostles, in the style of Gozzoli and the followers of Giotto. He worked by the light of an oil lamp, just like the early Christians in the Catacombs, so that he could reconstitute the exact colours, and look at him now—his eyes are positively bleeding! Do you know what the parish priest did while de Groux, who was completely exhausted, was resting in a field nearby? You can't possibly imagine!"

Mendès swept the tankards aside with his cane, and brought his fist down on the shoulder of the person nearest him.

"The priest thought his colours too pale," he declared, "so he had them touched up by a local painter. The filmy cloak of the Christ, the gossamer threads of the Virgin's robe, the gauzy wings of the angels, all repainted with washing blue and murderous red. Tell them about it, de Groux; go on, tell them about it. . . ."

De Groux held out one hand, a hand clothed in a black glove, through whose torn ends protruded fingers blacker than the glove itself, and in his reedy voice he affirmed,

"True, alas. Quite true."

* * * * *

"Rubbish!" Ibels, who knew de Groux well, said to me afterwards. "On the contrary, what probably happened was that, after doing the frescoes, de Groux got such a foothold in the church that the poor priest had to resort to any expedient in order to get rid of him."

For it must be admitted that every church in Flanders had reason to remember de Groux. He had literally lived in them for years. He would, for instance, go to visit one of them, and, hand on chin, shake his head in admiration over the stained glass, or the relics, or the high altar, or the architecture in general. And if he chanced to run into the priest in charge, he would say:

"What a magnificent church you have, Father! What a spiritual atmosphere it has! What excellent taste, the way everything is arranged! You will pardon me, I am sure, if I say so as an impious person—if, however, an artist can be impious in the House of God——?"

"No one is impious here as long as he respects these walls; an artist less than any other."

"That's very curious, Father, what you've just said about an artist—even one of little faith—feeling more at home than others in this place of final refuge. Is it because, from time immemorial, the Church has always called on artists to assist, through their art, in the understanding of religion? For example, Fra Angelico in Florence. . . ."

The priest would be won over and would listen to the learned discourse of the new disciple.

"Would you allow me to make a little sketch, Father, as an offering to the church? A little pencil-drawing of this capital here, which I am sure you are particularly fond of . . ."

De Groux would then do a sketch, followed by a pastel; then he would ask permission to set up his easel on a strip of oil-cloth so as not to dirty the flag-stones, and start on a picture of the stained glass windows. When he felt that the moment had come, he would say to the priest:

"Would you believe it, Father, I spent the whole night in your church—perhaps not in prayer, but at any rate in meditation. And I slept on the oil-cloth, beside my work, because I don't want to leave it for a minute until I have finished it."

And the priest would reply,

"You must have been very uncomfortable."

After that, it would not be long before the oil-cloth was replaced by a mattress, laid down next to a litle stove, on which de Groux surreptitiously cooked his potato stew; and he would install his canvases, palette, tubes of paint, smock, clothing, toilet articles and other belongings in a wardrobe nearby.

"You see that wall, Father," he would say. "I'm longing to paint a *Descent from the Cross* on it in the style of Cimabue or Simone Martini. Would you give me the pleasure of allowing me to sketch it in charcoal? It could always be wiped off easily enough with a rag."

When the worthy priest finally realised what kind of parasite—if such an ugly word may be applied to such an accomplished bohemian—he had on his hands, it was too late to put him out. By this time, de Groux would have made many friends, and even clients, among the congregation.

After the priest had exhausted his repertoire of polite hints and expressions of deepest regret and apology, he would be obliged peremptorily to order de Groux to leave. Whereupon the artist would give vent to a fine outburst of indignation. And he would go round the village and air his grievances in all the cafés, in the local school, at the town hall, in the lawyer's office and the doctor's consulting room.

"That priest is an absolute savage!" he would proclaim. "He understands nothing. Think of it: an artist of my reputation! I, Henry de Groux, son of the famous Charles de Groux. I wanted to do him the honour of immortalising his poor little church. I'm quite prepared to finish what will certainly be my masterpiece. And that man of God wants to put me out like an infidel, after having accepted my services, when everyone knows that from time immemorial the church has always been the protector of artists and sculptors."

He would walk up and down, his hands clasped behind his back under his ragged coat, and shake his greasy locks.

"Now, just consider, Monsieur," he would say, addressing himself to the school-teacher or the tax-collector, the doctor or the mayor, as the case might be, "who really built the churches? Was it a priest such as this one, with his weak and flabby hands; or an artist like me, with compasses and paint-brushes, setting the stones in their true positions, from the foundations up to the tower, whence shines the cross we are commanded to worship?"

And the old hypocrite would piously lift up his finger, cast his eyes aloft and add with a jeer:

"Perhaps the good Father thought I was invading his temporal domain by selling—in his church, I admit—a few pastels to some of his parishioners. Selling, did I say? I practically gave them away for the few francs people were willing to part with. Does the good Father—although he offered me some excellent wine, for which I shall always be grateful—imagine that I can do without earthly nourishment any more than he can? What a fine gesture he made in front of the crowd: but who is the poor merchant he drove from the temple? A merchant whose only wish was to increase the glory of his benefactor by his offerings, not to diminish it by commerce. . . ."

Things would eventually be straightened out. A little room would be found for de Groux, for which he paid with his drawings. But in his pride he would return to the church as a conqueror, his eyes flashing, his mane waving, and there would hold forth like a prophet to those sheep who were gullible enough to listen to him.

So it would go on, until finally the priest would decide that he was master in his own house; and de Groux would take to the road again, bag and baggage. And when he came to another likely village he would make for the church, and, with the same smile, begin looking around the nave as if he were inspecting a hotel room. Then he would start the same little game over again, and keep it up for a week or a month or sometimes longer, depending on the patience and forbearance of the priest.

⋆ ⋆ ⋆ ⋆ ⋆

How was it, one may ask, that Henry de Groux, whose work was already well known, should come to such a pass?

The Belgian Government had bought—cheaply enough, it is true—an extraordinary canvas of his, the *Christ aux Outrages*, which had established his artistic reputation. It showed Jesus, with his hands bound, in the custody of richly-costumed and impassive Romans, and surrounded by a furious mob. The whole scene was done with the passion of primitive painting; for de Groux had passed through the crucible of Constantin Meunier's school, and had doubtless known Van Gogh.

He had long since used up—or drunk up—the money he had received for the picture, and was bemoaning the trip he could have taken to Italy with the proceeds, when one evening, as he was dining with his wife and his young niece Cordelia, a friend came in to see him about a possible commission he had in view for the artist.

"You know, don't you," said the friend, "that I am one of the architects for the new Casino de Picardie?"

"Oh, yes. You're working for that millionaire who used to be a waiter, and is now putting up gambling-houses for silly fools at seaside resorts."

"I've been working for you too, de Groux, for I've got you a commission to do the decorations for the casino."

"What! Who? Me? De Groux work for that scoundrel, that bottle-washer, that panderer to human stupidity, when my only ambition is to decorate cathedrals?"

"Hold on! He'll give you thirty thousand francs for the job."

"Thirty thousand francs!" echoed the niece. "But, uncle dear, that's your trip to Italy, to the land of golden cathedrals. Indeed, for that amount you could even go to Greece!"

De Groux rubbed his chin thoughtfully.

"Well, after all," he conceded, "you go to the lavatory to relieve your mind as well as your bowels. I may as well go there to earn my trip. All right: it's agreed," he said, rising to his feet.

His friend gave him the address, and de Groux put on his old brown overcoat, which he had lugged all over Europe, crammed his *Tartuffe* hat over his stage-priest's hair, and went off to see the director. On arriving at the casino, which had just been finished, he was asked his name.

"Just tell the director to come here," de Groux replied.

The commissionaire took the message to the director, who happened to be talking with a contractor.

"Who's asking for me?"

"That queer fish over there."

The man inspected the "queer fish", from his enormous shoes to his crazy hat, the sides of which were resting on its owner's shoulders.

"All right. He's only a sponger. Let him wait."

De Groux waited fifteen minutes, half-an-hour, forty minutes, grumbling the whole time.

"A retired vintner, a bottle-washer, a table-wiper, to keep *me* waiting!" he fumed.

More than three-quarters-of-an-hour had gone by before the director finally decided to wander over to the door, and, seeing de Groux, said in an off-hand manner,

"Oh. Did you want anything?"

But our friend, exasperated by the other's tone, shook his head, raised his hand, and, throwing away his heart's desire and the thirty thousand francs, cried out in a strident voice,

"A beer, waiter!"

And away he proudly went, his shabby trousers flapping in rhythm with his hair.

★ ★ ★ ★ ★

"But what about the trip to Italy?" asked Cordelia, when he told her his story.

"Don't you worry about that," answered de Groux. "I'll go on foot."

He set out the very next day, his portfolio under his arm, his pencils in his pockets, his locks dangling on his shoulders.

From the start, of course, he tried to get permission to sleep in churches, paying for the privilege with his sketches, and to cadge his dinners in exchange for his gift of the gab. His progress was slow, and as the months went by he tended to loiter more and more.

One day, however, he received an unexpected windfall in the shape of a commission to decorate a private chapel. When he had finished it, he sauntered forth along the quays of the good town of Ghent with twenty-five thousand francs in his pocket. He wasn't interested in the waterside, only in the antique shops on the opposite pavement. Each one he came to filled him with the desire for possession. Among other objects, he was fascinated by a tapestry, and, following his usual habit, began talking aloud to himself:

"How delicate, how graceful is that young woman's body! What melancholy in her eyes: they remind me of stormy skies! What must her romance have been, that charming woman embroidered

Henry de Groux by U. Brunelleschi

in silk, and dead so long ago? What a pleasure if one could know her story! How wonderful it would be to own such a piece. Ah, if I were only rich! But—but——!" he exclaimed, "come to think of it, I *am* rich! Because I've got——"

He entered the shop, and, with all the arrogance of an English lord, demanded,

"How much is that tapestry?"

The shopkeeper stared at the poor wretch, at his worn shoes and his eccentric hat and coat.

"Very expensive," he said in an off-hand way.

"Yes, but how much?" insisted de Groux.

"Twenty-seven thousand," said the antique-dealer, turning his back.

"That's all right," replied the artist. "I'll take it." And he pulled out the money he had just earned. "I hope you will pardon me," he went on, "but I've only got twenty-five thousand francs with me. Would you be willing to trust me, and take an I.O.U. for three months from now?"

The dealer was only too willing to accept, and de Groux signed the I.O.U., which was to poison his life for years to come. He marched out of the shop humming a tune, while under his arm he carried the tapestry, which he hadn't even bothered to have wrapped up.

He sat down on a bench, unrolled his prize, admired it and called to several passers-by to share in his pleasure. Then, when he had admired it to his heart's content, he suddenly felt hungry. He searched his pockets but couldn't find a single sou.

The aroma of stew reached him from a nearby eating-house. Being a good Belgian, de Groux was never averse to a decent meal. After debating with himself for an hour in front of several restaurants he finally capitulated.

"I've had my joy of it," he told himself sadly, as he gazed at the tapestry for the last time. Then he went off to sell it to a second-hand dealer, for he did not dare to go back to the original shop. He managed to sell it for just enough for a meal and his fare back to Brussels.

His wife never heard a word of the story, but one can imagine the scene that ensued between his niece and himself.

* * * * *

All the same, the artist did eventually succeed in getting to Florence. It was the niece who managed to save enough money to pay the third class fare for them both. During the entire trip from Belgium to Tuscany de Groux did nothing but mumble to himself, as if he were saying his prayers.

At last they arrived in the land of their dreams, and went into ecstasies over the museums, the gardens and even the little hotel room they occupied together in the Piazza Donatello. But since they had to earn their keep, de Groux went down to the Piazza della Signoria with his pastels, got everything ready, put on a smile and waited for a customer.

Alas, in Italy, as everyone knows, beauty, like flowers, is over-abundant. The painter's most subtle appeals were fruitless; he sold nothing. Soon his meagre resources had melted away.

Yet the hotel bill had to be paid. So what did he do? He started by pawning Cordelia's coat; after the coat he pawned her dress; and then her slip.

"It's so hot," he informed her. "You can live here like a goddess on Mount Olympus."

"But I can't go out," she protested.

"You don't need to go out. I'll go out for you."

He did go out, in fact, only too often, and held forth in grand style in all the little *trattorie* he called at for a nip of *Grappa* or *Strega.* In a few days Cordelia was as wild as a caged tiger; and one morning, while de Groux was sleeping off the results of his previous evening's drinking, she seized *his* clothes. Then, draping herself in a curtain, she hailed an old-clothes' dealer she saw passing in the street, and sold him her dear uncle's beloved overcoat, trousers and shoes.

Presently the painter woke up with a start.

"My clothes! Where are my——?"

"They're at the same place as mine—in pawn."

"But, you idiot girl, how can I go out?"

"There's no need for you to go out. You can live here 'as if you were on Mount Olympus', like me."

"It doesn't matter," said de Groux, recovering his spirits; and getting up, he majestically took his seat in an old arm-chair covered with raised velvet. "Let us live as though we were on Mount Olympus. I'm Jupiter."

"If I were only Danaë!"

"Alas, I can't make golden rain. . . . If only I had a pair of trousers, at least! Yesterday I met an elderly Englishman who would certainly have bought—— Oh, well. . . ."

Henry de Groux "played Jupiter" for half-an-hour or so, and then, realising that this state of affairs couldn't go on indefinitely, he began to abuse his niece. For her part, she accused him of having inveigled her into leaving their native land, where at least she had a home and clothes to wear, and reducing her to nakedness in Italy.

He retorted that she was talking nonsense, that she should, on the contrary, be thankful to him for bringing her to this wonderful country, and to this little hotel where she had only to lean out of the window to see a corner of Brunelleschi's famous dome.

Cordelia answered that she didn't give a hang for that old stick Brunelleschi.

"Blasphemy!" shouted de Groux.

By way of a reply, the young girl snatched up his box of charcoals and hurled it at Jupiter's head.

"My daily bread!" shrieked the artist, his face turning purple under the splotches of charcoal, and he jumped up and made a grab at her. She fell back in terror against the window, which smashed behind her. Seeing the blood where she had cut herself, she screamed for help and took refuge in a cupboard. It was not long before the police arrived, and when they and the neighbours forced their way into the room they found a naked man running about foaming with rage. After a tussle they overpowered him, wrapped him in a bed-spread, and led him off to the lunatic asylum, where he remained for the next six months.

When he was somewhat better, he was allowed out, accompanied by a nurse and wearing the uniform of the institution. During one of these walks he ran into the painters Brunelleschi and Degaillaix and several other people he knew, and told them his sad story. They proceeded to get the nurse drunk and, taking de Groux off with them, gave him some money and a few clothes. But at that point he almost ruined the plot by refusing to leave Florence without his brown overcoat and hat, which, he claimed, were the only things that brought him luck. Not till they had been found was de Groux able to leave.

He went to Genoa, where he was given shelter by a rich lady who lived in a palazzo. It must be admitted that, after a week there, the artist began to grow bored, and, calling to mind his niece, whom he had abandoned in Florence, decided to send her some clothes he had picked up in a second-hand shop on the quayside, so that she could come and join him. The clothes, by the way, were nothing less than the habit of a nun.

* * * * *

Shortly after this adventure it was announced in the press that de Groux had died. *La Société Nationale des Beaux-Arts*, which was about to open its salon in Paris, decided to devote several rooms to a retrospective exhibition of de Groux's work, while several art revues—among them Karl Boès' *Plume*—put out special issues about him.

I well remember those large rooms in which his pictures were shown, and the Government ministers, critics, connoisseurs, artists and others all queuing up to have a look at the *Christ aux Outrages*, the portraits of Wagner, Leconte de Lisle, Villiers de l'Isle-Adam,

Baudelaire and so on, which had been set up in the middle of the main salon.

The night of the opening, after spending some hours at the printers of *Gil Blas*, I started to walk home to the place where I was then living on the Left Bank. It was not yet dawn, and the deep blue sky looked like a torn silk ribbon above the uneven roofs in the rue Bonaparte. The street was deserted, and the wind whipped round the closed shutters of the various art shops, making the weather-vanes creak and the cats mew plaintively under the moon. It was a perfect night in which to meet a ghost. And I met one!

For I suddenly became aware of a grotesque silhouette, whose shadow was elongated on the dry, white pavement by the light of the street lamp. It had crooked legs and a long overcoat, which flapped about like a flag, while under the dark, wide-brimmed hat two eyes glittered like steel points. Mystified and intrigued, I circled round the apparition. Presently he began to talk to me, and told me how a short while before he had been set upon by some roughs. He had taken off his hat and said to them with exquisite courtesy:

"Gentlemen, you are mistaken. I am not the one you are looking for."

They had talked to him a bit, for they didn't know what to make of this James Ensor character, who seemed like a walking, talking automaton. The joke of it was that, instead of being robbed, he had actually managed to wheedle a few sous out of them! On another occasion, de Groux had coaxed money out of a highwayman, who subsequently gave him a sound thrashing when he learned that his money had been give to the poor.

"It was the only way to get out of the predicament honourably," the old man concluded.

"But, de Groux," I said, "I thought you were dead!"

"Well—that's the official version, and, like most official versions, untrue."

"Why didn't you turn up in your shroud at your private view this afternoon?"

"To tell you the truth, I did think for a moment of doing so. But it would have been in rather poor taste, don't you think? Besides, I wanted to go to a lecture."

We managed to find a little café which was still open. When the painter had a big bowl of hot, sweet wine inside him his spirits revived, and after he had nibbled a crust of bread he gave a little silvery laugh and tipped back on his stool.

"De Groux," I said, "tell me about your death."

"Sh-h-h!" he warned. "That's a secret. Do you think for a minute that those people would have looked at my Villiers, my Wagner or my Rops in the same way if they had known I was still in my mortal form?"

He wrinkled his white, pointed nose. I ordered a steaming dish of mussels for him; and de Groux giggled again as he exclaimed:

"Rops! A combination of artist and commercial traveller: a braggart, a boaster who could hold us breathless for hours with his fantastic stories. How he lied! He lied with delightful ease, and so persuasively that he would have taken in any woman, he would have disarmed Germany. And how endearingly he would repeat to you the same story, with embellishments, that you yourself had told him the day before! Wagner I saw for the first time at Bayreuth, and I might sum up my impression of him in two words: titanic and malevolent; great power and great cunning. Villiers was a solemn chap; a spectral, ghost-like Bossuet, frightening at times. Verlaine? A delightful, spoiled child. But a shocking example! Yet how brilliant at repartee! I remember his quarrels with Moréas, and the latter saying to him one day, 'Verlaine, you're an ass'. Verlaine answered calmly, 'And you, Moréas, are merely an imbecile'. Then the Greek poet accused Verlaine of being drunk. The scene took place at a gathering of friends in the rue Descartes. Verlaine jumped up in a rage. 'Who said that?' he demanded. 'Someone you don't know,' I said, trying to restore order. 'Very well,' he said; 'hand me my hat and cane. I'm going down the street, and the first stranger I meet I shall murder.' "

"Tell me, de Groux," I said, "did you know personally all the people whose portraits you painted?"

"Of course I knew them—Nietzsche, Hugo, Zola, Napoleon..."

"Napoleon?"

The café-owner urged us towards the door. Outside, the pavement was beginning to take on a bluish hue in the early morning light. The artist grasped my arm and, slightly swaying, held out his hand:

"But the one who intrigued me most," he remarked, "was Dante Alighieri. Imagine a night like this, and meeting him in a street in Florence. . . ."

★ ★ ★ ★ ★

The First World War began. Late one night in August 1914, I heard a knock at my door. On opening it I beheld de Groux, carrying a huge valise—just like the one the famous clown Grock used. But Grock at least had a violin inside his. In de Groux' valise there was nothing, not even a stick of charcoal. He had come all the way from Brussels, on the eve of its capture by the Germans, and was hoping to go down to the South of France to join his wife and niece, who were ill with typhoid there. He had made the journey so far as best he could.

"The Germans must be in Brussels by now," he informed me.

"Good Lord!" I said. "And what about the six hundred canvases in your studio?"

"Ha, ha! It's not the Germans I'm worried about."

"Who, then?"

He hesitated a moment, then said,

"The Belgians."

For he was angry with his country ever since something that had happened a few years before. He told me the whole story that evening, temporarily forgetting his present distress.

"Well," he began, "it was all because of Victor Hugo's funeral. I was in the crowd that day in the Place de la Concorde, meditating on the fame of the great man who had just died. The head of the procession had already reached the Arc de Triomphe, and there were still a few groups about to start out for the Hôtel de Ville. I thought I was paying homage to the dead poet by being there alone, instead of joining one of the marching groups. But all at once I heard someone call, 'Hey, de Groux! de Groux!' It was a delegation of Belgian writers, and they cried out, 'Come along with us, *cher maître*; come and join our party!' I was young then and flattered by being called *maître*. I didn't wait to be asked twice. We hadn't gone ten yards before several of the group said to me, '*Cher maître*, you are more worthy than any of us to carry our banner', and they passed a shiny strap over my head and handed me the standard. It was a rather heavy honour, in the literal sense of the word. But it became even more so in the figurative sense, as it turned out. For some time I didn't realise the weight of the whole business; I was too busy with my own thoughts. In due course, we arrived at the Place de l'Étoile, along with the crowd, and went two or three times round the Arc de Triomphe. The Arc was hung with crêpe, while at each corner of the cenotaph were Horse Guards holding blazing torches. I went on marching round and round. We were pushed here and there, and suddenly I became aware that I had got separated from my Belgian delegation and that the ceremony was over. I was dead with fatigue, and the standard was killing me. I needed to collect my wits, so I went into a café to get a little rest and refreshment. I placed the banner in one corner, being careful not to crease it, and asked the waiter to bring me a drink and some writing-paper. And I sat there writing and writing for hours. When I had finished, I put the paper in my pocket and went out. And I walked round and round the square once more, still meditating.

"All of a sudden I ran into a band of students bearing palms. I struck my forehead. 'My banner!' I cried. 'I've forgotten my Belgian banner!' I retraced my steps. I went into one café after another, a dozen altogether, taking a little drink in each one out of politeness. But I couldn't find the place where I had left that cursed banner. And now those wicked Belgians accuse me of having sold it!"

On that tragic wartime evening, de Groux asked me to do something for him.

"I've written to several friends to ask if they could help me," he said. "But where are they? Have they even received my letters? Perhaps I was wrong in adding a postscript: 'Help me, and you will be astonished by my ingratitude'."

De Groux had often imposed on my friendship, as on that of many others. But seeing the fellow there without a sou, and knowing that his wife was ill and his niece at death's door, I did all I could for him. I persuaded a painter friend of mine, who was going away, to let him use his studio, a sort of maid's room on the sixth floor of a building in a little back street. Then I took de Groux to the Beaux Arts, where he was given two hundred francs; he got as much again from Rachel Boyer at the Union des Artistes.

Fasquelle, the publisher, commissioned him to do some drawings and gave him an advance of eight hundred francs.

Once he had his money, I saw nothing more of de Groux except when I ran into him by chance. I met him one day not far from his studio, and he begged me to come up for a moment to see something special. I climbed the six flights reluctantly, but before I had time to inspect the drawings he had put up all over the walls he feverishly unwrapped a long box, which had apparently come from Liberty's.

"Look at these," he said, holding up several tulle scarves spangled with gold, as well as an opera cloak and other finery. "There's more than five hundred francs worth——"

"What on earth is it for? A model? Are you going to paint *that*?"

"Oh, no. They're for my wife and niece."

"What! Those two women dying down there in the Midi, and you send them opera cloaks, and in wartime at that?"

"Why, yes," he said with his familiar smile, "and I've also bought a little donkey for them."

He was, however, in the midst of a frenzy of work in the small room, the bed of which remained untouched as he preferred to sleep on the floor, wrapped in a red plaid. He had been turning out enormous compositions and tacking up his pictures side by side on the walls all over the place, even out in the hall and down the servants' staircase. There were prints, drawings, lithographs, etchings and engravings on copper, wood and ivory. Along the corridors of the kitchen quarters there was a veritable Hell in pastels done for the glory of posterity: Joffre was shown decorating Albert I of Belgium in front of some of his troops, the King's figure designed as though for a stained glass window; General Castelnau was there, looking haggard and tortured; and there were scenes of the dead, with enough bodies to frighten the ghost of Edgar Allan Poe. Throughout the length of the corridor, de Groux had plunged into the trenches, watched operations and visited mortuaries piled high with corpses. With his charcoal he had "dissected" the countless anonymous dead, and had caught their most horrifying expressions with such relentless realism and vividness that when Degas saw the drawings he exclaimed,

"I can smell the stench of corpses!"

His living soldiers were even more frightening than the dead, for they looked like serried rows of automatons, whose clenched hands indicated their will to fight, though their eyes were distraught with fear. Out of the agony of those groups, those herds of tragic victims, what a gigantic, macabre monument in paint this visionary had erected for posterity.

Some nights de Groux would be picked up after he had fallen asleep or fainted on the stairs, a piece of charcoal still in his hand, and somebody would take him in and look after him. I persuaded the manager of the Palais d'Orsay Hotel to let him have a warm room with a soft bed, a carpet and a bathroom, because the artist had caught a bad cough in his freezing attic studio. I shan't go into the difficulty I had in getting him to accept new quarters. He eventually consented to move, but took no interest in the radiator, the running water or the silk eiderdown.

"I can't stand those mirrors!"

He turned round the wardrobes and the looking-glasses so that they faced the wall, and smeared the mirror over the mantelpiece with Spanish white. Each night his bed was prepared, the covers turned down and his night-shirt carefully laid out. It was no use. Each morning I found de Groux snoring away fully dressed on the bed, still in boots and his famous hat. And he even had the cheek to reproach me.

"You would make me come here," he complained. "I can't get a thing done. Ah, how much richer in sensations poverty is for the artist! How many ideas I had buzzing round my head when I climbed those dark back stairs to my little room! Whereas in this 'department store' . . .!"

* * * * *

It was about this time that the Bartholomé incident occurred. I have often wondered if the artist did it on purpose, for it was certainly characteristic of him.

It so happened that the sculptor Bartholomé, wishing to honour the Belgian refugee artists in Paris, decided to give a dinner for them. He decided to talk the project over with de Groux, whom he had recently met and taken a great fancy to.

"How many of them are there?" he asked de Groux. "About a dozen?"

"Oh, no," said the other. "Twenty at the very least."

"Then there won't be enough room in my house. I'll hire a private room in a restaurant. Would you like to make up a list for me?"

A week later de Groux brought Bartholomé a list containing the names of forty-eight refugee artists from Belgium.

"Oh!" exclaimed Bartholomé, on glancing at it. "The room I've engaged won't be large enough for all these people. I shall have to take the banqueting-hall at the Continental. What day shall we set?"

"You must give me at least a week's notice," replied de Groux, "because I think that when I write to them I ought to tell each one how much we think of his talent."

"That is very thoughtful of you."

De Groux spent two whole days trying to decide what colour note-paper would be most suitable in each case, finally choosing mauve for the Impressionists, white for the more classical, and so on. Then he sat up at nights writing the invitations by the light of a smoky lamp. Having composed and torn up three or more drafts of each one, the letters were finally done, and the date fixed for the dinner.

When the day arrived, de Groux put on dress clothes: that is to say, he called in various friends, people he knew in the neighbourhood, several artists, his concierge, etc., and asked them to help arrange his cravat, his cuffs and trousers. Besides, he wanted them to see him in all his glory.

"It's going to be quite an affair," he told them. Then he ordered a cab.

"Now, cabman," he said to the driver "take me to the banqueting-hall at the Continental. I'm a trifle late, but I shall be all the more welcome for that reason."

On arriving at the entrance, he called out,

"Come, pages and stewards, and conduct me to the banqueting-hall!"

Solemnly, his head held high, his ringlets curled by tongs, de Groux ordered the folding-doors to be opened for him.

And there, in the banqueting-hall, were fifty-two places laid at two long tables, with chairs conspicuously empty, while white-stockinged lackeys stood waiting for the festivities to begin. At the far end of the room, with their backs to the fireplace, stood Bartholomé in full dress, his *Légion d'Honneur* ribbon across his white shirt-front, and Mme. and Mlle. Bartholomé in evening-gowns, all three gazing at the scene in consternation. When they caught sight of de Groux they rushed forward.

"Well, Monsieur de Groux, where are the guests?"

"Er—— I—— Hm——"

"Did you send out the invitations?"

De Groux' little steely eyes opened wide. He felt in his pockets, stamped his heel on the floor and struck himself on the forehead.

"Ah—that's me all over! That's just typical of me . . .!" And taking out a packet of letters he threw them down on the table.

"Well, there you are, there you are," he said. "I simply forgot to post them."

★ ★ ★ ★ ★

The bridges of Paris. Drizzling rain, with night closing down. De Groux, homeless and without shelter, trailing after him the dejected pierette figure of Cordelia, whose gold-spangled black tulle scarf fluttered wanly in the wind from the Seine.

★ ★ ★ ★ ★

"Monsieur Henry de Groux requests the pleasure of your company at lunch in his studio, 9 rue Chaptal."

The sumptuous studio at 9 rue Chaptal, which the composer Nouguès had recently vacated, looked like a series of chapels, with its black and gold hangings, stained glass windows and statues of the Virgin in niches.

Among the people de Groux had invited for the occasion was the painter Louis Degaillaix, who explained to me that a trusting art-dealer had become excited about de Groux' work and had been persuaded to take everything the artist produced, in return for which he had agreed to rent this studio for him and pay two years' rent in advance.

"De Groux bought the piano on credit," said Degaillaix, "as well as all those ecclesiastical chairs, the Chinese vases and so on. He has already given several receptions, with princesses and Government ministers among the guests, his niece dressed up as a heroine out of Shakespeare, and he himself in a frock-coat and old slippers. And now it's half-past one, and everybody is here except our host."

It was getting on for a quarter to two when de Groux made his appearance, his hands thrust deep into his pockets.

"Well, well, friends," he said, "this is a pleasant surprise!"

"Surprise! Why, didn't you invite us to lunch?"

"That's so. I did. Quite true. But, you see——"

"What?"

"I haven't got a sou left."

"Now, look here, de Groux: you're not going to try your Bartholomé trick on us."

"Oh, no. Certainly not. Would you like some lunch?"

"It wouldn't be a bad idea."

"Very well. If that's all that's wanted——" And he went over to the wall, took hold of the black and gold hanging and ripped it off the curtain-rod with a single jerk. Then, rolling it up, he tucked it under his arm and said, as he walked out of the room,

"I'll be back in a minute."

He returned with some money, and took us to a nearby eating-place. We had quite a decent meal, in the course of which he recounted an experience with Loïe Fuller which was also in the de Groux tradition.

It seems that the celebrated dancer had often done de Groux a good turn. Among other things, she had wanted to buy a work of his entitled *Moonlight Sonata*, showing a scene in a German prison camp, with a soldier playing the piano for his comrades. However, when it came to fetching the picture, Loïe changed her mind and decided to take instead a portrait of a friend of hers which she happened to see in the studio. De Groux refused, claiming that the latter belonged to the King of England. Mme. Fuller was doubtless wrong to resort to such extreme measures to get her way, but one morning she arrived at de Groux', accompanied by a Miss B . . .

But let me quote the artist's own words:

"The slut! The virago! How dared she come to my house and demand a picture that I'd promised to the King of England and the Minister of Education, and for the same price that she'd paid for the other! Naturally I refused. She turned round, her back to the picture.

" 'You refuse?' she said.

" 'I certainly do,' I answered.

"Then what does she do but bang her huge rump against it, break the glass, slide the drawing out of the frame, and while I'm shouting, 'Stop thief!' make off with it to her car, with the help of her accomplice? But I'm going to hound her to prison, the harridan! I——"

All at once he smiled.

"Maybe it was a theft of love," he suggested.

He called the wine-waiter over, and said to him:

"You must have read *The Portrait of Dorian Gray*, my friend. Well, suppose it was a woman in the story, who, for love of another woman, stole her portrait, and you will guess the secret of the plot I was the victim of. You understand me, I hope?"

"Of course, *maître*. . . ."

"Good. In that case, you can bring us each a little glass of Calvados and a cheap cigar."

* * * * *

The War ended at last, peace came, and with it even harder times—at least for de Groux. One day in Cannes, I chanced to meet the architect Tissier, who asked me if I would go with him to Marseilles.

"We'll look up de Groux there," he explained.

"I haven't seen him for years," I said.

"You can't imagine how he's living now. A lady gave him shelter in Avignon several months ago. But he left her house and went to Marseilles, where he's taken refuge in the basement of the new opera house they're building there."

I went with Tissier to Marseilles, and the next morning we enquired for de Groux on the site. The foreman knew where to find him, and presently a figure emerged from under the foundations, covered from head to foot with plaster-dust and debris. Even his gaunt face was white with it.

He wiped his eyes, which were still bleary with sleep and badly inflamed, with the back of his sleeve, his face looking like some tragic old Pierrot. Then, as he slowly recognised us, he drew himself up and stood for several minutes motionless as a statue. At length he made a sweeping gesture with his hand all down the front of his filthy frock-coat, and, raising his head, exclaimed,

"Behold me in marble!"

* * * * *

I met him again one spring evening, all smiles, sitting on the terrace of a café in "Cubist" Montparnasse, surrounded by a number of creatures as extraordinary as himself. His chestnut overcoat had turned the colour of bird-droppings, in spite of his habit of carefully scratching the spots on it with his finger-nail. He offered me a seat and, pointing to the canvases hanging on the café walls, said,

"They look like lead franc-pieces someone has slipped into a church collecting-box, don't you think?" And, without pausing except to ask a passing waiter to bring a glass of *Vieille Tito*, he muttered "Excuse me" and leaned forward confidentially. I felt his locks brush my ear, and the edge of his soiled velvet hat touch my forehead.

"Did you know——" he began and then, as though he were telling a good joke, went on, "—that they want me to get married? And to a young girl too." He rolled his eyes.

"She's one of my pupils," he explained. "Of royal blood, though I'm not yet at liberty to reveal the name of her country. Sixteen years old. One must do the honourable thing, of course. I abducted her, as I once did my niece, and—weak man that I am—I have given in to her entreaties. Here she is now——"

A Hispano had just drawn up to the kerb, and out of it stepped a divine creature, with blond hair and sky-blue eyes. A light scarf half-hid her smile and rosy cheeks. She carried an armful of spring flowers. She almost tripped and fell as she hurried towards us.

"*Cher maître!*" she said, as she pressed her lips against de Groux' dirty forehead.

"Would you have believed it?" murmured the artist in an aside to me. And with an indulgent smile he added ruefully:

"To think that I might muck up my engagement by some foolishness or other," and he drew the lovely girl against his grimy coat, while she gazed up at him with admiring eyes.

* * * * *

About a month after our meeting, the Paris Embassy of a certain little country to the north felt that it should officially notify the young princess's family that she seemed to be leading a rather peculiar life, as she was to be seen not only every day but every evening in the company of an old man so filthy that even the poor in Montparnasse held their noses as he went by. That may have been an exaggeration, although it is certain that de Groux had a horror of bathing equal only to his aversion to mirrors.

The family sent a telegram to the princess's governess, asking her for a full report, and the latter, who loved Montparnasse as much as she did *Amer Picon*, replied that the gentleman in question was none other than a great painter; that he was the young lady's art-teacher; and that his morals were above reproach.

The Embassy took the liberty of intimating to the family that they would do well to look into the matter more closely; with the result that they decided not to call the princess home, because of the scandal it might create, but to send her maternal uncle, Aadge Hockren de Bloodjg, to investigate.

That worthy gentleman, complete with frock-coat and luggage, arrived shortly afterwards at the private house which had been rented for the young lady. Although it was one o'clock in the morning, he found all the beds unruffled except the governess's, which as a matter of fact had been left unmade for several days. Downstairs in the kitchen the only sign of life was a mewing cat. On the table were the remains of a meal and a half-empty glass of wine. The rest of the house was wrapped in silence and darkness. The newcomer poked with his umbrella at something he thought was a wig under a chair, but it proved to be only a mound of dust. He therefore sat down with a sigh and, in spite of the importance of his mission, fell fast asleep.

He woke to his disgust at eight the following morning, and hastened to one of the bathrooms. Seeing the bathtub full of stagnant water, he shrugged his shoulders and proceeded to wash as best he could. After putting on a clean shirt, he set out for Montparnasse on the stroke of nine, just ten minutes before his niece returned home and fell into bed, fully dressed.

Aadge Hockren de Bloodjg stopped before one of the cafés, in which, according to the information given him, his niece Edwige had been spending a good deal of her time; then, taking a deep breath, he went in.

He found himself in a long, narrow room, on whose walls three or four paintings with many-faceted forms had been hanging ever since the "heroic" era. There were also a hundred other masterpieces, which even a country barber would have hesitated to put up in the back of his shop.

Several waiters were mopping the floor. Seated in the rear of the place was a shifty-eyed, swarthy man, who looked like a turbaned ibis, or a caricature of Gandhi, or a fortune-teller from New York. A short distance away lolled a girl whose eyes were puffy with sleep. It was evident that both individuals had spent the night there.

"I only sleep one hour a year and I live on curds and whey," the turbaned ibis announced in response to a glance from de Bloodjg, who quickly turned his head away. But changing his mind, he decided to speak to the man.

"Sir," he said, "would you by any chance know—at least by sight—my niece Edwige Hockren de Bloodjg, and her art-teacher, Monsieur de Groux? My niece, I might add, is closely connected to royalty."

"I am the reincarnation of six hundred kings of Sweden and Persia," replied the other to let de Bloodjg know that he was not impressed by the reference to royalty.

Just then the girl who was lying on the other end of the seat suddenly came to life and called out:

"Yes. I know 'em. They eat in the same restaurant as I do."

De Bloodjg abruptly left the Indo-Scandinavian theosophist and went over to the young lady, who eagerly made room for him.

"A glass of milk" she said to the waiter, "and some *croissants.* And a sandwich, too, if Monsieur will allow me."

"Yes, yes. Of course," said de Bloodjg, gruffly.

The early morning customers began to drift into the café. The girl ate her breakfast ravenously.

"Where is the restaurant you mentioned, Mademoiselle? Would you mind telling me how to get there?"

"Don't you worry. I'll take you. For the moment you'd better wait here. They might come here first."

"Aren't they at the art school?"

"Oh yes. But which one? There are any number, you know. There are three in the rue de la Grande-Chaumière, for instance: Naudin's, Dufy's and Lhote's. Then there's Friesz in the rue Notre-Dame-des-Champs. And plenty of others. I know 'em all."

"Have you studied art?"

"No. I was a model. But I got peritonitis, and had to have an operation; and now I can't pose in the nude any more. It's too bad. They say my face is too ugly to sit for portraits; besides, I can't earn enough at it. So at present I'm waiting till I can find something better. Don't you want a drink?"

"I don't really know the drinks of your country."

"Waiter, bring the gentleman a double *Pernod*. That'll put new life into him."

"What's that?"

"A tonic. It's got an odd taste. But it'll cure you of the dumps and pick you up after your trip. You've just arrived, haven't you?"

"Who told you?"

"My little dog, Nabouchim-Péraf-Jebel. Now I think we'd better move on."

They "moved on" several times before lunch, and each time Aadge Hockren de Bloodjg took a dose of that excellent, health-giving tonic known as *Pernod*, the name of which he put down in his note-book for future reference.

When they finally reached the restaurant, there was no Edwige to be seen. Moreover, de Bloodjg was surprised by the modest atmosphere of the place. The French cooking, which he had heard so much about, struck him as rather mediocre. But then, he supposed, it was because of a slight headache he began to feel towards the end of the meal. After the coffee he thought he would like to have another glass of that tonic he had taken such a fancy to.

However, the girl, who was a good sort, persuaded him not to, and, taking him by the arm, she led him to a little hotel where she had once lived, and put him to bed as gently as a nurse. De Bloodjg slept until evening, when he woke with a queer taste in his mouth and a crick in his neck. As he gazed about him in surprise, a woman who was looking at him with wide eyes cried shrilly,

"A fine state you've got yourself in! If your niece could only see you now! Lie down again."

The word "niece" stirred some memory at the back of his mind, and with a heavy sigh he turned over towards the wall, which smelled of damp.

About one o'clock in the morning the girl, who had been lying beside him, woke him up, and suggested that it might be a good idea if they got up and went out for a bit.

He was astonished at all the lights in the streets and in the cafés, as well as at the crowds shuffling along the boulevards.

The girl led him from café to café, taking a little "breakfast" in one place and a little "supper" in another. They descended into several cellars, which had been converted into night-clubs, and pushed their way through such throngs of merry-makers as the good man had never seen before, even on Midsummer's Eve.

"I used to dance myself then," he told his companion.

"Is it Midsummer's Eve tonight?"

"Oh no."

"Well, it doesn't matter. Let's see if you can dance anyway. Come on. Everybody's dancing. You must do as the others do. This is Montparnasse, you know. If you don't, everybody will notice; and we can't have that. Finish your glass, and let's dance."

Aadge Hockren de Bloodjg started out by dancing very circumspectly, taking care not to strain himself. But towards half-past three in the morning he joined in a quadrille, kicked as high as the late Valentin, and tried to do the splits, in emulation of no less a personage than La Cimarosa, who had come down from Montmartre that night to grace the occasion. He succeeded, in fact, in executing an especially fine split, and as he sat in that position on the floor, he raised his glass high and shouted,

"Sko-o-o-oll!"

It was at this moment that he beheld in front of him a figure that looked like some sort of clergyman, with long hair and gleaming eyes, which drew itself up with folded arms and thundered,

"Sir, is this the way you normally behave?"

"I am dancing, sir. Have you any objection?"

"Have I any objection? What about this young lady?"

With that de Groux drew back, leaving Uncle Aadge still in the same posture, but face to face with the niece he had come to Paris to admonish and reform.

"Edwige!" he cried out, horrified.

"Avaunt, wretch!" declaimed de Groux, clasping the princess in his arms. "And God help you if you dare to touch my sweet young fiancée!"

* * * * *

"Then Gong-Tsu said to Fu-Tsu: 'There is good and there is evil. But what is good, and what is evil? Why is it evil to kill your fellow-man, if it gives you real pleasure, and if, furthermore, your fellow-man doesn't suffer enough in the process to be able to give you even a scratch in his last convulsive movement?' Monsieur Aadge Hockren de Bloodjg, I should like to kill you because I am a good man."

"Are you really serious, Monsieur de Groux?"

"Serious, yes, if you are willing to admit the generally accepted meaning of the word. Now, good, according to the egotist school (which I might have founded myself), is first and foremost the satisfying of oneself alone, nothing in the world being of the slightest importance, as the philosopher Tristum Bernardus pointed out, except what happens to oneself. He should have added, 'before death'; because after death you will see. . . ."

"What do you mean, 'I shall see'?"

"That's just a manner of speaking, for actually you will not see or hear anything again until your re-incarnation; and supposing you are re-incarnated in a few million years—— My God, what an atrocious-looking girl. . . ."

They were watching one of those cabarets in which the female entertainers, though far less naked than many a society-woman in the bars at Cannes or Juan-les-Pins, yet provoke cries of horror from one end of Europe to the other, even to the Shetland Isles and beyond.

De Bloodjg's eyes were glued to the stage, as de Groux proceeded with his discourse, while Edwige's head rested quietly on his shoulder, her two hands in one of his because the other was holding a glass of *Schiedam.*

For a whole week, now, for seven whole days—morning, noon and night—de Bloodjg had faithfully followed the painter and his pupil, hoping to be forgiven his previous conduct; and in return for a glass of Danzig *eau-de-vie* or a *Pernod* he stoically endured the philosophical reproaches, cruel threats and paradoxical apophthegms of the man who, on the very first day of their meeting, had declared:

"If I marry your niece, sir, it will be to save her from the ignominious debauchery into which her family and you, as their official representative, were, by your scandalous example, trying to plunge her. For two months this divine young girl has kindly entrusted me with her education and given me her heart, and I have initiated her into the ugliness of my miserable existence. While she witnesses these corrupting scenes, I talk to her in the purest language so that her soul will become more uplifted, and she will become more elevated in the company of a poor old man, such as I am, but whose spirit is rekindled by her youthful flame. The child born of our union will be another after my kind. And yet you wished to interrupt one of the finest works of destiny. Edwige is happy in her creative mission. And I am proud of having initiated her. It is entirely moral, in the best sense of morality. And you come along as a trouble-maker, trying to pollute the pure waters of this spring of happiness. Hold your peace; otherwise your Court shall be given irrefutable evidence. . . . Allow me to treat you to a glass of this *Mandarin*, which is, I believe, unknown in your country. Well, how do you like it? Can you not already taste that bitterness which precedes the physical and psychic pleasure inherent in such a drink?"

Meanwhile, the letters from the foreign Court began to accumulate on the table in Aadge de Bloodjg's little room in the Passy hotel; he went there scarcely more than once or twice a fortnight. De Groux advised him not to touch the letters, but to write home that everything was for the best in the best of all possible worlds.

Soaked in *Absinthe*, *Amer Picon*, *Armagnac* and different brands of champagne, de Bloodjg meekly tagged along after his new tutor and his niece. A month and a half went by in this manner. After a night out they would take rooms almost anywhere, perhaps in the rue Bréa or in Montrouge, though they rarely went beyond the Montparnasse quarter, "where," in de Groux' words, "a mystic fever reigns: all the more sacred because it increases every day. Woe to him who crosses the barrier and becomes submerged again in ordinary life."

Even so, it was necessary for them to pick up the cheques which were sent care of Edwige's governess. But she, having no reason not to cross the "mystic barrier", had already taken the money and disappeared. Sometimes the princess and her two companions would catch sight of her, perhaps in the midst of a crowd of dancers in some creole restaurant, where, dressed in a daffodil gown, she was whirling around with the best of them. But before any of the trio could descend from the balcony, the governess would have vanished, lured away, no doubt, by the muscular quadroon whose arms had been clasping her.

That was the reason (if any were needed) why one night de Groux, Edwige and de Bloodjg went on a tour of all the bars in the quarter. They even visited the *Iles Marquises*, which, contrary to popular belief, are not situated in the South Pacific but in the rue de la Gaîté, being a restaurant specialising in snails, uncooked ham and strong Breton brandy.

They sat down at a table in the back room, where the colour-prints on the walls, dating back to the era of the late President Sadi Carnot, enabled those customers with a lively imagination to feel as though they had escaped from the ugliness of modern times.

"In those days," observed de Groux, "this street had a charm that is difficult to imagine now. Eleven *cafés chantants*, not to mention five dance-halls, enlivened the scene, and there were none of those huge, oppressive tram-cars from the Halles. You could hear the organ bellowing over at Gangloff's; while the Bobino performers put on their little act right in the street itself, on a small platform arranged as a stage. And in the Impasse de la Gaîté, where they were building the Théâtre de la Rochelle, where Antoine was to win his first laurels, you could see cows grazing. They weren't a bit frightened by the car being tried out every day in the quiet street nearby. As for the fashions—why, that woman sucking shell-fish at the table in the corner will give you some idea of them."

Hearing his remark, the woman cried out,

"What insolence!"

"What do you think you are doing, Madame? Are you trying to blind me?"

A prawn had just hit de Groux smack in the eye, the one he usually winked with, he said.

Then something happened that no one could possibly have expected. Little Edwige, coming to the defence of her lord and master, hurled a carafe of water at the lady of the Sadi Carnot period. The latter slumped to the floor with a faint sigh. She was picked up and carried to the nearest police-station, where de Groux appeared shortly afterwards as chief witness. As Edwige and de Bloodjg had forgotten to bring their identity-papers with them, they were locked up for the night.

De Groux then slipped away on the pretext that he had to see his aggressor safely home. In fact, he did take charge of her. He got a horse cab—in keeping with the spirit of the times—and accompanied her out to Montrouge; and as they drove along they began a conversation which became unexpectedly prolonged.

"I must have known you in Brussels," the lady said, "and your father, too. I'm Bobette Lafèque. I used to be an intimate friend of dear old Leopold, you know."

"Who would have believed it!" exclaimed de Groux, in astonishment. "And what are you doing now?"

"I have a little house in Miramas."

"Ah, Miramas: the sun, the olive trees!"

"I cultivate my garden, play bowls with the men and argue with the village priest."

"What a sudden affinity I feel for you. Even in this old cab you bring with you all the perfume of Provence!"

"But how bored I am there! If only a man——"

"Ah, the Midi!"

"Could I persuade you to accept an invitation, dear fellow-citizen?"

"Heavens, it's tempting. . . ."

So it came about that, thanks to this little incident, de Groux left his fiancée, Edwige Hockren de Bloodjg, and two days later went down to the South of France with the one-time favourite of a king. As they sat together in a third-class carriage, she described to him how a year ago she had split the jack in a game of bowls.

"Oh, how marvellous!" exclaimed the painter, ecstatically.

PIERO TOLENTINO

He was known as a celebrity from Venice to Trieste and from Berlin to New York. A man with a mania for the Gothic, he could live in nothing but Gothic surroundings, and refused to tolerate any art alien to that period.

It was my friend Mme. Doyen who first took me to see him in his Palazzo degli Ambasciatori in San Barnaba, in Venice.

We climbed the stairs on tip-toe, partly out of respect and partly because the marble staircase was shaky, showing how damp the climate of Venice is. We knocked on the nail-studded door, and Antonio the valet, who might have come out of a Goldoni play, opened it for us.

We were ushered into a series of cathedral-like rooms, in which the walls were done in woodwork like an altar-screen, each fireplace was as spacious as a temple and each chandelier as large as the crown in the hall of Charles V at Aix-la-Chapelle.

At the end of the "suite", behind a double curtain of Sicilian velvet, lay the studio, whose bay windows provided a view over the Grand Canal and the Rialto, with gondolas moving about like toys on the green water. There we found the painter's wife, a Botticelli-like American, and Tolentino himself, a sort of Italian Pierrot. He was busy scraping the surface of a painting with a tortoise-shell palette-knife, and he had already brought to light the red and blue wings of a Carpaccio angel, which had been painted over by an unknown artist.

In addition to his various mediaeval chests, Virgins in niches and statues of saints standing on pieces of precious material, Tolentino had a collection of climbing-plants which screened the windows from the outside world.

"I can't bear to look at this dreadful town since the City Council was so misguided as to put office lights in the streets. There's not a Venetian who wouldn't have been glad to give an authentic old Venetian lantern."

Tolentino now lives in New York. He had one of his Venetian rooms shipped over there complete, and installed in a Sutton Place apartment house, where the decorations all happen to be Gothic and the East River serves as the Grand Canal.

He has carefully preserved his visitor's book, in which you can see all the names of the Italian and Austrian aristocracy, as well as many notable French and English ones. And he amazes the American aristocracy with his brilliant receptions.

Since I have included him in this book one might be prompted to ask if Tolentino is a real painter. I must answer that he most certainly is—at least, that is what he told me. One day, yielding to my insistence, he showed me one of his pictures. Or it would be more accurate to say that he led me into a darkened room, took a canvas out of a cupboard, asked me to stand a few yards away and, lighting a match, allowed me to look at the painting for three seconds, holding it towards me sideways.

He came to see me one day in a little studio I then had in New York, and I recall the face he made when he saw the modern canvases I had put up on my walls. It made me quite angry; or at any rate I pretended to be.

I made Tolentino sit down at an easel and, thrusting some brushes into his hands, said:

"Now. I've locked the door of this apartment, and I swear that I shan't let you leave here till you've proved that you can paint as well as those others whose work you so despise."

"But I've got a lunch engagement," he protested. "Besides, I can't paint without a model, or until I've had time to meditate. I'm never in a state of grace unless the atmosphere's right. What could I possibly paint in the midst of all this idiocy?"

I refused to give in, however. So Tolentino asked me to arrange the light, but he was more exacting about it than Isadora Duncan herself would have been. He made me hunt up some umbers and blacks of a kind no one has used, not even secretly, since the days of Jobbé-Duval's school. Finally, after more protests, he started to work.

It was then that I saw this great lazy fellow come to life, and the clown become a genius.

He began by smearing the whole canvas with a perfectly impossible tar colour, leaving only two or three spots which were scarcely less sombre. These spots gradually became shapes; the shapes, volumes; the volumes grew lighter or still darker, and suddenly a Rembrandt emerged, vivid, luminous, ready to step forth from its prison of canvas and colour. But Tolentino then darkened the beard of the old man he had painted, turned up the moustaches, put more warmth into the expression of the eyes, refined the contours, and—there was a Van Dyck. He asked me for white, then vermilion, then emerald green, and, as he swayed about on his stool like one demented, I watched him produce in succession a Rubens, with delicate flesh-tones, a Velasquez, and finally a Chardin. Like something supernatural, the pigment seemed to create the different faces and bodies as though under the influence of a magic wand, as Tolentino wiped off each image and formed a new one from the eyes, the flesh, the body, the light of the previous creation. And he kept this up for two hours.

At last he threw down his brush and said,

"There. That's enough."

I looked at the canvas again. There was very little left on it except a vague mask of a pale Beethoven. which seemed about to fade into nothingness.

"No!" I exclaimed. "You're not going to play Balzac's *Chef-d'œuvre Inconnu* on me. You must at least finish one face."

He picked up the brush once more, daubed about a bit, then relapsed into a sort of apathy.

"I can't do any more," he said.

So I let him go. And he left me with a shadowy form, compared to which a Carrière would be solid rock. And even today, and every time I meet Tolentino, I keep wondering if he did not hypnotise me, like some Indian fakir, and if his acrobatics were not better suited to a music-hall stage than to a gallery in the Louvre.

In the World of the Society Painters

LA GANDARA

I SHOULD LIKE to say something about Antonio de la Gandara.

Antonio de la Gandara was a painter of exceptional elegance. He was a gloomy and restless dreamer, a Parisian Spaniard who was, as he himself said, "inspired by El Greco and fascinated by Watteau". He began his career at a time when decadent literature was having its last flare-up: Goncourt was dying; Samain was fading away against the red-gold of his verse; Mallarmé was turning into a sphinx; and Jean Lorrain was tossing off his first jewel-like phrases. As the period required, La Gandara sought for poetry in the morbid (the fashionable kind, of course); for grandeur in melancholy; and for light in a glance or a precious stone. His studio became a museum of ghosts clothed in trailing silks; of automatons in frills and furbelows; of half-dead creatures, powdered, rouged and laden with rings. For a long time the devotees of the rare and the abnormal lived in a state of delirium. And there were plenty of them. The doctors had just discovered neurasthenia, the successor of the English "spleen"; and all the swooning beauties, American women frantic to be up-to-date, precious writers, drug-taking actresses and every neurotic in Paris rushed off to pose for "their painter", who would knock them off in three sittings, in shades of silver-grey and black, with a little pink thrown in for good measure.

Even the walls of his studio (which was in the old rue Monsieur-le-Prince), with its polished floors and antique furniture, were painted a dark grey.[1] He received his friends there in a velvet dolman, his back bent, his manner not at all affected but imbued with a touch of Spanish negligence, even to his patent-leather shoes, which he left unbuttoned. With his brilliant black eyes, hair and moustache, set off by his sallow skin, and his low voice, he was very much the *grand seigneur*, receiving all the gentry, from

[1] The studio now belongs to the artist Yves Brayer.

Arthur Meyer to Boni de Castellane (still very dapper), and la Cavalieri to the Duchesse de Rohan.

I recall the Duchess standing up while she posed for the portrait which André Rouveyre sketched of her in a note-book, if one may use the term portrait for the monstrous caricatures that this pupil of Gustave Moreau used to perpetrate in those days. They were much more extreme than the most ferocious Rouaults or the most incisive Lautrecs; yet for all their *outrance*, they were, paradoxically, astonishingly true to life.

The Duchess posed standing up because of a ruling La Gandara had established. For when he invited the smart set of Paris to come and admire his canvases, he never offered them "tea or a chair" because, if they were provided with either, the guests would inevitably spend their time chattering and gossiping instead of looking at the pictures.

But what a delightful man he was when one was alone with him! I often watched him as he painted. He worked slowly, but with an amazing sureness of touch.

"This portrait, which I have only sketched in so far, is of an Englishman. I'm going to begin at the upper left-hand corner and work down to the lower right. That is the way Velasquez painted. At present I'm painting a woman who has often spoken to me about you. Her name is Ida Rubinstein."

"Yes, I saw a very fine bust of her at the house of the Russian sculptor, Naoum Aronson."

"She's going to put on some interesting works of Verhaeren's and d'Annunzio's at the Châtelet. Claude Debussy is to compose the music. She read one of your articles on the Russian Ballet, and she would like you to write something about her and her productions. Would you do me a personal favour and go to see her? She's staying at the Hôtel Bristol, in the royal suite.

"Yes," went on the artist, "she really is a sumptuous creature. When she orders a coat from Worth's, for instance, she gets them to cut off the necessary amount of material, and then makes them destroy the rest under her eyes, just as a copper-plate is destroyed after a limited number of prints have been made. Do please congratulate her on what she is doing. As she is Russian, don't be afraid of paying her compliments; lay it on as thick as you can. When she's angry, she behaves like a llama: she turns her head to

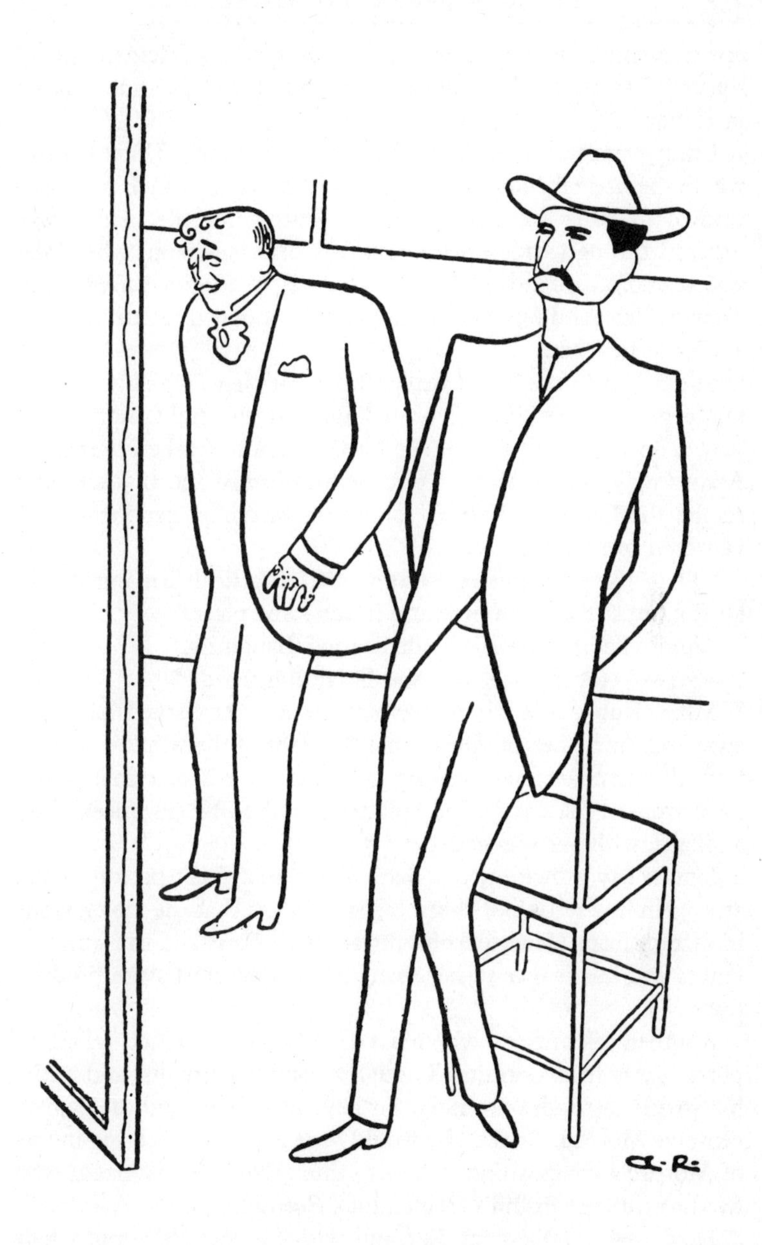

one side and thrusts out her chin. . . . But she's a fascinating person: she has hunted black lions in Anatolia and slept under canvas in Ethiopia."

I duly went to call on Mme. Rubinstein in the old Hôtel Bristol, where she had taken not one, but two royal suites, which had been thrown together for her. She was waiting for me, and I was ushered through wide-open doors to a drawing-room, where she was seated on a kind of throne. She was wearing a *zaimph* and, drawing her hand out from under it, she motioned me to sit down almost at her feet.

She talked to me about her professional plans, which were certainly most interesting. I waited for just the right moment to "lay it on thick", as the kindly La Gandara had asked me to do. Accordingly, when Mme. Rubinstein informed me that she had rented the Châtelet Theatre for her forthcoming productions, I ventured to remark,

"Then the two greatest stars in the theatrical firmament will be shining at the same time and in the same place."

"And who are they?" she demanded, haughtily.

"Sar—— forgive me: you and Sarah Bernhardt."

Mme. Rubinstein's mouth twitched, and she turned her head away, outlining her profile against the light of the window. Little by little her charming lower lip protruded to a degree that would have aroused the envy of any platter-mouthed Negro queen. My audience with her was ended.

I must say, however, that later I saw that great patron of the arts again in a setting of charming simplicity; that she took lessons in diction from Mme. Bernhardt; and that Paris and the world of letters and music owe to her many of their greatest stage productions.

Another celebrity of whom La Gandara did a much talked-of portrait was Jean Lorrain. Though a notable journalist and critic, his artistic tastes did not range far beyond Lalique and the painter Gustave Moreau. In fact, he would have enjoyed appearing in one of Moreau's compositions. And to think that it was Lorrain who tried to ridicule Rodin's tremendous *Balzac*! . . .

How well I remember Lorrain, with his lock of auburn hair falling over his deeply-lined forehead, his eyebrows contracted over his glaucous eyes, which gazed out from under lashes tinged, like his moustache, with flecks of gold. His chin was extremely long; his shoulders square; and he usually kept one of his hands, with its slender fingers loaded with rings, on his hip.

"Make me look healthy, my friend," he begged the artist. "Everyone thinks I'm ill, that I take drugs, just because I've written a few short stories. But I simply loathe drugs, just as I loathe chemist's shops. Opium and morphine nauseate me almost as much as all the society women I have to go around with. Give me a sea-port, with plenty of sturdy boys and girls—eh, Biscuit?"

"Biscuit" was Jean Lorrain's secretary. Most of the writers in those days seemed to have strange secretaries, Apollinaire and Salmon among them. Lorrain had picked up his somewhere along the banks of the Seine. Biscuit sported a sailor's shirt; but he also wore gloves that didn't match—one canary-yellow, the other with black stripes—as well as checked trousers and a top hat. He would sometimes disappear for a week, and eventually be found officiating as a preacher in the Salvation Army. Or Lorrain would get a tearful letter from him and have to go to the police-station, where his secretary had been taken for some minor offence.

While he posed for La Gandara, Lorrain would dictate one of his gossipy articles to Biscuit, send it off to the *Journal* and regale us with anecdotes until Robert de Montesquiou arrived, his elbow resting on the little finger of one hand, his shirt-collar hidden by a muffler and his voice pitched as high as the ceiling.

One Sunday, when I went to see La Gandara, I found him absorbed in a copy of the *Journal*, the front page of which was devoted mainly to Sem's latest book of drawings, in which the celebrated cartoonist, making fun of the current fashions, had caricatured the smart women of the moment, showing some dressed like taxi-drivers and others like sausages in a butcher's shop. Some he had pictured as mere girls, despite their seventy years, and still others were decked out in finery that would have made the old harridans of the music-halls weep, with waist-lines round their knees and ruffles on their shoulders.

The so-called "hobble-skirts" were in vogue then, and Sem had given the ladies not only horse's legs but horses's hooves as well.

"His talent is so great," asserted La Gandara, "that unless we firmly resist his influence we shall never be able to see a pretty woman except as Sem has depicted her, with all those minor imperfections he can insinuate so subtly. At the races I see people looking exactly like his portraits of them, and his visual and visionary power is so great that even after twenty years I'm sure they will still look exactly as he has sketched them, however much the fashions have changed."

Then we fell to talking of women's fashions in general, and, as he had been painting the portraits of most of the fashionable women for half a century, the artist declared:

"But often the caricaturist is wrong because of the nature of truth itself. Instead of making a synthesis of the styles of his period, as Guys did, for instance, or Velasquez or Goya in their day, he grasps only one phase in the development of a movement, a momentary aspect which is leading to something else. There is too much chiffon at present, of course, too many hoops and other accessories. There always have been. But all fashions are charming when seen through the eyes of great painters. People often swoon over the dresses in Watteau's pictures. But I should like to have seen a woman of the people or even a *bourgeoise* in such attire. Just imagine all the extras on a stage dressed like that. Naturally, then as now, there were terrible errors of taste in the non-essentials. We don't have to go back very far before we come to the bustle, for example, which will never attract us, in spite of Stevens, Rops, Chéret and Seurat. Naturally, the women themselves helped. It is a living paradox how a woman's body adapts itself to the prevailing fashions and to the gestures appropriate to them. Look how pink-fleshed and plump Boucher's models are, while David's are positively starchy. If sport became the vogue tomorrow, you would see every woman bulging with muscles. As for the errors, well, they disappear quickly enough of their own accord. But when all is said and done, the most beautiful dress will be the one which most closely follows the lines of the human figure, without any need of hoops, bustles or corsets."

On another Sunday shortly after, Marcelle Meyer came to my house and played a new piano work of de Falla's for Diaghilev, Fokine, Karsavina, Picasso and Massine. As she finished, Apollinaire came in, followed by Rouveyre, who whispered in my ear,

"La Gandara has just kicked the bucket."

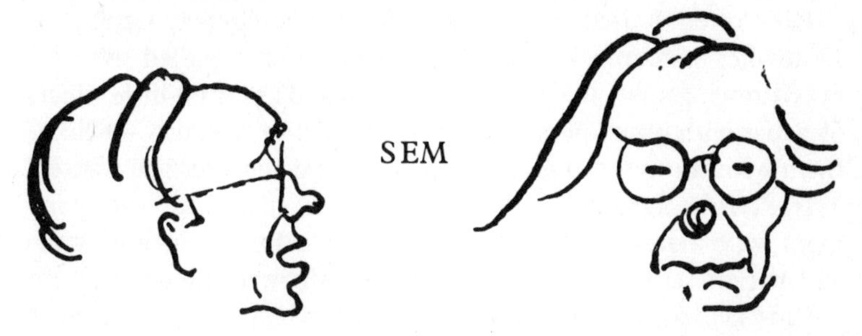
SEM

With his big umbrella under one arm, his brown raincoat and his rolled-up trousers, Sem really did look like a bespectacled marmoset going to the races. He laughed about it himself.

One day, as we were about to cross the street together, I caught his arm just in time to save him from being run over by a large car.

"I'd have sounded like a nut being cracked," he remarked.

He thought he was ugly, and, in the same pitiless way that he portrayed others, he used to caricature himself as a monkey.

Once, when I took the train for Deauville, I entered a compartment where there was a little man whose face was almost entirely covered by enormous dark glasses. He stared steadily at me, and I finally said to him, with a smile,

"Pardon me, but for a moment I thought you were Sem."

Sem removed his glasses, held out his hand, and replied,

"Do you think that's very flattering?"

He was never malicious, but he liked to make *bon mots*, just as his friend Forain did. He called Pierre Lafitte, the half-hearted sportsman who was always complaining of some malady, a *sportsmal.* When he heard that Coty, the perfumer, had gone bankrupt, Sem remarked, paraphrasing the Emperor Vespasian's *mot*,

"Odour has no money."

When he had an operation, some time before his death, I went with Fernand Vanderem to see him in hospital.

"Ah, my friends," he sighed, "they're draining my liver. I can't be peevish any more: I've no bile left."

"How do you manage to make people so unattractive, and yet make such good likenesses of them?"

"I simply try to make them better looking than they are, and that's how they turn out."

How often I used to lean over Sem's shoulder at Cannes or Deauville, watching him as he worked, his hat pulled over his eyes, drawing a lip, an eye, a nostril again and again on little pieces of paper with a tiny pencil. Later, at home, he would co-ordinate them with the aid of tracings, and finally get the effect he wanted.

In Paris he lived in the Boulevard Lannes, in a handsome apartment, with a drawing-room furnished with comfortable arm-chairs and wicker settees. On the light-grey walls were pictures by his friends Helleu, Forain and Boldini, with whom he often used to go for walks.

King Edward VII, whom Sem had frequently caricatured, expressed the wish to make his acquaintance; and when he met him, said to the artist,

"You have always flattered me."

When the King of Portugal was forced to leave his country, Sem told me that the caricature the artist had done of him was found on his bedside-table.

Yachts, trains, Casino dinners:

"All these people bore me stiff," Sem would say. For this man, who made others laugh, always gave the impression of being bored himself.

"I'd like to teach the ordinary people how to dress," Sem once remarked to me. "It really embarrasses me to see a working-man in a smock and a derby; or a clerk with a formal wing-collar and a soft shirt; or an official wearing brown shoes with a dinner-jacket. I'm going to do a book of drawings of them some time, and I'd like you or Marcel Boulenger to do the text for it."

"Why don't you write it yourself, Sem?"

"That's an idea."

"I have another idea: you should illustrate the text as well."

"I'll try. But, apropos of ideas, let's play a joke. Let's pick out some girl—not too bad looking, but unshapely—with a prominent chin, pop-eyes, awkward shoulders, big feet, a protruding stomach, and with her umbrella thrust under her arm."

"Like that girl there, for instance?"

"Yes. Then, with your articles and my drawings, we'll 'launch' her as the prettiest girl in Deauville. I'll bet you that for the entire season every single woman will carry her umbrella the same way, stick out her chin the same way, roll her eyes like an idiot, and wear a bow on her stomach."

For the entire season? It lasted the whole war, and even longer! And even ten years later fashionable women in South America were still trying to look like Mlle. F——, who had served as the model for our little joke.

But, in all modesty, Sem must be given the credit. . . .

BOLDINI
JEAN-GABRIEL DOMERGUE

Sem, Boldini, Forain and Helleu: I can still see the four friends striding down the Avenue du Bois de Boulogne each morning. Sometimes they were joined by a fifth: Abel Faivre. Sem I have already described; he looked smaller still when walking along beside the sallow, bearded Helleu, who was long and lean like the H in his name. Forain looked bent over, as if folded in three, with his hands clasped behind his back under his coat, making a kind of bustle; and his lips were always "set", ready for a caustic remark.

"It seems that they're going to change the name of the Avenue to Avenue Foch. X—— [a well-known parvenu] is furious about it. He told me the other day that he had decided to continue having 'Avenue du Bois' engraved on his stationery and visiting-cards. So when I write to him, I'm going to put 'Avenue Dubois' on the envelope."

Boldini was almost as deformed as Lautrec. He looked like a sort of hermit-crab, with his broad forehead, large eyes and quick gestures. And it was as a crab that Sem pictured him in one of his books of drawings. For his part, Boldini had done a fantastic portrait of Sem, giving him a nose like a corkscrew spiralling into infinity.

Boldini was misunderstood and sometimes scorned by the moderns, in spite of the quality of some of his work—such as his portrait of Verdi, in which he proved himself equal to the best. But a short time before his death he began to be bought by the more advanced among the collectors.

One of his pupils, Jean-Gabriel Domergue, had helped to bring about this well-deserved recognition.

How, you may ask, could Jean-Gabriel Domergue, the society painter, have any influence on——

Ah, but you don't know Domergue.

First of all, he is one of the wittiest of Parisians, and that counts for something, even in Paris.

When you talk to him about his painting, he is often frank enough to say:

"Oh, I'm *École des Beaux Arts.* I'm a stuffy old academic."

The result is that one is forced to respect him. For he is fond of Degas and Constantin Guys, and he proclaims Picasso a genius—on the wrong side of the fence, but a genius all the same. As for himself, according to his own description he is only a caricaturist, but instead of copying Hogarth he has gone back to the tradition of Giovanni da Bologna and the great animalists of the Renaissance. And, like the painters of the Renaissance—incidentally, his profile reminds one of Francis I—Domergue is both a painter and an architect and, one might add, a sculptor—at least through his wife, who models and makes her own castings. It was apropos of this that he, or one of his friends, composed a verse to the effect that

Domergue est assuré d'avoir un nom qui dure
Sinon dans le portrait . . . du moins dans la sculpture.

As an architect, he began by designing first a Venetian bed, then a summer-house, then a villa, and finally a château, the most beautiful on the Côte d'Azur, facing the Estérels, with gardens, terraces, fountains, dove-cots, servants' quarters and a tall chapel-like studio, a studio with great Venetian chandeliers, where every season society folk from three worlds—the Old, the New and the Demi-monde—come and rhapsodise over his canvases, which are as vivid and gay as life on the Riviera itself.

As I stood one day in one of his red and gold drawing-rooms, I could not help but admire the thrust of three brilliant columns, which reminded me of those in the setting for the ballet *Scheherazade.*

"Do you know how those columns are done?" he asked me with a laugh. "With drain-pipes; and a waste-pipe runs through this one here."

Domergue had, as the Slavs say, "fought so well" for Boldini that when Maurice de Rothschild came one morning to ask him if he would sell his Boldinis, the artist replied:

"Never! I've millions of francs' worth of them. But they're going up."

"I know," said de Rothschild. "One of his pictures was bought at nine o'clock yesterday for two hundred thousand francs, and sold for five hundred thousand at eleven, nine hundred thousand at seven in the evening, and a million and a half at midnight, to an Englishman."

"Not really?"

"It is absolutely true," concluded M. de Rothschild, "because I was one of the buyers and sellers."

"And what of the man himself?" I asked Domergue.

His Francis I beard quivered.

"A monster in mind as well as body. And a terrible flirt! One day I sent him a pretty model; a young girl, little more than a child. The first thing he said to her was: 'You get undress'. Good God, how bee-ootiful you are! I never saw a woman so *bella*. Von' you come vith me to Italia?' 'Italy, *maître*?' she said. 'You don' know Italy? Madonna! The Gulf of Genova, it curve aroun' like this,' and he put his hand on the girl's hips; 'the Gulf of Venezia go like this,' and he put his other hand around the nape of her neck; 'Napoli is like this pretty breast. . . . And the Lombardia plain is smooth like your stomach. . . .'

"He went on in this style for three-quarters-of-an-hour. Then, being somewhat wearied, Boldini said to the delighted girl, who was busy dreaming of blue waters and golden skies:

" 'Now you can get dress'. But vot is that you put on?'

" 'That? That's my corset, *maître*.'

" 'A corset! Ha-ha-ha-ha! Vot an ugly corset. You go away. I never take a girl to Italy with such an ugly corset.'

"On another occasion," went on Domergue, "I said to him, 'How are your amours going, *maître*?' (He had just turned eighty-four at the time.)

" 'Pooh. I don't even try any more. I know they'd be failures.'

"When the painter Sargent died, Boldini remarked:

" 'He was a man who was supposed not to have a heart. But after his death an autopsy was performed on him, and they found

Boldini in the manner of Sem

that he had a heart three times as large as the average. He had a heart, but nobody knew it.'

"And when he himself was dying, he said to his wife,

" 'What a pity God won't grant me just one more beautiful day. What a portrait I would do of you. . . .' "

* * * * *

Before taking leave of Boldini, I must say something about the quarrel he had with Sem. It occurred because of the caricature I have already mentioned. Not that Sem was offended by it. On the contrary, he wanted to keep it; but Boldini asked him to give it back. One day, saying that he wanted to "touch up" one eye a little, Boldini took it away with him, and never returned it. And the two friends did not see each other for a long time afterwards.

The years went by. Boldini grew old and melancholy. One evening he was sitting alone, without even the housemaid, who had left him because he was so difficult. There was a veritable mountain of dust on the floor and over all the furniture. He had just turned eighty-three, and he thought bitterly:

"Nobody comes to see me any more, not even Sem. Maybe I should give him back his portrait? No, that's impossible. All the same I should like to make it up with him."

He went to the telephone and rang up his old friend.

"Hello! Hello! Is that you, Sem? Guess who's calling you. It's poor old Boldini, who's going to die soon, and wants to see you. Do come over, will you?" And he hung up.

He waited.

A quarter of an hour passed, but no one came.

"If I were really about to die, he would get here too late," Boldini said to himself crossly.

Suddenly he had an idea. He did something that would have scared most people of eighty-three. He got undressed, placed lighted tapers around his bed, left the door partly open, lay down, crossed his arms over his chest and pretended that he was dead.

Another quarter of an hour went by, and still nobody came. At every little noise Boldini raised his head to listen, then resumed his pose.

Finally, he heard a sound, not very loud but more distinct than the others. It was Sem. He came in, saw the pathetic spectacle, made the sign of the cross and knelt down to pray.

Whereupon Boldini rose up, cried, "Boo!", and hopped out of bed like a Jack-in-the-box.

Sem fled; and the two never saw each other again.

Domergue had known the Lautrec family at Albi.

"Albi," he asserted, "is as beautiful as Toledo. But poor Lautrec was completely ostracised there. He was, in fact, driven away from the place. Yet today he is the boast of the town. It's a delicious irony. The archbishop's palace has been transformed into a Lautrec museum, and you can see there his works depicting the brothel houses where he used to spend his nights sketching, in the company of his friend Coolus."

* * * * *

Great news! J.-G. Domergue had been made an Academician! When Paul Léon, Fasquelle and several other old friends presented him with the ceremonial sword, engraved by Mme. Domergue herself, the old Parisian asked,

"Why should one be given a sword at an age when one has to begin to think of crutches?'

After the ceremony I accompanied Domergue back to his Paris home, which is as spacious and elaborate as his house at Cannes. It has a gallery of bronzes and a marble dining-room large enough to seat the whole Academy, similar to those depicted in Veronese's paintings. But on the walls are pictures which Veronese could not have shown: early Renoirs; Goyas of the Saragossa period; Canaletto palaces, out of which had probably come the gilded chairs in which we sat.

"I see you have a copy of the Botticelli *Virgin and Child* in the Louvre," I said.

"It is the Louvre *Virgin and Child* that is a copy," he retorted, "because it is painted in oils. Botticelli painted only in tempera. Mine is authentic. Look at it carefully. The things they have in these museums . . . !"

The painter chuckled in his short beard; his lips were very red, his teeth gleaming white. His Francis I nose twitched, and his eyes glinted.

"These museums!" he repeated.

For this man, who calls himself a stuffy old academic and a society painter, is in his way a fighter and a revolutionary.

"These art galleries. And your so-called 'moderns'. They are a hundred times more academic than I am; and far more prisoners of their technique. You'll see what is left of their colour a hundred years from now!"

* * * * *

"Well, now you are an Academician. Tell me how it happened."

"Why, it's the most fantastic story of my life."

We were sitting in another of the artist's studios, the one in which he exhibited his pictures. Looking at them, one would have said that Domergue had undressed women of every shape and class, and put them up, carefully framed, on his walls. There were hundreds of nudes, slightly elongated, in accordance with the "tradition of Giovanni da Bologna" and the great animalists of the Renaissance. For every painter of women is an animal-painter, whether he represents her as a parakeet, a greyhound bitch, an owl or just a simple female of the species—which is sometimes worse.

Domergue: Self-portrait

But Domergue is not given to cruel caricature, as his friend Van Dongen is. If he seems to harp on the worthlessness of certain ladies of the town or of the present generation of nobility, at least it is more out of relish than out of bitterness that he seems to crush raspberries on their lips, as though wanting to stuff them with the fruit. And with the same innocent relish he paints a peach-coloured skin under the transparent light of a parasol in stridently brilliant colours, and adorns his whores with bird of paradise plumes.

"The *Institut* is the logical climax of your career," I said. "You were born in Bordeaux; you are related to Lautrec; at fifteen you came top of your year's entry into the École des Beaux Arts; you were taught by Jules Levebre, who moulded such painters as La Fresnaye and Segonzac. At sixteen you won an honourable mention, and left all the others behind with your *Robe jonquille* canvas. You were awarded a medal at nineteen; the Institut prize at twenty; and the Grand Prix de Rome in 1913, with your *Rhapsody Singing the Praise of Heroes on the Outskirts of an Ancient Village.*"

"Joke about it if you like," replied Domergue. "It wasn't for any of this really. The fact is that during the 1914 war I published, under my own name, a book of drawings on 'German Atrocities'. I never gave it another thought until 1942, when a German officer came to see me. 'We believe that a foreigner used your name to sign a certain book of drawings,' he told me. 'Whoever he is, the person has already been condemned to death, and will be executed as soon as we find him. Meanwhile, you are requested to come to the Kommandatur's Office.'

"I didn't exactly feel like breaking into song on the way to the *Place de la Concorde.* After waiting there for half-an-hour, I was told that Prince Metternich wished to see me, and I was taken to the one-time residence of Talleyrand. I was ushered in between two rows of German officers standing to attention, and my knees were shaking pretty badly. A door opened, and I saw a queer little man, sitting behind the huge desk of the Prince of Benevento. He rose as I came in, and looked at me hard.

" 'Now,' I said to myself, 'he's going to read my death-sentence.'

" 'Are you Monsieur Domergue?' he asked.

" 'I cannot deny it,' I said.

" 'Sit down, then, and allow me to inform you that I, Prince Metternich, have nothing in common with the infamous Nazis who are in charge here.'

"For a moment I thought he was making fun of me. But he went on.

" 'Let's forget this affair of the drawings. Now what can I do for you? Can I help you to get out of Paris?'

" 'I should prefer to remain in Paris,' I said.

" 'That will be a more difficult matter. Unless you have an official position. You aren't a professor or a member of the Academy, are you? Or even a candidate for the Academy?'

" 'I could be that,' I said.

" 'Very well, Monsieur Domergue, you can begin your visits to the Academicians and, *as long as you are not elected*, you can remain in Paris. I will give the necessary orders.' "

* * * * *

"And that," continued Jean-Gabriel Domergue, "is how I began making my calls as candidate for the Academy, begging each member as hard as I could not to vote for me. The Liberation came; and all those whom I had visited during the bombing elected me, in spite of a thousand dirty tricks on the part of certain little pals, among them, those who had denounced my book of drawings to the Germans. I shan't mention any names."

"Are you glad now?"

"Yes, because I can still live in Paris, or go occasionally to Algiers or Morocco and paint the portraits of worthy industrialists, as a change from people like the charming Murat princesses or the Duchesses de Rohan and de Gramont, or the Goulds, or the Clarks. . . ."

"Speaking of the latter, wasn't Clark the American senator who owned as fine a collection as the late Richard Wallace's? I remember he was so furious because of the capital tax they wanted him to pay here that he took his pictures over to America instead of bequeathing them to the Louvre."

"Yes, that's the one. And this was after the Government had missed the boat over the Wallace Collection."

"Have you started attending any of the Academy meetings?"

"Oh, yes. As in most Academies, they have a 'Right' and a 'Left'. The 'Right' isn't bad because it includes among its members the best of the so-called 'Rightist' painters. But on the 'Left' you won't find Derain or Braque or Rouault or Segonzac or Matisse. . . ."

At that moment our conversation was interrupted by the arrival of the director of a gallery. He had come to offer the artist a contract.

"Why?" asked Domergue.

"Well," said the visitor, "because a painting that is put on the market brings in more than one that is sold privately."

"Certainly," replied Domergue; "but I should prefer that it brought me more than it did you!"

"But suppose there were another war. Everything you have might be taken from you. You yourself might be persecuted."

"Nonsense," said Domergue; and, pointing to the pictures of the slender, graceful women on his walls, he went on, "And if they applied the law of retaliation, they would have to sentence me to end my days in a nudist camp."

ALBERT BESNARD

Albert Besnard, president of the Société des Artistes Français, Director of the École des Beaux Arts, and later of the École Française in Rome, was a most excellent man. He encouraged young artists, and in his own work tried out such bold experiments that he was nicknamed "The *Pompier* Who Wants to Start a Fire".[1]

I had gone to see him one day with Louis Vauxcelles, and we were rather taken aback when he said,

"As a matter of fact, I'm expecting the King of England. . . ."

The King of England was as yet only the Prince of Wales; but the future Edward VII (who admired Detaille!) liked to pay visits to well-known painters.

"Oh, well you might as well stay," said Besnard, who, incidentally, was dressed in a very odd fashion. He had spent the whole morning trying to decide what to wear for the occasion, and whether he should put on a jacket or just his artist's smock. He had finally compromised by pulling his white smock over his jacket, while Mme. Besnard had also slipped one over her silk dress.

A secretary came to announce the Prince's arrival, and, to his embarrassment, was introduced to us. Besnard gave us a wink and then hastened to welcome the royal visitor. His Highness appeared, all smiles, bowed to his hostess, and, gloves, hat and cane in hand, began his tour of the studio. In the back of the room Besnard had placed an immense panel, and the Prince stopped to examine it with his host and hostess. For a moment no one uttered a word; then the Prince of Wales took a cigar-case out of his pocket and held it out to Besnard, saying,

"Do you smoke, Monsieur Besnard?"

Mme. Besnard came forward, and the artist replied,

[1] A play on the word *pompier*, which means fireman as well as anything banal or academic in art. [*Trans. note.*]

"Yes, and my wife smokes too."

The Prince passed her the case without batting an eye; and the three, cigars in hand, continued to look at the panel. Then something unexpected occurred. It may have been a draught, or perhaps the picture was not fastened securely; or the emotion in the room may have been highly charged: the fact remains that the canvas suddenly fell flat on the floor in front of them. Despite the royal presence, the painter could not prevent himself from crying out,

"*Merde!*"

Aghast, Mme. Besnard looked from her husband to the Prince, and as if to confirm what destiny had evidently ordained, she raised her cigar and repeated,

"*Merde!*"

Finally, the Prince, with immense gravity, removed the cigar from his mouth and, with a gesture of the hand, exclaimed,

"*Mince!*" [1]

CAROLUS DURAN

Carolus Duran, the father-in-law of the playwright Feydeau, and for a time the teacher of the American painter Sargent, was the most self-possessed man I have ever known, and the most diplomatic.

It so happened that a beautiful foreigner, among many others, once commissioned him to do her portrait. Unfortunately, for all her elegance she was insufferably high-handed, like so many of her compatriots, who are accustomed to driving men to work as animals are driven to the slaughter. And as for the way they treat artists. . . !

The *maître* had given in to all the pretty lady's whims. In spite of his easy-going disposition, he would not have put up with such behaviour had she been a Frenchwoman. However, as she was something new in his experience, she rather amused him. He even agreed to paint the portrait at her house, which was a considerable concession, as it meant that he lost much valuable time. Moreover, she was often late for her appointments, and she would tell lies to

[1] Euphemism for the word *merde*, meaning "Dear me!" [*Trans. note.*]

excuse herself, heap reproaches on him and indulge in all sorts of whims and tricks, even to the point of wanting to change her dress in the middle of a sitting, or suddenly remembering an engagement with her hairdresser, or asking the artist to alter the size of her eyes or of a jewel in the painting.

At last the portrait was almost finished, and ready for framing.

When Carolus Duran arrived at the lady's house one Saturday for the final sitting, the maid informed him that Madame was ill and could not see him; but she hoped he would come back the following Wednesday or Thursday.

The next Wednesday he returned punctually, but, just as he was about to mount the stairs, the concierge ran out and stopped him.

"Are you going to Miss X's?" she asked.

"Yes. Isn't she any better?"

"Any better? Why, she's gone away!"

"Gone away? Will she be back soon?"

"Why, Monsieur, she's gone to America. She sailed last night."

"Good Lord. But my picture——"

"Oh, don't worry, Monsieur. It was well packed. I helped to crate it myself. Madame was very anxious about it."

"And you never heard from her again?" I asked Carolus Duran.

"I learned, after it was too late to do anything about it, that the picture had been exhibited all over the place, and that she had sold it and then bought it back again."

"And what became of the lady?"

"Oh, I met her subsequently at a reception in Paris. She smiled and held out her hand."

"And what did you do?"

"I kissed it. After all, ours is a wretched profession, in which we take our profits as we can, and our losses without complaint—unless we are caddish enough to demand payment in advance. If I'd started a lawsuit or made a fuss, I'd have got the reputation of being a trouble-maker, which is even worse than being a bad painter. I shouldn't have got any more commissions. Whereas in this case.... You won't believe me, but she actually had the cheek to ask me to come to her house and do another portrait. And I consented. That portrait brought me three others, for which I was well paid. I was still young then, and it was worth my while."

"And did you get paid for the second portrait?"

Carolus Duran took out a cigarette, lit it, and—made no reply.

HARPIGNIES

Harpignies was not a "society painter", but rather a painter whose work was bought by "society people".

I met him through Vauxcelles; and what tales he used to tell me about the old boy. How, for instance, the *vieux chêne*, who was still good for two *Absinthes* a day at the age of ninety-seven, used to assert that he would not die during the War unless he was deprived of his favourite beverage.

He had lived for almost a century, and had always refused to see a doctor—except once, when he fell seriously ill in his eighty-fourth year. On that occasion he said to the doctor,

"I warn you: I won't take any medicine."

"And I warn you, sir, that if you don't keep to your room for at least a fortnight——"

"A fortnight! Are you pulling my leg?"

"And if you don't take this medicine tonight, it will be all up with you."

"I don't believe in doctors or in medicine."

"On my word of honour, you'll be done for."

"All right, all right. I'll take your drugs."

"I'll come round and see you in the morning."

Next morning the doctor returned, and found Harpignies up and working at his easel in the garden.

"What? You're up?"

"Of course. You can see for yourself that I'm perfectly well."

"Did you take my medicine?"

"Oh, yes. I promised——"

"It wasn't so bad after all, then?"

"Ugh! I chucked it all into a good strong *Pernod*, and I didn't taste a thing. . . ."

* * * * *

"I went to see Harpignies one winter's night," continued Vauxcelles. "He was probably about ninety-three then. He kept me until one o'clock in the morning. As I thought it was high time for him to go to bed, I got up to leave.

" 'Stay just a little longer,' he begged. 'What time is it? I'll go with you as far as the corner.'

" 'What, at this hour? Besides, it's snowing.'

" 'Nonsense. Nonsense. The snow's lovely.'

"He got up and wrapped himself up well in a big cape.

" 'You can do me a little favour,' he informed me, once we were out in the street. 'Let's go this way.'

"We had walked for perhaps half-an-hour, when he stopped in front of a tall house.

" 'I'm all right except for my eyes,' he said. 'That's why I wanted to ask you—— You see, I have a little friend who lives up there on the sixth floor, and we've agreed on a certain signal. Will you look at the third window from the left and tell me how the curtains are fixed?'

" 'White curtains?'

" 'Yes, that's it. How are they fixed?'

" 'They're drawn.'

" '*Merde!*' exclaimed Harpignies, sending the snow flying with his cane. 'She's got her "old man" with her tonight.' "

* * * * *

Poor Vauxcelles. He died during the war, half-blind. My friend Waldemar George told me of one of his last *mots*.

The great critic was standing in the street one day, looking at a poster of a German soldier kicking the behind of a poor non-Aryan.

"What do you think of it?" brusquely demanded a German officer who had come up behind him.

Vauxcelles looked round at him, and said calmly,

"It's very badly drawn."

PAUL CHABAS

As an art critic, I had occasion, in 1935, to attend one of the dinners the Société des Artistes Français gave each year before their private view. It was held in a restaurant in the Champs Elysées. All those around me seemed to be decent enough people, and even sincere painters. But when the speeches began my fellow-critics and I were appalled. And when Paul Chabas, the president of the Society, rose to speak, our dismay became stupefaction.

Every year Paul Chabas exhibited his work, which consisted mostly of graceful, naked young girls bathing in a lake, against a background of misty mountains. And this same gentleman had the impertinence to say at the end of his speech:

"——but we are all eclectic here. We welcome 'everyone'—even Signac. Yes, even Signac," and he repeated the phrase three times, each time stressing the name—which was doubtless scorned by most of those present, for was he not the man who emulated Seurat, the man who had written that little Bible of art, *D'Eugène Delacroix au Néo-Impressionnisme?*

"*Even* Signac"! With the words still ringing in my ears, I ran into an old painter standing in the door of that respectable Salon; on seeing me, he threw up his arms and said in a lugubrious tone,

"Well, I've done it!"

"What have you 'done', my friend?"

Then, as though he were some society woman confessing to an amorous intrigue, he whispered:

"It's too bad, but I've gone 'modern'. Come and look at it. After all, this is 1945; and one has to live." And he led me up to an Impressionist canvas in the style of 1875.

WERBOFF

M. Michael Werboff, whom I have often met in Cannes, Biarritz and New York, has painted kings, queens, Royal Highnesses, millionaires, even artists. He has counted among his patrons Gustav V of Sweden, King Carol, Alphonse XIII, Grand Duke Dmitri, Grand Duchess Marie and the Duchess of Mortemart; also Vuillard—yes, Vuillard himself—Romain Coolus, Courteline, Léon Blum, Boncour, Harold Vanderbilt, Titta Ruffo, Jos Straus, Tristan Bernard, Henri Torrès, Mrs. Osborn and many others.

If he ever wrote his memoirs, it would be a most interesting book. But M. Werboff is as discreet in his talk as he is in his art.

"I have been received by sovereigns, just as the artists of the Renaissance were welcomed to the tables and homes of Popes and Tyrants. Should I not appear to be an ungrateful guest if, for instance, I were to reveal that Gustav V has such big teeth that I felt I should paint him with his mouth closed? 'Come, come,' he said to me. 'I know I've got ugly teeth. But they've been exaggerated so often in caricatures. Make them just as they are: they're my teeth, aren't they?'

"Apropos of Alphonse XIII, I was once invited to a formal dinner given by a new Spanish grandee. The King had sat himself down next to a very pretty woman. Whereupon the host came and showed him the place reserved for the royal guest. 'The place for Royalty is wherever I happen to be sitting,' declared His Majesty. 'And what is more, let it be understood here and now that, as a Spanish grandee, you must *tutoies* me, or else call me "Your Majesty"; but not "you".'

"Carol was much simpler, and Madame Lupescu kept her distance. One day I asked if they would allow me to take a photograph of them together, and the King obligingly called her to come and stand beside him. But she refused, saying, 'No. I must not be photographed with you when you are wearing your uniform.'

"It was Coolus's opinion that 'a portrait should reveal the subject to himself, and explain him to others'.

"Titta Ruffo often used to fume at present-day audiences, and maintain that 'singing is not shouting. An artist is not a vocal phenomenon. But people today don't really listen; they don't appreciate a *mezza-voce*. All they are looking for are the high notes.'

"As for Courteline, what a fine fellow he was! To give you an idea of his character, I must tell you an anecdote about his wife and their dog. His wife wanted to give the dog some medicine, but, being unable to manage by herself, she asked her husband to hold their pet while she administered the dose. Courteline was furious. 'What!' he said. 'Do you think I am mean enough to fool a little animal that trusts and loves me; and betray it even for its own good?'

"The last portrait I did," concluded Werboff, "was of Torrès, the lawyer and senator. Unlike most people I have painted, he wanted to pose standing up. He chatted away fifteen to the dozen the whole time. And he was indignant because, so he said, he was being urged to betray his fellow-men."

JAN STYKA

Jan Styka was known in France chiefly through his celebrated portraits of Tolstoi, Maxim Gorki and Chaliapin, whom he painted seated together at the same table. He also did the illustrations for Sienckiewicz's *Quo Vadis?*—a work, by the way, which owes a good deal to the elder Dumas's *Acté*.

With his big moustache and side-whiskers, his high boots and his fat stomach, Jan Styka looked like the embodiment of General Durakin, who comes in the Comtesse de Ségur's tales. But whenever anyone took him for a Russian, he would make a furious gesture and thunder in his burring voice:

"Russian! I've been a Pole for almost eighty years now, and I'm as solidly built as the oldest brothel in Warsaw, where a rosewood leg caressed by Napoleon hangs over the main window. What do you think of this rainy weather? It's all the fault of these stupid people in the casinos. How idiotic to dress up that way, and drink the stuff they drink, and look at cabaret girls, and throw streamers about—all the dreary amusements you see in the films when they want to show you what gay life is like in high society. I'd rather go round the Riviera dressed like a fife-player, as in Hébert's *La Malaria*—the way I dress in Capri, which I became king of. It was there that I received the poor Spanish Infante, whom all the ragamuffins threw stones at one year because he tried to be even more original than his confrère in the Villa Tiberius. You know, the one who died last year at the foot of the fresco he had commissioned the painter Brunelleschi to do for him. He was the descendant of a lover of that queen of France who ended up on the scaffold. You know who I mean: her fichus are famous. Well, to cut a long story short, the Infante conceived the idea of recreating Paul Delaroche's picture *Sicilian Grape-gathering* in the Quisisiana gardens. He started out by getting together all the young models in the island, *bambini* 'more beautiful than della Robbia's', with curly hair, golden skin and sensuous lips. He stripped them naked, as in Virgil, and set them to ravaging all the vineyards on Monte Solaro. And at sundown they began a bacchic dance above the Gulf, which lasted till the moon rose. Their parents all applauded happily, and their older brothers and sisters brought mandolins and lanterns. The whole island was enchanted.

"The scene took on another aspect when it came to paying the bill. The Infante sent the enraged owners of the vineyards to his steward. The steward pleaded for time. Next day the Infante was nabbed on the wharf, as he was trying to slip away from the island, after the manner of Ulysses. He was taken back and shown the ruined vineyards with their vine branches still green.

"Each of the children had meanwhile been given a thrashing. Now it was the Infante's turn; he was undressed and put into a vat, where he was kept long enough to acquire an aversion to grapes, as well as to the painting of Paul Delaroche, for the rest of his life. He was finally rescued by a *marchesa*, who settled his account. That was no worse, believe me, than what goes on in France. I'm thinking of doing an enormous picture. . . ."

Adam and Tadé, the charming Styka's two sons, are in America. Both of them are first-rate portrait-painters, and they earn a great deal of money—which is just as well. . . .

Lithographers and Engravers

HOW MUCH SPACE I should like to give to the different illustrators among my friends. For example, there was Bernard Naudin, who did the illustrations for our *Cri de Paris.* He used to frighten us every time we lunched at Baty's by coming disguised as a National Guardsman and flourishing a sword; or as an acrobat and walking on his hands from one table to another. And then, suddenly, he would start talking in a frenzy of enthusiasm about the "Art of Drawing", about discovering a certain "line", a certain style. Unfortunately, he ended his life among people less wise than himself. . . .

Then there was the aristocrat Cappiello, who first modelled his faces in clay and afterwards drew them in pencil, often using a window-pane, or the window itself, to draw on.

"But to get the exact volume," he would say, "and to replace tonal modelling by the use of line, I have to distort, not follow, the contour. It is a question of art as opposed to artifice."

There was also the *Assiette au Beurre* crowd, who came down from Montmartre, and the "Edgar Allan Poe-ish" Gus Bofa, and the *Araignée* group: Chas-Laborde, Orsi and Guy-Arnoux, the Naval painter, who went out every evening to argue in all the bars of the Marbeuf quarter, wearing riding-boots and carrying a crop under his arm, followed by his dog, which tugged like remorse at his coat-tails. ("Just one more glass, old man. Not a drop more.")

And there was Bib, with his wit: "That woman has had her face lifted so much you can't even put a pencil into her snub nose any more. Where is her nose, anyway? You can hardly recognise it except by the smell."

I recall Rabajoi, too. He was a professor at the Polytechnic; but he could draw those women in the casinos with a quiet ferocity.

And there was Paul Colin, the poster artist. He had left Nancy with Lurçat, "who had 'flunked' medicine in order to go in for painting". Colin's name is on every wall; he is a Commander of the *Légion d'Honneur* and, as a supreme tribute, the Government put on an exhibition of his work at the Pavillon de Marsan. Whenever you meet him, he is surrounded by women of an extraordinary and exotic beauty. Nevertheless, Colin is inclined to be melancholy, and he is tormented by that noble discontent which plagues all great artists: "Have I done my task well? Could I not have done better, aimed higher, done something else?"

Paul Colin: Self-portrait

"So you're satisfied with your car, are you?"

I stared at the scatter-brained fellow who had asked me the question, looking at me with large eyes which appeared even larger through his glasses. As I was in a bad humour, and we were in the middle of a crossroads with taxis hooting all round us, I answered him sharply. He got hot under the collar; and I did too. But all at once he burst out laughing, introduced himself as Régismanset, and with that we made friends. He threatened to "knock my block off" if I didn't come with him to Tartine's. Tartine was the young lady with turned-up nose and mocking eyes who was sitting beside him, and had been doing her best to calm him down. Just then Galtier-Boissière came along, and we all went off together and wound up in Tartine's kitchen. A month after that, Régismanset went round with me getting material for *L'Illustration*. If we stopped anywhere for more than a minute, the white pages of the artist's sketch-book would be covered with drawings, thirty or more sketches appearing with the rapidity of an animated cartoon, the proper setting for each one emerging at the same time.

VERTÈS

I must not forget those two virtuosi, the fashionable designers for New York magazines and Paris stores, Vertès and Touchagues.

"Last week," Vertès told me, "I went to see a well-known critic, who lives in a sort of garret without heat or running-water or bathroom; and I shouldn't be surprised if it weren't still lit by paraffin lamps. When he saw my car he said, 'That isn't yours, is it?' And when I politely assured him that it was, he shook his head and raised his hands. Yet he's an intelligent man. He writes about modern painting, and contributes to a dozen big newspapers. It really is extraordinary. There are still plenty of people about, even artists, who think of painters as they were thought of fifty years ago, and can't conceive of an artist having a car like any ordinary tradesman."

This conversation took place in Vertès car, a Buick, which was running smoothly along at sixty miles or so an hour on the road from Deauville to Paris, where the artist was going to see a publisher about some book illustrations he was doing.

It was through my dentist, a charming fellow named Breger, that, ten years previously, I had made the acquaintance of the artist who since 1935 has been a great favourite in America.

"One of my patients is a young refugee," Breger had told me. "He says he comes from Hungary, that he is a painter, and that he has no money. I asked him to let me see some of his work. I have been to his place, and seen the kind of thing he is doing, and I believe in him. Here is one of his drawings."

"You are right to believe in him," I said. "That is the work of an honest man."

An honest man, indeed. With his gloved hand on the wheel, Vertès told me more about the job he was working on.

"The publisher commissioned me to do the illustrations for a book of Zola's, which he intends to sell at twenty thousand francs a copy. To be exact, the book will be sold in a set with three others, and so each purchaser will have to pay eighty thousand francs for the lot."

That was in the days when there was an enormous amount of speculation going on both in books and in pictures.

"When I asked the publisher how he wanted me to do the illustrations he replied, 'It doesn't matter. Other artists have done line drawings for me, and I had blocks made.' 'But,' I said, 'you can't sell a book with line-block illustrations for a price like that. I'll do some engravings for you.' 'All right, if it won't take too long.' Well, I worked on the copper plates for two years, and as I wasn't satisfied with them, I destroyed them last year and began all over again. And if I could, I would still do two of them over again."

We reached Paris and went straight to the publisher's. Ten minutes later Vertès reappeared looking rather pale.

"What's the matter?" I asked.

"That swine!" he expostulated. "Do you know what he did? I thought he'd be anxious to see the work I had done so carefully. You can appreciate how much it means to an artist to see a publisher take up the proofs one by one, and watch his eyes light up and a smile come over his face. But this fellow put my work in a pile, counted them without so much as a glance, shoved them all into a drawer and handed me my cheque. He didn't even give me time to thank him. I must say I prefer André——"

The André he was referring to was the intelligent owner of the casinos at Deauville, Cannes, La Baule and several other places. We had lunched with him that day, and when Vertès had mentioned to him that he was going to Paris to collect some money owing, André had remarked:

"We three are lucky to have found a way of keeping alive without having to work at the bottom of a mine, or staggering to an office on time even if you've got the gripes. I have my casinos; you your books; and you, Vertès, your drawings."

* * * * *

"I love the circus," Vertès said. "If you're fond of horses, you like to draw and paint them. You like seeing them even at the circus—especially at the circus. What a marvellous opportunity the circus is for the painter, those wonderful bodies, in that wonderful light. You can paint human bodies there much better than you can in an art-school. I remember one pair of acrobats who had more the grace of swallows than of aeroplanes, as they literally flew from one trapeze to the other. I asked the female member of the team to come to my studio one day. She was only a tiny girl, yet she seemed like a goddess when she was up in the air. She had a perfect body, supple and strong, but you had no idea of that from the way she dressed. So as to make her feel at home I talked to her while I made sketches.

" 'When you're "up there",' I said to her, 'suspended between life and death, I suppose it must always be an exhilarating and terrifying moment, in spite of your being used to it."

" 'No. We're used to it, as you say.'

" 'But you talk to each other sometimes, don't you? I saw you talking last night when you stopped for a second.'

" 'Oh, that was nothing.'

" 'But I'm sure you said something."

" 'It wasn't anything, I tell you. My partner said that the coat a woman in one of the boxes was wearing was made of fur, and I thought it was monkey. When we were on the ground again, we found out which of us was right.' "

* * * * *

Vertès doesn't go to the circus any more. Nor does he run races on all fours with Fujita and the charming Dora on the promenade at Deauville, as he used to. As I write these lines, the artist, who delights the readers of *Harper's Bazaar* each week with his novel and amazing ideas, has retired to the studio of his home at Northport, Long Island, where he has been working on a large panel for a house in Dallas, Texas. And what beauty, gaiety and style he has put into the painting!

To the right is a mauve Harlequin, leaning on a grey horse and playing with a gold coin; in the centre a slim young woman places a garland of roses on her head; while on the left a young child holds out his arms towards a flock of birds.

He painted the woman's head no less than seven times. After adding a few more touches, he laid down his brushes. He was already in his bathing-trunks, and we went across the road and down to the beach.

"I don't much like doing panels," he said. "I really prefer

lithographs to anything else. I learned how to do them when I was young. One painter who made superb lithos in those days was Willette."

"I knew him," I replied. "I often went to his studio in the Batignolles, on the ground floor of a little house there. I almost always arrived just as he was finishing his weekly drawing for the cover of the *Courrier Français*. He did his work standing at a large high desk. He drew from memory, but with the aid of casts of arms, legs, necks, etc. He was always bewailing the times we lived in, for he belonged to what I used to call the 'generation of grumblers'.

"On the other hand, what times those were. Do you remember the *Chat Noir* cabaret, with Willette's famous painting *Parce Domine* on the ceiling; and all our friends there, including Lautrec? . . ."

TOUCHAGUES

For all his dark face and high cheek-bones and chameleon-like eyes, Touchagues was neither Hungarian nor Mongolian. He came from Toulon, via Cannes; and almost immediately he

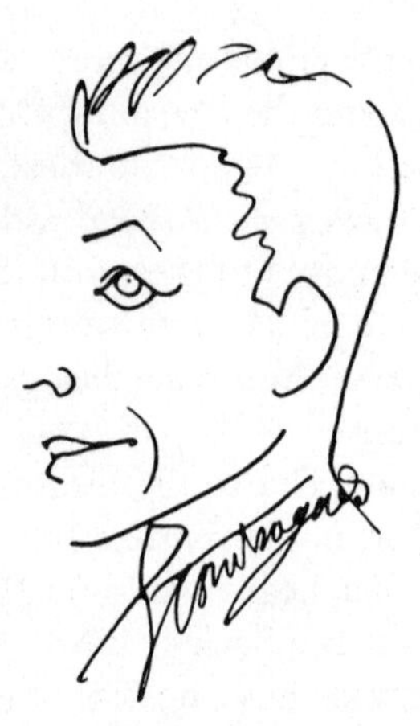

Touchagues : Self-portrait

arrived in Paris he found his niche in the Rue de la Paix, in the salons and dressing-rooms of the mannequins, or "models", as they are called nowadays. He usually lunched at the *Cabaret*, or at Berkeley's.

He was truly bewildered by all the models and women customers. So much the better for him, if he was!

Just as Soutine abstained from meat in order to paint it more sensually, I imagine that Touchagues remained chaste the better to savour visually the delights of the breasts, legs and hips that were continually being displayed before him.

I once went with him on a trip to Italy, which he was visiting for the first time, and I tried in vain to get him to look at the old palaces and mediaeval towers and bridges. Whenever I called his attention to some historical site, he would invariably answer:

"Look at the way that woman walks. She moves her legs as nervously as a cat." Or: "Just look at that young woman with her child at that window. Watch how her stomach moves under her red dress when she breathes. Here: hand me your pencil. If I could only—— Yes, I think I can get it. . . ."

In the Shadow of Utrillo's Tragic Drunkenness

I WANTED TO wait until now before giving an account of my many meetings with Maurice Utrillo, a painter who was erratic yet always himself, unrestrained yet disciplined, a bohemian yet a furious worker; the artist who brought perspective back into painting with a child-like naïveté, whose genius was primarily intuitive, but who painted with scientific exactitude.

Discipline was his foremost quality, even at the most difficult periods of his life—and he had many such periods, including poverty and confinement in institutions. Yet he never abandoned the principles of his métier, or was careless in his technique.

It is a curious fact that great artists who have been on the verge of madness, or mortally ill, have nevertheless been able to keep their genius intact when at their work-table or when painting, no matter how disorderly or exhausting their lives may otherwise have been.

I shall not attempt to repeat here all the details of a life which has already been described so often by others; or go over again

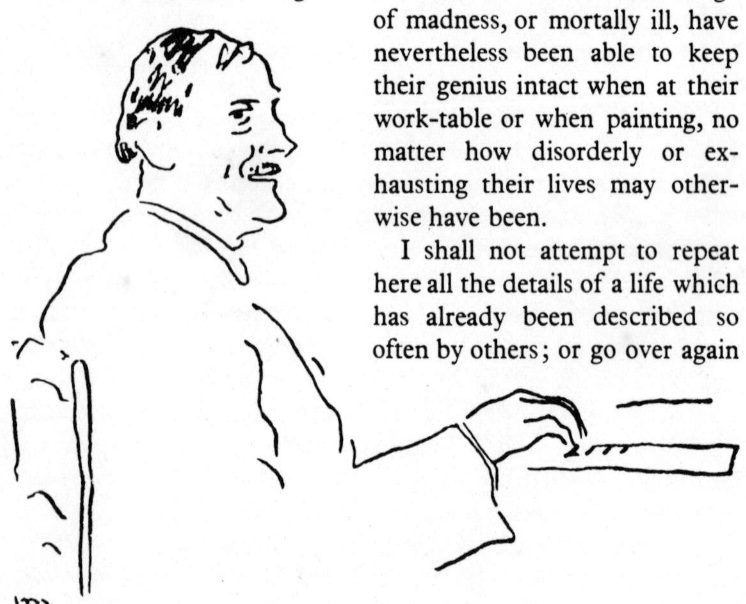

Utrillo at the Piano

the early years, spent mostly in the bistros of Montmartre, tied to the apron-strings of his mother, Suzanne Valadon, the former model of Degas, Lautrec and Gauguin—from all of whom she inherited a love of beautiful design and vivid colour.

Dorgelès, Carco, Pierre Mac Orlan, André Warnod, Armand Ziwès, René Barotte, Basler, Pierre du Colombier, Ch. Terrasse, Maximilien Gauthier, Georges Charensol, Mosellan and many others have written of Utrillo's youth and early beginnings; of his friendship with the masons who got him into the habit of drinking; and how his fortunes rose in 1939, when he was awarded the Carnegie Prize; and again, in 1951, when he received the rosette of the *Légion d'Honneur*.

One wonders whether, at any stage of his life, Utrillo was ever very far from the days when he used to make faces at passers-by and yell,

"No, I'm not crazy. I'm just an alcoholic!"

"He would go wild," his father-in-law, the painter André Utter, told me, "when he saw people sitting outside cafés; and we had to drag him over to the other side of the street. He was jealous of their drinking."

His charming wife Lucie said to me not long before his death:

"He doesn't need to drink to get tight nowadays. His imagination is enough to intoxicate him, all the more so now he has enough to eat. For I realised that his drunkenness needed something solid under it, so I always make him eat first. And look at the home I have made for him. Did he ever have one like it before? And it wasn't old Bourdelle who arranged the villa this way. It was I, Lucie, who did it," she insisted, with embarrassing candour. "Old Bourdelle was a great sculptor; but the good taste and the cleanliness of this house are due to Lucie, and no one else."

Lucie is a plump, well-dressed woman, with eloquent eyes and expressive hands. She always used to call the painter "my jewel of a husband, my child husband". And he would reply, as if repeating a litany, "My darling, my dear Lucie".

"There is no greater painter in the world," she would assert.

True, she should be the first to think so, but the last to say it. Is she to be blamed or admired? She dedicated her life to the "freak", as his father-in-law called him, and had as her reward the satisfaction of personally exploiting (and why not?) all the advantages of his money and fame.

She played more the role of mother to him than nurse. She bought his cravats, and took as much care of the "Utrillo legend" as she did of his pocket-book.

"The master can't see you," she would tell intruders. "He's in his oratory, saying his prayers."

The "oratory" in question was a small room full to overflowing of Joan-of-Arcs in marble, bronze, plaster, paintings, stained glass, even in the form of picture postcards.

"I kiss all my Joan-of-Arcs several times a day," Utrillo once informed me, adding, "It's hard work, but very holy." Even as he was speaking, he suddenly remembered to kiss one of the numerous medals he wore on a little chain round his neck.

Almost to the end of his life his hair was black and smooth; and he wore his moustache in the Charlie Chaplin style.

"Tell me," he once asked in a hoarse, faltering voice, "do I look my age? I was born in 1883, and I still haven't a single white hair. And I'm pretty strong. Yesterday I played billiards with that big milkman from Croissy. You ought to see what a stocky lad he is. Well, I beat him. Have you seen my parakeets? I've got seven of them. And we've got palm trees and magnolias and cedars that my Lucie ordered from the Midi. I didn't care how much she had to give for them."

He smiled, but did not try to hide the habitual look of melancholy that lurked in his light blue eyes.

On that occasion I went over to examine one of his frescoes, which covered the entire wall of his living-room.

"That's the Montmartre Jungle, the whole Jungle done from memory," Lucie told me; "from the Sacré Cœur to the 'Lapin-Agile'. It's just as good as his Montmagny period or his 'white' period, don't you think?"

"All my periods are good," put in Utrillo. "Just now I'm painting in new orange tones, with lighter and lighter greens, and working in one thin layer over another. But you've got to know how to use it. I've achieved a euphoria of colours that ignorant people dislike. People are always wanting painters to do something new, and yet they prefer their earlier work. Why? As if their older canvases weren't 'new' at the time they were painted! As if my present canvases won't be 'old' some day! I'm very proud of having been given the Carnegie Prize for a picture I did in 1938. But if I were a collector, I should want to exchange all my earlier canvases for those I'm doing now."

And how did Utrillo paint?

There are very few who ever saw him at work; for he liked to be alone, in a state of ecstasy bordering on a trance, with no one looking on—just like his mother Suzanne Valadon. I remember once going to see her with some American friends who wanted to buy one of her pictures, or at any rate talk to her. There was no one at home when we knocked at the door of her house in the rue Cortot. We were told we should find her in a little wine-shop at the corner of the street. And there, huddled on a cane chair at a table, was an old woman with grey hair done in a little bun on top of her head, her heavy-lidded eyes peering out through steel-rimmed glasses, dressed in a jacket and a blue and white apron.

One of my American friends went up to her and said,

"Pardon me, Madame, but can you tell me if Madame Valadon is here?"

"Madame Valadon? What do you want her for?"

"We should like to talk to her."

"Yes? Well, you can talk to me."

I came forward then, and introduced everyone.

"My friends would like——" I began.

"Oh, yes," she answered. "The Americans don't buy anything. They just come to see you."

"Yes, but if they're friends——"

She got up, and we followed her. She took us to her house, pulled a large key out from under her apron, led us up a narrow wooden staircase, and opened a door. We entered a big square studio, with a view of the grey plain to the north.

"That's the landscape poor Georges Michel, the first Montmartre painter, used to paint. He died in poverty in 1843. Almost all the Montmartre painters died in poverty, even in those days. You want to see my pictures? What for? I know you didn't come to buy anything from us. Maurice's canvases? You don't want much, do you? Come along; I must go back downstairs. Have you seen enough? No, none of that is for sale: they're souvenirs. Come this way. My apron's undone; it's lucky I discovered it. I mustn't ruin what's left of my appearance. Look out for that second step."

★ ★ ★ ★ ★

How did Utrillo paint?

Petridès, Utrillo's art dealer, used to take the artist into the woods in his car. Maurice would choose a site, and, with ruler and compasses, draw meticulously inside the car, which was fitted up like a film studio.

By way of contrast I remember Vlaminck, with his nose in a muffler, his feet in sabots and his sabots in the snow, brushing in with heavy, careful strokes his wonderful landscapes, as romantic as those of a Courbet or a Ruysdael, but entirely his own in their lofty conception. I recall the poor, half-mad Modigliani out in his shirt-sleeves in the Montmartre winter; and Utrillo, too, at one time, his nose and fingers red with cold, numbly gripping his brush as he shivered in a village street. He certainly had a right to the car he had "earned" for his art dealer—who loved him, understood him and cared for him.

First, Utrillo would trace with long, straight lines his perspective scheme in his big sketch-book, then put in, as he worked from the ground up to the sky, the thick lines of the trees, tapering off the branches and rubbing in the leaves lightly. His lips would contract when he was concentrating on what he was doing; but his fingers remained calm and sure in their touch.

In the evening (but only after a glass of red wine, of course) Utrillo would prepare his canvas himself, making his ground with a base produced by mixing all the scrapings on his palette together; this gave a fine unity to the whole canvas, from the sky down to the foreground.

The next morning, when the canvas was almost dry, he would take a heavy black pencil and draw with the utmost precision the smallest details, even a lamp-post, which would look afterwards as if it had been done with brush-strokes.

Then he would set about preparing his palette. The colours, the contrasts, which he wanted were already part of him; and his palette would, therefore, remain astonishingly "clean".

He used zinc-white, not flake-white.

"Look," he would say, "I had to pay fifty francs a kilo for this white, and it used to cost two and a half francs!"

Next he would choose yellow-ochre, burnt-sienna, cobalt-blue, vermilion and pure emerald-green.

What a simple vocabulary for such richness!

And, in contrast to Corot's principles, he would always start with the sky to establish his values.

"Lucie dear," he would call, "come and look at these values!" And he would begin his work rapturously, without further hesitation.

Utrillo always cleaned and prepared his sable brushes himself, and lined them up on the table. There were fifteen of them; in the same way, the figures in his pictures were always an uneven number, generally five.

He would put aside his original design and nearly always work from memory, rarely making use of a reference-note of any kind. As a rule, he turned out at least one canvas a week.

As a relic of his bohemian days, he used to get up late, about eleven-thirty; there were prayers until twelve-thirty; then conversation with his dear Lucie, followed by lunch.

Like Rodin, Utrillo was fond of tripe *à la mode de Caen*; but he had a special weakness for Russian squirrel, roast chicken and garlic sausage. No coffee. A Manila cigar. And so to work.

At half-past four he would often fetch himself a glass of red wine from the dining-room, and return to work on his canvas by artificial light.

"He is so sure of his colours, of his values, of just what he wants to do," Lucie would boast, "that he could almost paint in the dark! The inner light: that is the whole truth. . . ."

They usually dined at nine, either in their villa *Le Vesinet* or out somewhere, often with friends. When he was in company, Utrillo scorned compliments, unless they came from one of his neighbours or an impoverished artist.

"Because," he explained, "if he is poor and not jealous, then it is all right."

He would grumble when people reproached him for not being pleasant to this or that person.

"They all say the same thing!" he complained; and an ugly look would come into his eyes, and he would frown. He would fidget with his hands, put his elbows on the table and sulk. But after the dessert he was "allowed" to sit down at the piano. Then the famous painter, who growled when people complimented him on his pictures, would smile beatifically, glance from right to left, launch forth into a rendering of *The Moonlight Sonata* with one finger, cover up his mistakes, improvise, accompany himself in syncopated time, and think himself in the Seventh Heaven of delight whenever anyone applauded, or when the proprietor of the bistro said to him,

"Go on, Monsieur Maurice. You're a great musician."

He would rise modestly from the piano, serene once more, and mumble a few verses. For he had a penchant for poetry, and had written a poem about his mother, another about Joan of Arc and a third about Modigliani. And when he pronounced the latter's name, he would say:

"We had our differences, but he was a god. May the Lord keep his soul in grace. . . . When we met for the first time, back in those bohemian days, to prove our admiration for each other we could think of nothing better to do than to exchange overcoats. Then we got drunk. Then we fought. And, finally, we were found lying almost naked in the gutter because thieves had stolen practically everything from us."

* * * * *

I never saw Utrillo in a more complete state of bliss than on the evening of the private view of an exhibition of flower-pieces by Suzanne Valadon and himself, put on by Petridès in his new gallery in the Avenue Matignon. Everyone in the art world was there. Utrillo had come, accompanied by his priest—the "guardian of his conscience", as he called him—who restrained him in his drinking.

"Just one more glass, Father, so that I can explain better what a wonderful artist my mother was."

"Very well, *cher Maître*."

Scorning the champagne and the fruit juice that were being served, Utrillo slowly sipped the cheap red wine that had been specially provided for him, and then he led us to the pictures.

"Look, look," he said. "My flowers are nothing compared to my mother's."

The two artists' paintings had been hung alternately on the walls. Utrillo's lilies, poppies, corn-flowers and carnations seemed as if casually and capriciously tossed on to the canvas against their solid backgrounds; whereas Suzanne Valadon's pansies, primroses and anemones looked serious and demure in their circles of light.

"They're different; but why should one be better than the other?"

At this, Utrillo's mouth twisted in anger and his eyes blazed. He grasped each of us by the sleeve in turn, and shunted us from one canvas to the next.

"She had a better sense of design, of form, of volume!" he declared. "We should get down on our knees. . . ."

It was a far cry from the rows between mother and son in the little bistro on the corner of the rue des Saules, where the old jade used to splutter so hard that the spray splashed her spectacles, while she rumpled her hair with one hand and her apron with the other. But they would always end by kissing and making up and, of course, sharing a good bottle of wine.

That night, as we were all gathered together, Utrillo suddenly raised his hand and asked for silence. He wanted to read us a poem he had written for the occasion in honour of his mother:

Créature d'élite et de bonté imbue
En ce monde elle fut l'âpre vérité nue.
Lors, prodiguant le bien d'un sûr discernement
Aux humbles accordait son parfait dévouement.

Las ! le sort fut cruel à l'âme disparue
Qui de mille tourments fut la proie ingénue
Me chérissant toujours de son doux cœur aimant . . .

"And Honegger is going to put the poem to music!"

Utrillo the poet; Utrillo the pianist. . . . !

When the evening was over and the last cocktails drunk, and the beautiful ladies and their escorts had departed in their cars, we found ourselves alone under the lovely chestnut trees in the Avenue Matignon. Feeling somewhat lachrymose from his red wine, Maurice surrendered to his sadness and, putting his hand on my shoulder, said,

"I'm a poor sort of chap, aren't I?"

"You're a splendid fellow," I assured him.

"Nevertheless, a poor sort. . . ."

Out of the tail of his eye he watched the last of the visitors drive away. They had come there to fête him or, as he said bitterly, "to make my canvases go up in price".

As his wife joined us, he added quickly,

"Now I'm not a poor sort of chap any more, thanks to Lucie."

But the expression in his eyes did not change. He wasn't fooled.

All at once he said to her,

"Leave us alone." And though Lucie still followed us, he went on:

"I want to like everybody now—even Utter, who so often gave me good advice. Let's walk a little faster. My wife doesn't like me to say so, but I shall, just the same, because——" He cast a hasty glance over his shoulder, and took my arm again.

Poor, great man. . . .

* * * * *

Yes, poor, great man.

Some years later I chanced to run into him in the lobby of the Hôtel Majestic in Cannes. His wife was in evening dress, and he had on a dinner-jacket. She was drinking a glass of champagne; he was having his usual red wine, but in a crystal goblet. I sat down with them.

"Just one more glass," he begged, timidly.

"No. And it's not because your friend is with us. You've had your ration, you know. If you take any more, you'll be complaining of feeling ill again tonight."

Maurice looked at me.

"Do let him have just a spot," I said. "It won't do him any harm, and it will make him happy."

"No. He'll want still more," replied Mme. Utrillo. But she poured him out a few drops, nevertheless, while the poor wretch gave me a grateful look.

A crowd of fashionable people were moving about in the lobby.

"What a pity there's no photographer here to take a picture of you two," said Lucie.

"That's easy enough to arrange," I assured her. "All I have to do is to call up the *Avenir de Cannes*."

"Oh, please do."

I went out to the bar, called up the offices of the paper, and was told that a photographer would be round in five minutes. But as I was triumphantly returning to our table, a horrible spectacle greeted my eyes; for there was Utrillo, foaming at the mouth, his eyes starting from his head, being dragged to the lift. The minute he saw me, he shook a trembling finger at me.

"Go away!" he raged. "You're no true friend. You've been betraying me for the last forty years. I don't like false people!"

"Quick. Quick. Get him into the lift," said Lucie; then added, raising her voice, "—with a bottle of Bordeaux."

"But what have I done?" I asked her, when Utrillo was finally "stowed away".

"Nothing," she replied. "It's just that he saw you go into the bar to telephone, and thought you were going to have a drink without him."

Two Methods in Oils

GOERG

WHEN YOU RING the doorbell at the home of Edouard Goerg (who paints Hoffman-like figures with brilliantly lacquered faces), a valet in an immaculate white coat opens the door and takes you to the artist's studio through a hall decorated with Negro masks. There you are welcomed by a man wearing a pair of sandals, a loose velvet jacket and a raw-silk shirt with an open collar, above which appears the most smiling face imaginable. It is a healthy pink, and the eyes are light and sparkling behind the spectacles, while the domed forehead is surrounded by blond curls. Goerg is at once joined by his wife, a Botticelli-like creature with eyes even lighter than his. This sylph makes an astonishing contrast to the round-headed, round-eyed, doll-like figures which look out from Goerg's canvases, holding flaming bouquets of flowers, or shrinking in fright from the gentlemen who would be grotesque if they didn't look so convincing.

"I am becoming more human, much pleasanter," he says.

"Do you think so? In any case, your colour has improved, and that's what matters most."

"Yes, that's the most important thing. There's been too much 'sketching' these last few years; personally, I want to paint in oil, using no turpentine, and explore all the possibilities of that medium, from the most fluid transparency to the most solid sort of pigment."

"But the man in the street—that is, the average man who visits the art galleries—is apt to ask: 'Why do you paint these fantastic, unreal figures?' Don't answer as Rouault or Matisse did, and tell me it's because you see them that way. There's some good reason or explanation, just as there is with Chagall."

"Yes, perhaps. But I have no idea what it is. I was born in Sydney, but I'm of pure Champagne stock. In everything I paint I am seeking.

"At the beginning of my career I wanted to escape from what we all considered then a horribly bourgeois atmosphere, and for a while I thought of becoming an actor. I was haunted by the faces of two people: Little Tich and Grock. For a time I was a pupil of a painter named Lauth, who had married Aurore, George Sand's grand-daughter, whose round pink face and brown hair contrasted sharply with the velvet collar of her dress and her jade buttons. That, perhaps, made an impression on my painter's subconscious, even after I had left Lauth, who wanted to make a society painter of me. You can imagine what I should have made of my sitters. But I kept working away. My father once said to me, 'You want to be a painter so that you can spend your days in cafés with a model on your knees', and that produced a violent reaction in me. I took a definite dislike to cafés, though I couldn't do without models. In addition to that, I went on a most fantastic journey. I was in love with a young woman who had gone to live in India, and I followed her there, although I was under age, and had no passport and almost no money. When I came back, I entered Maurice Denis's painting-class at Ranson's. He made us paint from imagination or memory, just as Gauguin, his teacher, had made him. He talked very little. We all dreaded Saturday, which was correction-day. I finally summoned up courage to show him a large canvas I had done, a sort of synthesis of Paris and its 'fauna'. After all, Maurice Denis was the painter of the ceiling in the Champs Elysées Theatre, and the author of *Théories*, which contained the famous maxim: 'Remember that before a picture is a naked woman or a landscape, or some anecdote or other, it is first and foremost a plane surface. . . .' So I waited, trembling, for his verdict. Denis singled out a corner of my canvas, and, pointing to a woman's foot, he said, 'That shoe isn't bad'. A teacher little knows what harm a remark like that can do, and how long the harm lasts.

"For that reason, in the course I am now giving at the Grande Chaumière, I am always careful what I say to even the least talented of my pupils. But I have known many older men who have been helpful: Laboureur, for instance, who introduced me to the world of engraving. For it is a world in itself, I assure you.

"Do you remember the meals we all used to have together? Pascin used often to be there."

"Yes, with a bowler hat on his curly head."

"With a tulle veil fastened to it, like an Englishwoman in Cairo. But we never dared to smile. What an odd man: very difficult to figure out. And always followed by a group of admirers. A woman left her husband one day in the hope of converting Pascin. The young painters pestered him too. 'Am I a good painter?' one of his compatriots once asked him. 'Am I?' he retorted. At times he would take flight, and cross frontiers and oceans, trying to get away from people and places; he kept running away, always fleeing from something, until he made his final tragic escape. . . .

Goerg: Self-portrait

"We'll skip the war of 1914: five years of mud, filth, glory, heroism—much of it in vain, alas. Let's talk of painting instead. I give precedence to expression; to beautiful pigment. Among the painters, I like Rebeyrolles, who is worth watching, and Lorjou, with all his grandeur and naïveté. Lorjou seems to think that he's the first artist since Goya. Villon? Well, yes. He has become too much a man of 'taste'. His subtlety lessens his value for those who can't grasp the richness underlying his apparent timidity. Derain? People don't do him justice. Like his friendly rival Vlaminck, he is one of the greatest painters of our time. I very much liked a young painter named Gruber, a pupil of Jacques-Émile Blanche. He knew very little about the art of the past, but what tremendous power there was in him. I talked to him about Grünewald, and he went all the way to Colmar to see his work. He was entranced by it."

We resumed our discussion of Goerg's own pictures, and the artist argued lucidly, while his "sylph" stood beside us, rolling *Caporals*.

"I have tried to express the essence or spirit of human beings in plastic terms. I am accused of being a 'literary' painter. I don't give a damn. After all, poetry and imagination aren't such bad things in painting. You can't escape them any more than you can escape your own times. Not one of us is entirely free. There are all sorts of influences—obvious ones, and secret, mysterious, unknown ones. And we are forced from time to time to borrow from others or even from ourselves. My figures often resemble each other, don't they? Well, they're my children, so it's hardly surprising."

YVES BRAYER

Yves Brayer's success was assured within the space of a few years. Is it because his canvases are almost conventional, despite the fact that his palette range is quite his own? Does he perhaps represent a certain tendency among the young to try to satisfy the taste of the public? In his clear and intelligible landscapes, there is a tempered audacity, a technique that is both austere and appealing, and a reaction against what today may seem objectionable in other, apparently more daring, painters.

Yves Brayer is a big, blond fellow, who still wears a little beard that frames his mouth, the *collier de barbe* so popular at the École des Beaux Arts. His wife, who is tall and straight like an Ancient Greek statue, is named Hermione, so he has every reason for returning to the classical tradition. His paintings, done in light ochres, with bare foregrounds almost entirely devoid of detail, his sweeping horizontal lines, and his palette, on which the cold tones often predominate, have all caused him to be accused of monotony, in spite of his technique, which is so perfect as to be sometimes disconcerting.

But in his studio in the rue Monsieur-le-Prince, not far from the one La Gandara had, I saw huge, vital, chaotic, tortured compositions, with houses and buildings hurled, as though by a storm, against the dense skies of the background.

When I asked him what these pictures were, he answered,

"My rough drafts."

"Your what?"

"Yes, just that. I know that nearly all painters start out with a small canvas and end up with something vast, but I do just the opposite. I brush in a big canvas out of doors or in my studio, and then reduce it to the smaller kind of pictures I've shown you."

"But my dear Brayer," I said, "these large canvases that you call 'rough drafts' are really finished works, and to me infinitely more interesting than your cold, condensed, geometrical arrangements, which are much too perfect. Your so-called rough drafts, which you do in one session, have real resonance! Each colour pleases the eye, each perspective delights it, each contrast attracts it. This Siena church, here, looks like an immense whiteness placed upon the city's wounds, whereas in the perfect painting it is only a perfect church. The larger version is really 'inhabited': its windows

Yves Brayer : Self-portrait

are open, its campanile reaches towards the clouds like an outstretched arm. It all speaks, sings, even shouts, at times; it stirs and moves us. The light effects are all varied; each detail smiles at us; the distances call to us; and we actually 'live' in the foreground of your picture."

"I rather thought so too. But then I wasn't sure. . . ."

"Oh, that eternal doubt, that everlasting inability of artists to trust the inspiration of their own souls! How infinitely more human, more alive and true are these larger paintings!"

"Well, I thought of including that canvas in my show in London. But I felt it my duty to react against the disorder that prevailed between the two World Wars, against improvisation, against——"

"When improvisation produces *that*?"

Then Brayer brought out of his racks a picture of a skinned lamb, all dark and bleeding; a nude whose muscles seemed about to burst through the skin; scenes of the Camargue ("where nothing ever happens", but on what a plane of despair!); views of Rome and Venice, in which the touches of ivory black were like iron masks on tender flesh; and Spanish cities smelling of fire.

"You were pregnant with all that, you had to give birth to it, and yet you hid it? Or you made one of those perfect paintings out of it. . . . Oh, Jivaro of painting! You reduce your works to such an extent that you almost desiccate them."

Protests from Hermione. I have gone too far, of course. But the artist's gaze wanders from one canvas to another. He shakes his head. Tomorrow he will do just as he likes. . . .

And yet he had been brought up in a hard school. He had been taught not only by the kindly Lucien Simon, but also by Forain. The young Brayer had often gone to study under that ferocious draughtsman.

Once Forain asked him,

"What are you doing at the moment?"

"A portrait of a model," Brayer replied.

"A portrait of a model?" echoed Forain, his lip curling sarcastically. "Indeed? It is possible to do a portrait of your concierge, or of some passer-by, or of a laundress; but not of a 'model'. A model has no soul—any more than a 'lady'. A model is only a body, a subject for study, an image; not a portrait."

Brayer smiled as he told the story. "I was rather angry with him. But Forain was right."

Forain by Sem

The Salad Generation

BERNARD BUFFET

BERNARD BUFFET: THE infant prodigy of post-war painting; winner of the Critics' Award in 1948; and fought over ever since by collectors and museums all over the world.

And yet, how harsh his work is: a desperate "aestheticism", desperate in its stiffness, its discipline, its ugliness, in the bourgeois sense of the word. But it is faultless in its architecture, and—when he suddenly enriches his vast compositions with immense sombre tones, which enable him to escape from the cage which he has built round himself—remarkable in its technique.

More than all the other young painters—even those who seek a new form of interpretation in the "abstract" or non-figurative—he is that rare artist who throws himself headlong into the fight. The expressions of admiration and abuse written in the visitors' book at his exhibitions are reminiscent of the controversies that raged before 1914 around the innovators of those days.

Certain critics, when they see his elongated, tragic faces, so devoid of any romanticism, have gone so far as to call them "inmates of a concentration-camp"; this only makes the painter laugh.

For the creator of these works from an icy Hell is a smiling young man, with sparkling eyes and a fresh complexion. He is quite slim (though not as thin as the figures he paints!); and, like a former Prince of Wales, orders his clothes from Sigvald's or Dorian Guy's (which has often made me want to psychoanalyse him).

He was born in Paris. In 1944 he studied at the Beaux Arts, under a teacher named Narbonne, who was "intelligent, and liked Picasso, but had nothing to teach".

"I learned far more in the evening courses in the Place des Vosges from a teacher from the Ville de Paris by the name of Darbefeuille, who showed me how to draw 'honestly'. I was already interested in the architecture of a picture, the rigid lines which give it its spirit, its balance and its buoyancy. I put my figures in and, of course, their construction harmonises of its own accord with that of the picture. Was I interested in the 'Golden Section'? Oh, it quite excited me. But I didn't use it. Taste and instinct are sufficient. Otherwise, what prison bars those numbers are, no matter how enticing they may be. You ask about Abstraction. I have a horror of the Menessier, Lapique and Pignon kind of thing, and especially of odd literary titles given to works of art—not that that is anything new: Picabia was doing it in 1901 . . . Hartung? Yes, his black lines give me a certain feeling. The same holds true of several painters from Pierre's gallery. I liked the Cubists; and Juan Gris's reserve; and La Fresnaye's stylisation. Where is the new painting going? Or, rather, what is its future? I believe in the future of a kind of painting that is less 'debauched': I believe in more careful drawing. I think that David should be rehabilitated—though not if it produces what I have seen at certain Salons. (We won't mention any names.) That's a real catastrophe. And so is this idea of going back to Ingres. In the Musée de l'Armée, which is nothing but a magnificent collection of odds and ends (I'm speaking from the point of view of 'painting'), there is an emperor by Ingres which would make you prefer any other painter, especially the work of one man whom I admire: Gros. The Spaniards? I don't care for them so much. Piero della Francesca? Not much. Raphael? No. El Greco? Too mannered."

"Well, in heaven's name, whom *do* you like, Buffet?"

"Apart from Gros—Courbet, Degas, Derain, Vlaminck, even Gruber; and also those I mentioned before; and, above all, the Avignon *Pietà*."

Why hadn't we thought of it before? That is the key to Buffet's work.

"Not entirely," Buffet said. "I painted in my present style before I ever saw it. I use as few colours as possible, on a white or grey ground. Black and zinc-white or flake-white. Recently I've added ochres and earth colours, cadmium-reds, lemon chrome-yellows. I like that very cold colour."

In three months Buffet painted the ten enormous panels he showed in his last exhibition, with stiff tapestries hanging over divans, on which his amazing figures lie, their flattened stomachs balancing their long faces. He worked directly on the canvas without any preliminary sketches, putting in his main values, the harmonies of which he had planned in his mind before he started. The encircling black lines round the subjects were added afterwards.

"Certain canvases 'come along' of themselves; others, never. Then for a while I'm in despair, like Gros. I like drawing, you understand. That is why I prefer, for example, Valadon to Utrillo. But expressiveness also moves me, as in Van Gogh's work, and Soutine's, although their point of view is the opposite of mine; or, perhaps, because of it. The Impressionists, on the contrary, scarcely move me at all. Cézanne's *Baigneuses*, yes: the unchanging aspect of the subject. For the subject does count, of course—after the actual painting, after the architecture of the work."

And he smiled, this painter of iron cages, this young millionaire, whose brushes had earned millions of francs by the time he was twenty-five. On that very day he was calmly awaiting the visit of an eminent member of the Government. . . .

Bernard Buffet : Self-portrait

The Sculptors

RODIN

THE CLOCK IN the tower of Saint-Germain-des-Prés struck two. I had not yet had lunch. There was no restaurant open in the neighbourhood except one of those "chain" eating-places to which the well-known dandy Alexandre Duval gave his name.

I casually entered the half-deserted place. In one corner the waitresses were going over their accounts. Near one of the windows was a solitary diner, a robust old man with a wrinkled forehead, a flowing beard and a napkin tied round his neck like a baby's bib.

Whenever the napkin slipped out of place, one could see the tiny rosette of the *Légion d'Honneur* on the silk lapel of his black frock-coat.

I went towards him. There was something familiar about that square forehead beneath the hair *en brosse;* the large, full eyes beneath lowered lids, like those one sees in paintings by Filippo Lippi; that pink skin; that nose, which was slender at the bridge and broad at the end; and that wavy beard, with amber glints in it.

"Why, it's Rodin!"

The diner raised his head. From under the light-coloured lashes the clear blue eyes gazed out at me. Rodin tightened his napkin, held out his hand and, without further preamble, said:

"I often come here. I don't care for the larger restaurants. You can't get broth in them any more. And I love broth. I like the old-fashioned soups: beef-soup, without that burnt taste or artificial colouring. That's the kind of dish I used to have when I was young. And cabbage-soup. And bread-soup. Ah, the virtues of a good bread-soup, thick and digestible and health-giving! A bread-soup is a panacea. It is a national monument. And that is, too——" he added, as the waitress brought him a dish of tripe. The sculptor's smile became positively Gargantuan. Pointing to the tripe, he went on:

"Doesn't that look like stone, the stone of cathedrals? The

cathedral of Beauvais, for instance. Do you know the cathedral of Beauvais? Few people do. Yet it towers over France, over the whole world. The deep, warm colour of this tripe, with its crenellations, makes me think of the cathedral of Beauvais."

What an epicure, Rodin, and how whimsical!

The sculptor then ate a whiting cooked in wine, and a dish of stewed prunes; and, after a half-bottle of Graves, he half-closed his eyes as he sipped a well-sweetened cup of coffee.

When we had finished lunch we strolled along in the mellow sunshine under the leafy chestnut trees, which held up their flowers like tiny candles. Then we got into his waiting car and drove off to Meudon, Rodin expressing his approval or disapproval of different places as we went along.

"The Place de la Concorde has beautiful proportions, although the little columns are somewhat squat. The roof of the Grand Palais is horrible: it looks like an Arab tent. There shouldn't be anything in cities but domes, like Santa Sofia. I make an exception for the Medici palace, of course, and a few fifteenth- and sixteenth-century houses."

Every other minute he would return to the phrase "the proportions are beautiful". And he would describe a circle in the air with his hand before bringing it back to rest on his knee.

From time to time he would take a boiled sweet out of his pocket and munch it. Then his face would become still. Under the heavy, arched brows, behind his glasses, his sea-blue eyes remained fixed. The large nose stood out firmly between his slightly flushed cheekbones. Only his white beard stirred majestically in the wind.

His left hand, resting on the handle of his umbrella, twitched and stretched, as if too confined by its grey glove. His ungloved right hand, the fingers of which were powerful at the base, rather thick at the joints and squarish at the tips, was still.

Our first stop was at the Dépôt des Marbres, where Rodin picked up some mail and got back into the car. Glancing at a copy of the *Courrier de la Presse* he was carrying, I asked the artist if he read everything that was written about him and his work.

"I certainly do," he replied. "The press is a very great force. And it is only because of the liberal press that I have been able to live. It has kept me from being completely crushed by the academic art that has always oppressed me, and still does. Yes, it is the press that has enabled me to live. And it is thanks to the press that my *Thinker* stands in front of the Panthéon today. It is placed a little too high, but I shall have it lowered."

Rodin's eyes sparkled, grew malicious; and he began to reminisce about his career.

"At first I was far ahead of the ideas current at the time. I was so much in advance that I and all those like me were treated as madmen. It took 'them' forty years to understand me. And now academic art, which fought against me and plagued my life, wants to give me a seat in the Academy. I am above bearing a grudge. I don't have to revenge myself, even by showing contempt. I shall accept the flower or the palm which the conquered enemy wants to offer me. Actually, my great official victory was the unveiling of my *Thinker*. You were present, weren't you? We went back to my house together. Do you remember the fine solemnity of the occasion, and the splendid figure of Madame Weber, with the peplum of her Greek dress and her bare arms outlined against the colonnade? Since that day I don't believe a single soul has shown hostility to me."

We arrived at Meudon, where the land, with its winding footpaths, slopes gently down to the Seine. The dark, straight poplars are sharply silhouetted against a background of paler trees, the hills are tinged with red, and the woods are suddenly cut by the black line of a train.

"Don't the trains worry you?" I asked, as we walked out on to the terrace.

"No. They are like enormous pythons boring through the forest, diving into the greenery, reappearing, and diving again. . . . This way."

We went round the summer-house and past a colonnade, behind which were numerous white forms in marble and stone. In a pond nearby several swans were lazily floating, pecking at the golden leaves that fluttered past them.

Rodin led the way to his studio and, installing himself in a large arm-chair, sat there musing with half-closed eyes, his hand stroking his beard, a satisfied expression on his face.

"People used to plague me about the silliest trifles," he said, "without understanding the meaning of my work. The public and some of their servile critics have reproached me all too often for exhibiting sculptures of separate parts of the human body. I have even been the victim of impudent cartoonists. Couldn't those people understand anything about sculpture or the studies for sculpture? Couldn't they realise that an artist has to work just as hard to make a hand or a torso expressive as he does a face? And that it is perfectly logical for an artist to exhibit a single arm instead of a 'bust', which arbitrarily has no arms or legs or abdomen? The thing to aim for is expression and proportion. The means of achieving it is by the modelling; for it is through the modelling that flesh is made to live, to vibrate, to fight, to suffer. . . . But enough of that. The truth will prevail, or is beginning to prevail. The truth will always prevail. Look there, for instance——"

I raised my eyes. In the autumn sky a spot of gold near a white cloud began to grow larger. It became a line, then a sail, turning alternately from grey to white and from white to black, as it was borne into the shadow or into the light, on the waves of the wind. The rigid wings, the roaring propeller, seemed to form an aureole of grey around the breast of the bird.

"There is Leonardo's dream going by," murmured Rodin.

The plane passed over us, without even casting a shadow.

"That," resumed the artist, "is the yearning of a whole people, which has taken shape in the sky. It makes me very happy. Those planes going by are a Renaissance. They have the greatest kind of beauty; that is to say, the beauty of courage and sacrifice. Even before the War the aeroplane had rehabilitated the country in the eyes of its citizens. It had restored their pride and confidence. It had kindled the spark of ambition in the eyes of the young, making them resolve to conquer the clouds. I have often talked with aviators, and what pleased me most about them was that they spoke of their 'birds' just as engineers do of their locomotives, or as real sculptors do of the texture of their marble. And for that reason, because they were, in a sense, fellow-artists, I regarded these young men as if they, too, were creators and demi-gods. Formerly, I used to wonder what it was that enabled one to recognise this glorious fraternity. But now I know. It is something which, since the days of antiquity, has united heroes and artists. It was this surge of patriotism, a surge of ideas like upraised swords, which sent a thrill through the whole of France. Indeed, at the most terrible moment of danger, the artist gripped his pencil or his pen more firmly while he sought inspiration in the skies of France. And as love for his country grew inside him, the aviator felt his wings grow larger too."

Rodin fell silent for a moment, his head thrown back, his eyes fixed on the distant blue. Then he gently took me by the arm.

"Come with me: I want to show you my biplane. You will be the first to see it."

We went back through the studio where stood the slender, white figures of young heroes: *Leonidas*, *Icarus*, *Apollo*, *La Patrie*, *Inspiration*, *The Sun*. We threaded our way among fawn-like nymphs of marble, with limbs contorted in a frenzy of passion; unfinished busts, whose lips already seemed to smile, the eyes to speak. Presently I found myself in a large room containing only a single monument. It was a bare column, crowned by an elongated sphere, which seemed to tremble under the touch of some unseen being.

You must know Houdon's *Diana*, poised on one toe, so alive in her grace that you almost expect her to come running up to you. You must often have seen Giovanni da Bologna's *Mercury*, with wings on his heels and arm outstretched. You must at least have heard of the wonderful *Nike* of Paeonius, in front of which virgins were warned to hold their breath.

But if only you had seen Rodin's *Biplane*!

It is composed of the figures of two vigorous young men in marble, curved like reeds. The light is reflected on their foreheads, which are lifted towards the sky; it plays over the torsos, with their broad yet subtle modelling, and spreads out across the wings. The two figures are back to back, one foot just barely touching the sphere.

As for the wings, you might think, perhaps, that Rodin would have made them as they look in real life. You might imagine them widely extended, in the classical style. Not at all. They are partly folded, the feathers quivering and ruffled, the frames intermingled, almost awkwardly, but beating energetically; pushing, aiding, shattering each other. One wing is drooping, as if broken; and I was actually surprised not to see the feathers falling.

The studio, the walls, the ceiling—everything disappeared before those twin shapes of white. And from the two vibrant, ecstatic bodies, so frenzied in their ardour that their arms bent back to touch their heels, the blue air seems to bound and rebound. . . . The air shimmers at the tips of the wings, at the young men's finger-tips. From wherever I looked, the group on the column seemed to be in flight, harmonious as light.

Standing beside me, calm and smiling, Rodin changed from his frock-coat into a smock, clothing himself in whiteness also. And only a short while before he had been extolling the virtues of beef-stew!

★ ★ ★ ★ ★

When he returned from Rome, I went to see him at his new studio in his home, the Hôtel Biron. On one side of the large entrance-hall there was an amazing bronze doe, on which sat a squat Nippon god, laughing with his mouth and his eyes and his ears. And the deer's horns cast a tracery of shadow on the white woodwork.

A little further on, framed by the wide arch of the window, a nude *Eve*, with bowed head, was weeping her eternal sorrow into her lovely arms, in front of the melancholy garden with its bare trees.

On the floor were several hollowed-out stone basins, in which fawn-like, full-bodied nymphs twisted their marble torsos. And there on a cloth-wrapped pedestal, like some flower coming out of the ground, was a radiant, smiling face just emerging from a block of stone which still bore the marks of the quarryman's pick.

The door opened, and there appeared the harassed face of Mario Meunier, the sculptor's learned friend. I followed Meunier along the hall and entered an even lighter room, where a thousand drawings were hanging on the walls in faintly gleaming, unobtrusive frames of gold.

Meunier drew aside a screen, and I beheld the imposing spectacle of Rodin sitting motionless, a velvet cap on his head, his white beard rippling down his chest. His nose looked more angular than ever, his cheeks more flushed; and his eyes gazed out serenely but with a certain mischievousness from under his heavy brows. Two locks of white hair had escaped from beneath the black velvet cap. His hands rested inert on the arms of the chair. His legs were wrapped in a wool rug from the Pyrenees.

The head was the living image of Michelangelo's *Moses*; the covering over the knees reminded me of Denys-Puech's *Meissonnier*.

I waited for the statue to speak, and finally it did.

"I am nailed to this chair as the result of bronchitis," Rodin told me. "But I'm almost better. The climate here is certainly not as mild as it is in the country I've just left, although it did rain a good deal there. Contrary to what people say, I was given a delightful welcome in Italy. I superintended the placing of my *Walking Man* in the courtyard of the Farnese Palace, which is our Embassy in Rome. Its modelling goes well with the impressive architecture. The modelling is the dimension that really counts. The modelling is the diapason, the proportion. It is that which gives the 'impression', much more than the height or breadth. I am very glad that my *Walking Man* has been put there.[1] It was a demonstration of something I wanted to prove. For I wanted especially to do a modelled piece of work, a powerful example of sculpture. It is not 'complete'. It has neither head nor arms. But that is of little importance to artists. In commercial art they never forget to put the arms and heads on statues, whether they sell for five francs or ten or two thousand; and sometimes each individual hair is shown."

Rodin's calm face with its rosy skin showed not the slightest sign of a wrinkle. An inexpressible serenity had relaxed the muscles of his leonine countenance. He spoke placidly, his eyelids drooping a trifle; yet beneath their shell-like transparency his eyes were as alert as ever.

"I looked at Rome with the eyes of a young man. I was seeing it again; or, to be more exact, I was seeing an entirely new city. One's first impressions fade with the years. This time I had the profoundest impressions. And I recaptured beauty—the three most beautiful aspects of Rome.

"The first of its beauties is its antiquity, the immortal power of which strikes deep into our hearts and eyes.

"The second, which is also very appealing in its fecundity and richness, is the rococo style of the sixteenth and seventeenth

[1] The *Walking Man* has since disappeared from the courtyard of the Farnese Palace, just as the *Thinker* has disappeared from its emplacement in front of the Panthéon. No one knows who took these great works or what has become of them.

centuries. True, the size of the monuments, the bronze *fasces*, the gold of the columns, never let you forget the dignity of antiquity; but I love the rich setting, the varied shapes of the fountains, the many palaces which make up this second of Rome's beauties.

"And the third of Rome's beauties is by no means negligible. It is the great monument to Italian Independence by the architect Pio Piacentini. It is not ugly—from the point of view of our time; and, although it is enormous and dominates the city, it doesn't shock you. It represents a new trend in Italy. And the aesthetics of the palace are very agreeable."

"And what about the fourth beauty of Italy?"

"Which one is that?"

"Futurism."

"Oh, I saw it. I saw it. Their pictures look like something out of a child's kaleidoscope—the bits of coloured glass which always look exactly the same. That's true of Cubism, too. It is a pity. Those young fellows must have a certain artistic temperament, and they could put it to better use. Nowadays, when it isn't nonsense, it's simply showing off. After all, 'The Past', which some moderns scorn, includes the Greeks and the Romans, and they were really something. . . ."

What paradoxical blindness on the part of one who fought for his own "too advanced art"!

"The unfortunate thing," Rodin went on, "is that there are no crafts any more. If they still existed among the common people, the common people would have more understanding. An old cabinet-maker will always prefer, say, the well-turned foot of a chest of drawers to any whole piece of furniture made for a cheap store. In the same way, an artist prefers a well-modelled head or arm to a complete statue of the commercial variety."

Night was falling gently over the silent formal garden: a silvery reflection of light, dimmed by the black sky, clung wanly to the sad branches. We looked out at the scene. The fire leaped in the fire-place. The old Master rose to his feet abruptly. He pressed his grave face against the window-pane, and murmured,

"It is beautiful, very beautiful. . . ."

* * * * *

I saw Rodin for the last time during the 1914–1918 war. The twilight over Paris that evening had been exquisite. It is not such an unusual phenomenon, but you have to walk across one of the bridges over the Seine, and along the Place du Carrousel or the Invalides Esplanade, really to appreciate it. I ran into Rodin just as I was crossing the Esplanade.

His hand on his beard, his umbrella under his arm, his pince-nez wobbling on his thick nose, the famous sculptor was standing looking at the sky. Sombre violet clouds were piling up behind the base of the Eiffel Tower, while higher up the heavens had taken on a rosier hue. Overhead a little purple island, followed by a patch of gold, swam slowly through the limpid blue.

"You know, in Italy," remarked Rodin, "the skies are very beautiful, especially in Rome. But the tones are more intense. It is only in France, in the Ile-de-France, that you see these lilac shades, these extremely pure pinks, which blend harmoniously with the other tones, however varied they may be. They cast an enchantment over the whole city. Even the walls are delicately tinted by the reflections of light. They play a ceaseless, gentle game, chasing and catching each other. They mingle without confusion, like layers of gauze; from one end of the horizon to the other, they play in harmony—a symphony which no art, not even music, has ever rendered."

The great artist folded his hands over the handle of his umbrella. A beam of gold flashed on his glasses, and he said softly, though without despair,

"Ah, to be able to sculpture that——!"

BOURDELLE

Bourdelle: I recall his round brown face, framed by a soft *collier de barbe*, and his voice booming as if he were in a cathedral. His studio was in a blind alley, which today bears his name. His little apartment, which was quite bourgeois in character, was one flight up in a shabby house in the Avenue du Maine. On the walls, still covered with nondescript paper, were photos of Greece; on the mantelpiece a terracotta head the artist had brought back from Crete. There was an oval table, and near the window an old lady busy mending clothes.

Was this the birthplace of his huge *Heracles*, the bas-reliefs in the Théâtre des Champs Elysées, the great statue of France gazing anxiously towards the horizon?

"I was an architect before I took up sculpture. Moreover, I always want to know where my sculpture is to be placed so as to be sure that it fits in well with the 'landscape'. Now, during the Renaissance——"

I met him again in St. Mark's, in Venice. He was studying the mosaics in the great cupola, where dozens of saints are shown seated side by side.

"What magnificent proportions!" he exclaimed. Then, nudging me, he added:

"What would happen if all those saints suddenly stood up! . . . Shall we go to Torcello tomorrow?"

Torcello is the ancient cradle of Venice. In order to reach it, you have to go via Burano, an island famous for its lace-making. Burano has a Northern appearance, with its brick houses, its still canals and its sunburnt, sad-eyed needle-women. We lunched there in the sunshine, pestered by flies and ragamuffins sucking melon-rinds and grape-skins, and surrounded by a collection of cats and dogs with eyes more pitiful than those of the beggars. And how many there are in that blessed land!

It was not a gondola but a flat-bottomed *sandolo* that we took in order to cross the short stretch of lagoon separating the two islands.

Torcello, the island of fire, is deserted except for a few little thatched houses, where antiques are sold. Everything in and around Venice is antiques, for that matter. Everything is "period".

A visitor to one of the antique-shops was stroking a kitten which had jumped into her arms.

"How pretty it is!" she said.

"Authentic fifteenth century, with a full guarantee," declared the shopkeeper, who had not even bothered to raise his eyes from his account-book.

But in the Torcello church, with its bare brick walls, there are the most beautiful mosaics in the world, more beautiful than at Ravenna, more beautiful, even, than those in St. Mark's.

"Only in France are there any more beautiful," asserted Bourdelle. But as we entered the basilica, the sculptor grasped my arm and whispered,

"They *have* stood up here!"

They were tremendous, those saints; quite overpowering. Curving under the vault, it seemed as though they were leaning down from Heaven over the Faithful, and about to annihilate them.

"They must have frightened the early Christians as badly as the ancient idols did the pagans."

Directly opposite there was an enormous Virgin, extending from the altar to the top of the dome, her head and shoulders curved in an infinitely gracious gesture. And she was all gold and purple, azure-blue and fiery red.

"What a lesson," Bourdelle said to me as we departed. "And I thought that the four chief pillars of Italian art were Michelangelo, Raphael, Correggio and Titian. But *that* is the chief pillar."

Here was the inspiration for his *France Veillant*. The day it was unveiled he nudged me in his familiar way, and said,

"Do you remember the Virgin of Torcello, and how she seemed to rise up to Heaven?"

BARTHOLOMÉ, THE VICTIM OF BARTHOLOMÉ

The painter and sculptor Bartholomé derived his fame primarily from his *Monument to the Dead*, which was set up in the Père La Chaise Cemetery. It must be admitted that the work owed a good deal of its inspiration to the tomb of Canova. Nevertheless, when Degas was doing his sculpture, he went to Bartholomé to ask him for technical advice.

The sculptor was a rather austere man and very decided in his opinions. I recall a conversation I had with him in his studio, where I had gone after Rodin's funeral. Speaking of his late confrère, he remarked,

"They made him a member of the Academy, and he meekly allowed them to, like a steer being led to the slaughter."

On the way to his house he had fumed the whole time about one thing and another.

"I wish we had a tyrant, an intelligent tyrant, at the Beaux Arts, who would pull down such atrocious agglomerations of stone and bronze as the monument to Victor Hugo (the one in the Place Victor Hugo), and the one to Jules Ferry. Yes, a responsible tyrant: there was one, for instance, in Michelangelo's day."

"Yes, and he preferred Bandinelli!"

Unfortunately for Bartholomé, he was the first, if not the only, victim of the very "demolitions" he had demanded so fiercely. The Government had commissioned him to do a statue of *The Defence of Paris*, to be placed in the Cour du Carrousel. Bartholomé executed a monument that was really beautiful in its expressive simplicity; but, since it did not harmonise with the statues around it, it was removed after the sculptor's death.

ARISTIDE MAILLOL'S LAST "WORK"

Dear Maillol: as robust and firm on his feet as his own large-hipped, thick-ankled statues, which he certainly did not skimp. How well I recall his discussions with Picasso at Céret, not far from his own Banyuls, in the Basses Pyrénées!

A follower of the classical French tradition, Maillol gave this advice to the artist who had just broken with academic form:

"You must do as everyone else does."

To which Picasso replied,

"You must do differently from everyone else. You must do everything afresh."

Maillol

"You must do better than anyone else: that is the way to do it differently."

"You must do it differently, and do it better."

"It is more difficult to do as everyone else does, and yet do it better."

They went on in this strain, but ended by embracing. Picasso had a great admiration for the older man. And Maillol sensed what was boiling up inside Picasso.

For sixty years Maillol worked away almost in silence, even when he was visiting his friend Renoir. Both men loved full, ample forms; and their only joy was that of the gods: to create.

Why were Maillol's last days saddened by secret slander? Some people even went so far as to speak of his "regrettable attitude" during the German occupation of France. I asked Lucien

Maillol about it, and I recall his very just indignation when he told me.

"Aristide Maillol did not go to Berlin, and for several good reasons. First of all, his old friends who had received him in Germany in 1926, including the millionaire Kessler, had died, victims of the Hitler régime. He had been deeply grieved by it. Secondly, his villa and studio at Marly had been occupied and sacked by the Germans in 1940, and his works scattered. That certainly didn't encourage him to fraternise with the enemy. Though some people made slighting allusions to his two visits to Arno Breker in Paris, he deserves only praise for it. For Maillol was eighty years old when he left the safety of his home, and he first requested and then demanded that his little model Dinah and her husband should be released from the prison at Fresnes, where they were being held, pending deportation to the salt mines in Poland. Maillol undertook the trip knowing full well that he would be exposed to criticism from people ignorant of the facts. And he had to wait a long time before he accomplished his mission—and then only by sheer force of courage. Since Dinah, who was of Russian origin, had been working for an English underground group for two years, it was a very risky business. Maillol won, finally, and saved the lives of two people who were very dear to him. He died in spite of the care given him by Nicolau and Tallez, who were the soul of the Resistance Movement in Perpignan. For this reason he deserves a halo for being a great human being as well as a great artist."

It is an open question whether or not Count Kessler helped Hugo von Hofmannsthal in the writing of *Elektra*, for which Richard Strauss composed the score. It is of little moment. It is sufficient that Kessler took Maillol to Greece. On his return, I went to see the sculptor and asked him to give me an account of his impressions of that country.

"Yes, it is very beautiful," he said. "But what did I learn there that was useful for my work? Almost any woman in my native Roussillon, with its harsher skies, moves me as deeply—though differently—as the Greek statues. Perhaps even more. Of course, under the pellucid skies of Greece contours seem to move, to live, to melt away like sugar, only to reappear immediately and more sharply, especially in certain lights and at certain times. It is very moving. But here, you see, I can feel the sap mounting from the ankles to the head of my peasant women, the young ones, and this naturally helps to make my clay and marble live."

ARCHIPENKO · LAURENS · ZADKINE · MATTEO HERNANDEZ · DESPIAU · LIPSCHITZ

In the exhibition of sculpture at the Petit Palais there were no works by Archipenko, who had gone to America. I had been told the most fantastic stories about the way he had tried to flout social conventions, and his efforts to avoid the commonplace in sculpture.

There were no Laurens, which was a pity. The moderation of his constructive innovations was wholly French. There were no Zadkines either. A sculptor in wood, Zadkine's studio, filled with tree-trunks, was like an enchanted forest, with roughly hewn nymphs aspiring to a new kind of grace, very different from that of ballerinas, with their smooth, round arms, or Dianas with "elegantly posed" hands.

A salute to the black granite sculpture of Matteo Hernandez, cut out of the raw rock, the most massive animal representations that any sculptor has attempted since the Egyptians. And yet Despiau, blinded by his fine sensitivity, unjustly condemns them.

And there is Lipschitz, whose work bursts out of him with such power that the forms he creates seem to tear open the solid volume of traditional sculpture.

"Have you seen the Bourdelles?" he asked me. "The days of the big-wig who did the *Monument to the Dead* are over. Nowadays, it seems as though Bourdelle is himself influenced by his Czechoslovakian pupils. But, after all, it is Rodin who still dominates here, as everywhere else."

"I thought you didn't like Rodin."

"I didn't like him before because I didn't understand him. In 1911, when I first exhibited my head of a young Italian girl, Léon Cladel came to me, very excited, and said, 'Rodin stopped to look at your head. He asked for your name. He said that the piece was really good.' I immediately felt depressed. For if Rodin, whose work I didn't like, took to my sculpture, I was sure that my work couldn't be much good. To me, he seemed anarchic. It was only when I saw some of his work in the rough ten years later that I suddenly understood it. In some of the pieces he had put aside, there was such a freedom of execution that all at once I grasped the great richness of his tremendous personality. I had simply mistaken liberty for anarchy. A man must cling to order as a base for his own security, and use that as a point of departure. What about my cubism, you ask? and cubism itself? It is a point of view. One must free oneself from natural forms. An aeroplane flies. But just because of that you don't have to represent it with feathers and feet like a bird. Take my *Europa and the Bull*, for instance. The bull is not an exact copy of a bull, yet it is more 'bull-like' than a real bull. I tried to interpret its strength, its bestiality, and also Europa's tenderness. But the important thing is to win the contest between volume and light. If you achieve the volume, then you have won. Of course, you must have a subject. But when you have chosen the subject, the contest between light and mass remains. And the victory! The rest is nothing but words. . . ."